The Silverplate Bombers

The Silverplate Bombers

*A History and Registry of
the* Enola Gay *and Other B-29s
Configured to Carry Atomic Bombs*

RICHARD H. CAMPBELL
Foreword by PAUL W. TIBBETS

McFarland & Company, Inc., Publishers
Jefferson, North Carolina, and London

> *The present work is a reprint of the illustrated case bound edition of* The Silverplate Bombers: A History and Registry of the *Enola Gay* and Other B-29s Configured to Carry Atomic Bombs, *first published in 2005 by McFarland.*

LIBRARY OF CONGRESS CATALOGUING-IN-PUBLICATION DATA

Campbell, Richard H., 1928–
The silverplate bombers : a history and registry of the Enola Gay and other B-29s configured to carry atomic bombs / Richard H. Campbell ; foreword by Paul W. Tibbets.
p.   cm.

Includes bibliographical references and index.

ISBN 978-0-7864-6907-9
softcover : acid free paper ∞

1. B-29 bomber — United States — History.
2. B-29 bomber — Registers.   I. Title.
UG1242.B6C368   2012   940.54'252 — dc22   2005010583

BRITISH LIBRARY CATALOGUING DATA ARE AVAILABLE

© 2005 Richard H. Campbell. All rights reserved

No part of this book may be reproduced or transmitted in any form or by any means, electronic or mechanical, including photocopying or recording, or by any information storage and retrieval system, without permission in writing from the publisher.

On the cover: The *Enola Gay* on Tinian
(photograph by Robert E. Krauss)

Manufactured in the United States of America

*McFarland & Company, Inc., Publishers
Box 611, Jefferson, North Carolina 28640
www.mcfarlandpub.com*

Frederick C. Bock
1918–2000
(USAF Historical Research Agency)

This story of the Silverplate B-29 Superfortress
is dedicated to Frederick C. Bock
and the men of the 509th Composite Group.
They served their country at Wendover, on Tinian, and at Roswell.
Their efforts and this airplane brought an end to World War II
and opened the Atomic Age.

Acknowledgments

*When you steal from one author, it's plagiarism;
if you steal from many, it's research.*
— Wilson Mizner

Writing this book taught me that an author needs all the help he or she can get, and the more the better. When I started out, it seemed to me that all I had to do was gather the facts and figures and then sit down and put them on paper. After nine years of research and writing, I now realize that it takes the contributions of many people to produce a book like this one, and I will try to acknowledge their assistance as best as I can.

I am indebted to many individuals for their help in researching archives and document files and for finding and providing photographs that add so much to the text. I must also thank those people who had the patience and forbearance to edit many versions of the text and the many friends who provided advice and suggestions on how the history of the Silverplate B-29s should be presented.

I owe a huge debt of gratitude to Archie DiFante and his colleagues at the U.S. Air Force Historical Research Agency at Maxwell Air Force Base in Montgomery, Alabama. They spent many hours extracting information from aircraft record cards and translating it into a form that I could understand. Archie, Joe Caver, and others at this facility also helped me find mission data, aircraft accident reports, photographs, and many other documents that filled in missing details.

I am very much obliged to John Coster-Mullen, who has graciously granted permission to use material from his book regarding physical and operational details of the Little Boy and Fat Man bombs. He has also been kind enough to offer suggestions on how to describe the bombs and has provided photographs of the Little Boy atomic bomb. His book, *Atom Bombs: The Top Secret Inside Story of Little Boy and Fat Man*, on the atomic bombs used in World War II is the result of a massive research effort and should be considered the most comprehensive description of these weapons ever published.

Alwyn T. Lloyd of the Boeing Airplane Company in Seattle provided me with the initial list of Silverplate B-29 serial numbers, which made the research task so much easier. His books on the B-29 Superfortress, included in the bibliography, have been valuable sources of information.

Roger A. Meade, historian and archivist at Los Alamos National Laboratory, located and provided copies of many documents and photographs relating to the Manhattan Project and the Silverplate B-29 project. David Menard, while he was with the Research Division of the Air Force Museum near Dayton, Ohio, supplied information on the plane known as *Bockscar*, which is on display at that museum. He also provided valuable suggestions on how to write this history.

Some of my early collection of documents came from M/Sgt Roger Hooker, then historian for the 509th Bomb Wing at Whiteman Air Force Base in Missouri. John Spiller came to my aid with valuable data on the general-purpose high-explosive bombs dropped by Silverplate B-29s during their initial operations on Tinian. Sam Bono of the National Atomic Museum in Albuquerque, New Mexico, was very helpful in locating and copying documents in that museum's files.

There is an old saying that a picture is worth a thousand words. If that is the case, I must express my appreciation to Leon Smith for providing the photographic equivalent of thousands of words. His images, particularly those of 509th nose art and crew members, are superb and their reproduction herein does not do them justice. My thanks also go to Robert W. Krauss, who supplied copies of photographs from his large collection of 509th pictures. I am beholden to Mel Foley, a member of the 509th at Roswell after the war, for several photographs from his collection.

I am grateful for the editing efforts of Clay Perkins and Tom Mathewson. Their critical reviews of various versions of the manuscript have helped eliminate errors and have greatly improved the text. At the same time, they are absolved of any responsibility for the content of this book. That responsibility is mine alone.

Finally, I am indebted to Brigadier General Paul W. Tibbets (USAF-Ret) and Gerry Newhouse for their support and advice.

If there are others who provided assistance in the writing and production of this book and I have not mentioned them, I apologize. The oversight is unintentional.

And to my wife, Beverly, thank you for always supporting and encouraging me in this endeavor.

Contents

Acknowledgments	vii
Foreword by Paul W. Tibbets	1
Preface	3
1 The Beginning	5
2 Development and Production	8
3 Combat Operations	25
4 The Los Alamos Test Program	42
5 Silverplate Accidents	47
6 Places and Units	56
7 The Bombs	70
8 The 509th Composite Group	96
9 The End	103
Appendix A: Chronology of Events	109
Appendix B: Silverplate B-29 Mission List (Tinian, 1945)	113
Appendix C: Crew Information	119
Appendix D: 509th Composite Group and Project Alberta Roster (Tinian, 1945)	143
Appendix E: Project Alberta	155
Appendix F: Silverplate B-29 Summary	159
Appendix G: Individual Silverplate B-29 Histories	161
Chapter Notes	217
Bibliography	223
Serial Number Index	227
General Index	229

Colonel Paul W. Tibbets, Commanding Officer, 509th Composite Group. August 1945, Tinian. (Robert W. Krauss)

Foreword

Much has been written about the development programs that produced the atomic bombs and the Boeing B-29 Superfortress bomber. There also have been many books and magazine articles published that describe how we prepared for the atomic bombing missions and how they were carried out. What has been lacking until now is a history of the development and life of the special version of the B-29 that carried the atomic bombs. This history of the Silverplate B-29 fills that void.

I was chosen to organize and command the unit that would be responsible for dropping the atomic bomb on Japan and Europe. This was in 1944. I was told I could have anything I needed to get the job done by using the priority code word "Silverplate." A specially modified version of the Boeing B-29 Superfortress bomber would be the airplane we would use, and it eventually became known as a Silverplate B-29. I had been testing the B-29 for almost a year when I was picked for the job. I knew the weaknesses of the plane, and I was convinced I knew the cure for those weaknesses.

We began to organize the outfit that later became the 509th Composite Group at Wendover Army Air Field in the fall of 1944. Special modified B-29s were received on a sporadic basis, after being modified to what is known as a "Silverplate" configuration. These airplanes had fuel injection engines and fast-acting bomb bay doors, and with the removal of all turrets and armor plate, they were 7,200 pounds lighter than other B-29s. (The tail guns remained.) These changes permitted these airplanes to fly above 30,000 feet at an average speed of 260 mph while carrying a payload of 10,000 pounds a distance of almost 2,000 miles. This performance put them above the capabilities of any known fighters, just as it put them above peril from anti-aircraft fire.

The modifications to carry the atomic bombs consisted of changes in the bomb bay. An H-frame was installed to hold a bomb shackle by a single lug, and sway braces were added to steady the bomb in rough air. The most important change was the replacement of the carburetor-equipped engine with a fuel injection engine. These new Silverplate B-29s were also equipped with Curtiss-Electric propellers with reversible pitch capabilities that improved the plane's stopping power.

We now had the best B-29 in the entire Army Air Forces, and we were ready to go do the job directed of us. We went to Tinian, flew our missions, and the war ended. The Silverplate B-29 did what was asked of it, and it went on to be our nuclear deterrent for several years after the end of the war.

Brigadier General Paul W. Tibbets (USAF, Ret.)
Commanding Officer, 509th Composite Group

PREFACE

This is the story of a special version of the Boeing B-29 Superfortress bomber. Its name, the Silverplate B-29, refers to the code name for the project that produced it.[1] The goal of that project was to create a plane capable of delivering atomic bombs. The Silverplate B-29 was the result.

Only 65 of these airplanes came into existence; yet they played a crucial role in events that altered the course of mankind. Some of the Silverplate B-29s were in service for only a few months, while others became the backbone of America's nuclear deterrent force in the years immediately following the end of World War II. The two most famous of these distinctive bombers, given the nicknames *Enola Gay* and *Bockscar*, are the only two that remain, 59 years after the missions they flew into the history books.[2]

The story that follows is about an airplane. The focus is not on the men who flew it, the bombs they dropped, or the morality of their use. It simply tells the history of how 65 Silverplate B-29s were produced, used, lost in accidents, converted to other configurations, and finally sent to their graveyard to be turned into scrap. It is somewhat ironic to think that possibly some of the aluminum pots and pans used to cook meals in the 1950s were originally parts of Silverplate B-29s.

The initial research to gather data on the Silverplate B-29s actually began in 1994 as a broader search for information on the 509th Composite Group and its crews, aircraft, and missions. The reason for that research was to compile material for a commemorative booklet for the 50th anniversary reunion of the 509th, held in Albuquerque, New Mexico, in August 1995.

The commemorative booklet was written and published by Frederick C. Bock, one of the Airplane Commanders of the 393rd Bombardment Squadron of the 509th. Bock was the chairman of the 50th reunion planning committee, and I had the honor to serve as his co-chairman responsible for support arrangements provided by the National Atomic Museum Foundation.[3]

The Silverplate material included in the 1995 reunion booklet was limited to facts and figures regarding the fifteen B-29s used by the 509th on Tinian Island, but the research that produced the original information indicated that there were many more Silverplate B-29s and that their history might be uncovered. The response to the 1995 commemorative booklet, and to an updated version prepared by Bock for the 509th reunion in 1997, told me that there were many people who would like to know more about the B-29s called Silverplate. And thus was born the notion of doing the necessary additional research and then writing a history of these special airplanes.[4]

As noted in the dedication of this book, this history of the Silverplate B-29s is intended as a memorial and tribute to Fred Bock. Not only did Fred share information he possessed, he also provided the desire and motivation to learn more about these special B-29s and to put it all down on paper. Fred Bock was a friend and a true gentleman, and I feel honored to have known him. Fred died 25 August 2000.

The entwined evolution of the atomic bomb and the Silverplate B-29 is briefly introduced in chapter 1. The basic history of the development and delivery of the Silverplate B-29s is set forth in chapter 2. The deliveries and operations of the aircraft are grouped into phases, beginning with the prototype and ending with the follow-on program known as Saddletree.[5]

To enhance the historical perspective on these airplanes, chapters on their combat operations, the test program in which they were used, accidents that occurred, the bombs they carried, the places and units to which they were assigned, and the 509th Composite Group have been included. In addition, appendices have been included to present a chronology of events, information on missions flown, the personnel that were present on Tinian, the flight and ground crews, and milestone dates for each airplane. The individual histories of all 65 Silverplate B-29s are presented in serial number sequence in Appendix G.

This book does not pretend to be a detailed history of the development of the atomic bomb or of the original B-29 Superfortress. The telling of the Silverplate story requires the inclusion of some details of the Manhattan Project, the atomic bombs, and the B-29 bomber, but the body of published works on these subjects is enormous and any additional words on my part would be redundant. The references mentioned below are but a few of the books on these subjects. The bibliography provides an extensive list of references for anyone wanting to know more about how the bombs and the basic B-29 were developed.

Comprehensive treatments of the atomic bomb program can be found in *The Making of the Atomic Bomb* by Richard Rhodes and *Racing for the Bomb* by Robert S. Norris. The personal recollections of General Leslie Groves are set forth in his book, *Now It Can Be Told*. Two books on the activities at Los Alamos are *Critical Assembly* by Lillian Hoddeson and others, and *Project Y: The Los Alamos Story* by David Hawkins and others. An excellent account of the assembly of the bombs on Tinian can be found in *Project Alberta: The Preparation of Atomic Bombs for Use in World War II* by Harlow Russ. A detailed technical description of the Little Boy and Fat Man bombs is *Atom Bombs: The Top Secret Inside Story of Little Boy and Fat Man* by John Coster-Mullen.

Books on the B-29 program include Bowers' *Boeing B-29 Superfortress* in the WarBird Tech series, Lloyd's two volumes on the B-29 in the In Detail and Scale series, Pace's *Boeing B-29 Superfortress* in the Crowood Aviation Series, Birdsall's *Saga of the Superfortress*, and *Building the B-29* by Vander Meulen.

A few of the books that tell the story of the operations of the 509th Composite Group and the use of the Silverplate B-29s include *Target Hiroshima* by Christman, *Rain of Ruin* by Goldstein and others, *Enola Gay: Mission to Hiroshima* by Thomas and Morgan-Witts, and *Return of the Enola Gay* by Paul Tibbets.

1 THE BEGINNING

At the time of the 50th anniversary in 1995 of the atomic bombing of Hiroshima, there was renewed controversy as to whether the bombing was necessary and whether the United States was guilty of some crime against humanity. A slogan that appeared on a bumper sticker and in other forms took the position that "If there hadn't been a Pearl Harbor, there wouldn't have been a Hiroshima."

An extension of that slogan that seems appropriate to the story told in the following pages suggests, "If there hadn't been an atomic bomb, there wouldn't have been a Silverplate B-29." But there was an atomic bomb, rightly or wrongly, and the history of the airplane developed to carry it is an account worth telling.

The programs to develop and produce the atomic bomb and the B-29 bomber began and progressed together along remarkably similar timelines. Both programs had their beginnings at about the same time in 1939, they passed major milestones at the same time in 1942, and their paths converged in late 1943. A list of milestone dates is included in Appendix A.

The Air Corps (the U.S. Army Air Forces after 20 June 1941) drew up requirements for a new heavy bomber in December 1939 and mailed them to potential bidders the following month. Professor Albert Einstein's famous letter to President Franklin D. Roosevelt (dated 2 August 1939) was delivered to the president on 11 October 1939, and modest efforts to investigate the possibilities of an atomic bomb were set in motion the following month.[1]

It is interesting to note that while Einstein envisioned the construction of bombs based on the uranium fission phenomenon, he went on to offer his opinion that "such bombs might very well prove to be too heavy for transportation by air." His view was that "a single bomb of this type, carried by boat and exploded in a port, might very well destroy the whole port together with some of the surrounding territory." Had his thoughts in this regard been proven accurate in future years, the story that follows might well have been about a Silverplate ship instead of a Silverplate bomber.[2]

A contract was let with Boeing for the first two XB-29s on 6 September 1940. The first flight of the XB-29 took place a year later on 21 September 1941, a little over two months before the attack on Pearl Harbor. Meanwhile, Brigadier General (later Major General) Leslie R. Groves took over the newly established Manhattan Project on 17 September 1942 and efforts to develop the atomic bomb were immediately accelerated. One month later, Los Alamos was selected as the site for a laboratory to design and develop the bomb. Known as Site Y, the location was selected by Groves and J. Robert Oppenheimer, the director of the laboratory.[3]

Oppenheimer and the initial cadre of scientists and engineers arrived at Site Y to begin work on the design and development of the bomb in March 1943. In October of that year, Group E-7 of the Ordnance Division of the Los Alamos laboratory was formed to manage the integration of the bomb design with a delivery vehicle. Norman F. Ramsey was the Group Leader and one of his principal engineers was Sheldon Dike. The reports of Ramsey and Dike on their work are primary sources for this story.[4] Coincidentally, the first production B-29 was accepted by the Army Air Forces on 7 October 1943.

When Group E-7 was established in October 1943, sufficient progress had been made in defining the dimensions of the two bomb types then under consideration to begin thinking about an airplane that could deliver the bombs.

Both types of bombs then envisioned used plutonium as the nuclear material. One version, given the nickname Thin Man, employed the gun method for bringing the plutonium sections together for detonation. It was estimated it would be 17 feet long and have a diameter of 23 inches. The second model, called Fat Man, used an implosion technique for squeezing the plutonium into a critical mass for detonation. Its dimensions were estimated to be nine feet in length and 59 inches in diameter.

In October and November 1943, Ramsey and Dike analyzed the features of the only two long-range bombers thought to be capable of carrying the estimated weight of the bombs. The Boeing B-29 Superfortress was selected on the basis of its expected availability, the payload it could carry, and the size of its bomb bays. The alternative, the British Avro Lancaster, was eliminated from consideration because its bomb bay was not wide enough. It has also been written that General Henry H. "Hap" Arnold, Commanding General of the U.S. Army Air Forces, was adamant that if there was to be an American atomic bomb, an American bomber would deliver it.

The B-29 Superfortress was a four-engine, long-range bomber with a wingspan of a little over 141 feet, a length of 99 feet, and a vertical stabilizer/rudder height of nearly 28 feet above the ground. Its empty weight was 72,000 pounds while its gross weight with a nominal fuel and bomb load was 120,000 pounds. Powered by four Wright R-3350 radial engines that developed 2,200 horsepower each at 2,600 rpm for takeoff, the B-29 could carry a bomb load of 20,000 pounds with a range of over 5,800 miles. The service ceiling was 31,850 feet for the standard version of the B-29, while its cruising speed was rated at 220 mph with a nominal top speed of 365 mph.

The total production of B-29s, including prototypes and test versions, totaled 3,965 aircraft.[5] The cost of a fully equipped B-29, including government furnished equipment, was about $782,000 (in 1945 dollars).[6] This figure obviously does not include the operating and facility costs associated with B-29 operations in World War II, but it does include development and spare parts costs. Additional information on the estimated costs of the B-29 program, the Silverplate project and the development of the atomic bombs is included in chapter 9.

On 1 December 1943, Army Air Forces Headquarters in Washington directed the Materiel Command at Wright Army Air Field (now Wright-Patterson Air Force

Base) near Dayton, Ohio, to undertake the modification of a B-29 bomber in great secrecy and with the greatest possible priority. The letter also noted that the 58th Bombardment Wing at Smoky Hill Army Air Field in Kansas had been instructed to deliver a B-29 to Wright Field without delay.

The December 1943 directive had as its subject, "Silver Plated Project." Subsequent communications shortened the title to Silver Plate, and the code word for the project and its priority eventually became one word, Silverplate. The B-29s modified and produced to carry atomic bombs soon became known as Silverplate B-29s.

To relate the timing of the B-29 bomber and atomic bomb programs with events in World War II, it should be remembered that Einstein's letter to President Roosevelt was written a month before the Germans invaded Poland, but was not delivered to the president until a little over a month after the war in Europe began. The first flight of the XB-29 took place over two months before the Japanese attack on Pearl Harbor and General Groves assumed direction of the Manhattan Project shortly before the Allied invasion of North Africa. The first drop test of a prototype atomic bomb shape and acceptance of the first production B-29 by the U.S. Army Air Forces took place at about the time the invasion of Italy began.

Other events included the delivery of the prototype Silverplate B-29 from Wright Field six months before the Allied invasion of France, activation of the 509th Composite Group just before the Battle of the Bulge, and arrival of Silverplate B-29s on Tinian at about the time of the surrender of Germany.

The focus of this story is on the history of the Silverplate B-29s, and to a lesser degree, on the 509th Composite Group and the atomic bombs they dropped. Since the 509th was created specifically to use this airplane and this airplane was produced specifically to carry the atomic bomb, numerous references to the 509th and the atomic bombs are included in the pages that follow. Because of this interrelationship, separate chapters are devoted to the 509th and the bombs.

2 Development and Production

Silverplate B-29s were in operational service for over six years, beginning with the prototype in January 1944 and ending in 1950 when the last of these special airplanes were modified to remove their Silverplate features. After a standard B-29 was modified at Wright Field to produce the prototype, 64 more airplanes with the capability to carry atomic bombs were produced. They were delivered in phases over the years, as is described in this chapter.

Phase One — The Prototype

In response to orders from headquarters, a B-29 from the 468th Bombardment Group of the 58th Bombardment Wing at Smoky Hill Army Air Field in Kansas was delivered to Wright Field in early December 1943 for modification to the initial Silverplate configuration.[1] The aircraft, serial number B-29-5-BW-42-6259, was produced at the Boeing plant in Wichita, Kansas, and delivered to the U.S. Army Air Forces on 30 November 1943. Wright Field assigned project number MX-469 to the modification effort and gave it a short title of "Pullman."

The modifications incorporated into 42-6259 from December 1943 to January 1944 primarily changed the bomb bay arrangements so as to accommodate the size and shape of the Thin Man bomb. At 17 feet in length, the Thin Man was longer than the length of a normal B-29 bomb bay. The center fuselage structural section between the bomb bays and under the wing spar was removed and separate bomb suspension and release mechanisms for the Thin Man and Fat Man shapes were installed in the front and rear bomb bay areas. The resulting single bomb bay was about 33 feet long and used two sets of lengthened bomb bay doors.[2]

Figure 1 is a photograph of the prototype taken at the site of the initial tests, Muroc Army Air Field (later Edwards Air Force Base). As can be seen in the photograph, the prototype retained the four turrets normally installed on B-29 bombers.

Figure 2 shows the modified bomb bay and new bomb bay doors, looking from the rear toward the front. A Fat Man model can be seen mounted in the front bomb bay. To carry the Thin Man bomb, two glider tow cable attach-and-release mecha-

1. Prototype Silverplate B-29. (Los Alamos National Laboratory)

nisms were modified and installed in the front and rear bomb bay areas so as to connect with the two attachment lugs of the Thin Man bomb. In addition, the radome normally mounted between the two bomb bays was removed and provisions for operating the bomb release mechanisms were added.

The Wright Field crew assigned to fly 42-6259 in the test program included Major Clyde S. Shields as the airplane commander and Captain David Semple as the bombardier.[3] The first drop test series was conducted at Muroc Field in California in February and March 1944. One test in this series resulted in severe damage to the bomb bay doors and the prototype was flown back to Wright Field for repairs and additional modifications.[4] New bomb bay doors and three new engines were installed and the bomb release mechanisms were modified to eliminate problems with the release of bombs.

The second set of bomb drop tests was conducted at Muroc in June 1944. At about the time these tests were concluded, the scientists at Los Alamos determined that plutonium could not be used in a gun-type bomb and development work on the Thin Man bomb was terminated.[5] The Thin Man bomb is shown in Figure 3. In lieu of the Thin Man model, the Los Alamos scientists devised an alternate gun-type bomb known as Little Boy that used uranium as the active material. The Little Boy bomb was ten feet long, had a diameter of 28 inches, and weighed about 9,700 pounds. Los Alamos also came to the conclusion that although the dimensions could be kept

2. Bomb Bay of Prototype Silverplate B-29. (Los Alamos National Laboratory)

about the same as originally planned, the weight of an operational implosion-type bomb might be considerably heavier than was first thought.

After the June series of tests, 42-6259 was flown back to Wright Field for the modifications required by the Los Alamos decisions. To accommodate the estimated 10,000-pound weight of the Fat Man model, a decision was made to replace the glider tow cable attach-and-release mechanisms in the front bomb bay with the British type F release and type G attachment. In addition, with the elimination of the Thin Man design there was no need for the single, long bomb bay. Therefore, the prototype was modified back to the original two bomb bay configuration in which the rear bomb bay was of the standard B-29 design.

After the latest modifications to 42-6259 were completed at Wright Field, it was flown to Wendover Army Air Field in Utah, where the 509th Composite Group was about to be activated. At Wendover it was assigned to the 216th Base Unit, the organization established to support the Los Alamos test program.[6]

Drop testing of Fat Man and Little Boy models with the prototype aircraft resumed in September 1944 and its use continued until it was damaged in late 1944 in a landing accident at Wendover.[7] It was never used again for Los Alamos drop tests and after a period of storage at Davis-Monthan Army Air Field it was assigned

3. Thin Man Bomb in Prototype Bomb Bay. (Los Alamos National Laboratory)

to Fort Worth Army Air Field in Texas for use as an instructional aircraft. It was scrapped in May 1948.

Phase Two — The First Batch

The second phase of Silverplate B-29 deliveries began in August 1944 when two key decisions were made. One was to form the unit that would be trained for combat delivery of the atomic bombs, the 509th Composite Group. The second decision was to modify additional B-29s for training of crews and continuation of the Los Alamos drop test program at a much greater pace.

The 393rd Bombardment (Very Heavy) Squadron, in training at Fairmont Army Air Field in Nebraska as an element of the 504th Bombardment Group, was selected to be the combat squadron of the yet to be activated 509th Composite Group. The Commanding Officer of the 393rd was Lieutenant Colonel Thomas J. Classen, who was later named Deputy Commander of the 509th. Personnel of the 393rd moved to Wendover on detached duty in the middle of September 1944, but deliveries of the first group of Silverplate B-29s from the Martin Omaha plant did not begin until mid–October.

The engineering and modifications for the first group of Silverplate B-29s were accomplished at the Glenn L. Martin Aircraft Plant in Omaha, Nebraska. The changes made in production aircraft were primarily to allow for carrying and dropping the atomic bombs. Thus, they were essentially the same configuration as the prototype as it existed in September 1944. The B-29s delivered to Wendover in this group did not include the performance improvements incorporated in the later models used on Tinian. The aircraft were delivered to Wendover with the four upper and lower turrets installed, but they were removed soon after they arrived at Wendover.[8]

There were 17 Silverplate B-29s delivered from the Martin Omaha plant to Wendover from October to December 1944 for use by the 393rd and the 216th Base Unit. The aircraft were modified to the Silverplate configuration at the Omaha Modification Center under Project 98146-S. Three of these aircraft were assigned to the 216th for use in the Los Alamos drop test program:

B-29-15-MO-42-65234   B-29-15-MO-42-65235   B-29-15-MO-42-65258

The remaining 14 aircraft were initially assigned to the 393rd Bombardment Squadron for use in training the air and ground crews:

B-29-5-MO-42-65209   B-29-15-MO-42-65238   B-29-15-MO-42-65261
B-29-10-MO-42-65216   B-29-15-MO-42-65239   B-29-15-MO-42-65262
B-29-15-MO-42-65217   B-29-15-MO-42-65240   B-29-15-MO-42-65263
B-29-15-MO-42-65236   B-29-15-MO-42-65259   B-29-25-MO-42-65264
B-29-15-MO-42-65237   B-29-15-MO-42-65260

4. Wendover Army Air Field in 1945. (Robert W. Krauss)

The 509th Composite Group was activated at Wendover on 17 December 1944 with Lt. Colonel Paul W. Tibbets as the Commanding Officer.[9] At the same time, the 393rd was released from the Second Air Force and assigned to the 509th. Other elements of the 509th were manned with personnel already assigned to Wendover and with officers and enlisted personnel drawn from Army Air Forces units around the world.

Some of the 393rd aircraft were flown on Los Alamos drop test missions to target areas at Wendover and at the Navy Salton Sea bombing range in California to further the development of bomb components and ballistic tables.[10] These missions also enhanced the 393rd training program. At least ten of the aircraft delivered to the 393rd during this period were deployed to Batista Field in Cuba in January of 1945 for a month of long-range over-water navigational training. Frederick C. Bock, one of the airplane commanders deployed to Cuba, confirmed that he and his crew used aircraft 42-65238.

On 21 February 1945, the number of aircraft being used by the 216th in the Los Alamos test program was reduced by one. An engine fire on aircraft 42-65235 during a test mission resulted in an emergency landing at Wendover with the crew evacuating the aircraft as soon as it came to a stop.[11] The damage from the fire was considerable and this aircraft was not used in the test program again. It was finally repaired at Wendover and flown to a storage site where it was eventually declared surplus and scrapped.

In the latter part of February 1945, the schedule of Los Alamos drop tests increased significantly and the Test Section of the 216th desperately needed additional aircraft. Arrangements were immediately made to transfer 42-65236, 42-65259, 42-65260, and 42-65262 from the 393rd to the 216th. Drop test and crew training activities using the Silverplate B-29s delivered in this phase continued into the spring of 1945 until the new and improved aircraft of the next phase began arriving at Wendover.

Most of the Phase Two aircraft were transferred from Wendover to other units temporarily before being placed in storage in late 1945 at either Davis-Monthan Army Air Field in Arizona or Pyote Army Air Field in Texas. Four of the aircraft assigned to the 216th (42-65234, 42-65258, 42-65260, and 42-65262) were retained at Wendover for use in the Los Alamos drop test program until after the end of World War II.

By the end of 1944, numerous changes were being incorporated into all newly produced B-29s to correct problems encountered in combat and training operations. One of the most important of these changes was the use of a new version of the Wright R-3350 engine that had vastly improved cooling features and utilized fuel injection in place of the original carburetor system.

In January 1945, Tibbets and Sheldon Dike from Los Alamos met with Boeing officials at the Wichita plant to discuss a project for bringing the 393rd and 216th aircraft up to the latest possible configuration by recycling them in small groups through a modification center. Instead of entering into a modification project, a decision was made to incorporate all improvements and other bomb-related changes into a new group of Martin Omaha production aircraft.[12] Thus, the stage was set for the third phase of Silverplate B-29 deliveries.

Phase Three — Improvements for Test and Tinian

Immediately after the meeting at the Wichita plant in January 1945, Tibbets and Dike visited Wright Field and Army Air Forces headquarters to finalize arrangements for the new Silverplate B-29s and to reach agreement on their configuration. Project 98228-S was established by Wright Field to cover production of the improved aircraft.

The decision to replace the initial Silverplate B-29s with improved versions included replacement of the aircraft used for the Los Alamos drop test program as well as those for the 393rd. Delivery of the improved B-29s to Wendover began in April 1945 and continued until shortly after the war with Japan ended.

Although a total of 28 Silverplate B-29s were produced in 1945, a somewhat arbitrary definition has been adopted for this phase and the next regarding which B-29 serial numbers are included in which phase. This phase includes the five Silverplate aircraft delivered for the Los Alamos drop test program and the fifteen aircraft delivered to the 393rd that were later deployed to Tinian and used there in combat operations.

Deliveries of the additional eight aircraft after the last 393rd B-29 had departed for Tinian are covered in Phase Four.

The basic Silverplate configuration established for the 28 B-29s delivered in this and the next phase included the latest improvements in aircraft performance as well as modifications for loading, monitoring, and dropping the two types of atomic bombs to be used in combat. These aircraft were also equipped to carry general purpose high-explosive bombs as well as the Fat Man shapes filled with 6,300 pounds of high explosives, which were called "Pumpkins."[13]

The most significant change in the new Silverplate B-29s was the use of a vastly improved power plant, the Wright R-3350-41. This engine incorporated better cooling features, fuel injection, and a fuel flowmeter/manifold system. In addition, Curtiss Electric propellers with reversible pitch capabilities were installed to improve braking power on landings. These improvements probably contributed more to the success of 509th operations on Tinian and the atomic bombing missions than any other feature of the new configuration.

Another modification included in the aircraft delivered in this and the next phase was the use of pneumatic bomb bay door actuators in place of the hydraulically operated actuators used in earlier models of the B-29. These devices enabled the rapid opening and closing of the bomb bay doors.

The Silverplate B-29s delivered in Phase Two were delivered with turrets and armor protection installed, but 509th personnel at Wendover removed these items to reduce the weight of the aircraft. The Silverplate B-29s delivered in Phases Three and Four were either assembled at the Martin Omaha plant without the turrets and armor protection or modified immediately after leaving the production line. As in Phase Two, the tail guns and armor for the tail gunner were retained in these aircraft.

In addition to the aircraft performance enhancements included in phases three and four, improvements in the aircraft structure associated with carrying the atomic

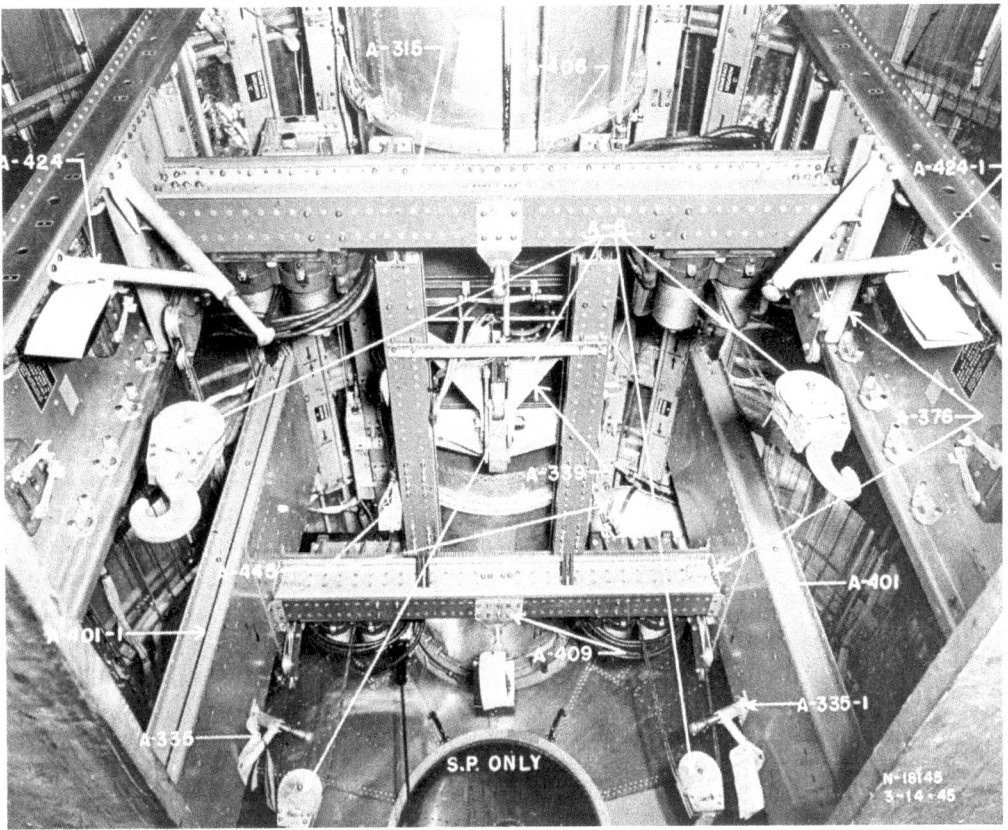

5. Front Bomb Bay of Silverplate B-29. (Los Alamos National Laboratory)

bombs were also included. The H-frame installation was modified to correct deficiencies found in earlier versions, and improved sway bracing components for both Fat Man and Little Boy shapes were provided.

The British type F bomb release and type G attachment used in the later version of the prototype were retained, and dual electric and mechanical bomb release systems were installed.

An additional modification in these aircraft was the addition of an electronics test officer position and related equipment in the forward pressurized compartment next to the radio operator's station.[14] Electrical cabling from the monitoring equipment at this position to the forward bomb bay enabled the electronics test officer to monitor the condition of an atomic bomb mounted in the bomb bay during flight.

As noted above, this phase covers the 20 Silverplate B-29s delivered to Wendover during the first half of 1945, with the last aircraft in this phase being the last of the fifteen B-29s deployed to Tinian by the 509th. The additional eight aircraft delivered to Wendover after the last 509th B-29 had departed Wendover for Tinian are included in Phase Four.

The first five aircraft delivered in this phase were assigned to the Test Section of the 216th Base Unit at Wendover for use in the Los Alamos drop test program. The first four B-29s in this group were taken from the Martin Omaha plant assembly line in the standard B-29 configuration and accepted by the Army Air Forces in February 1945. They were then placed in the Omaha Modification Center adjacent to the Martin plant, converted to the Silverplate configuration, and delivered to Wendover in April 1945. The fifth aircraft of this group, 44-27295, was produced on the assembly line as a Silverplate model and delivered to Wendover in March 1945. The five serial numbers were:

B-29-30-MO-42-65384
B-29-30-MO-42-65385
B-29-30-MO-42-65386
B-29-30-MO-42-65387
B-29-36-MO-44-27295

All of the five aircraft listed above were reassigned to Kirtland Air Base in New Mexico after the end of World War II, where they were used in continuing drop tests for Los Alamos (see chapter 4). Two of the aircraft, 42-65385 and 42-65387, were destroyed in crashes during test operations at Kirtland. The remaining three were eventually stripped of their Silverplate components, assigned to other locations and operations not related to the atomic bomb program, and finally declared surplus and scrapped in the latter part of the 1950's.

It should be noted that the block number of 44-27295 was originally 35, but the number was changed by one digit to 36 after delivery from the production line to indicate a difference in configuration from others in block 35.[15] The same situation applied to the first nine B-29s listed below in the group of 15 aircraft assigned to the 393rd Bombardment Squadron.

B-29-36-MO-44-27296
B-29-36-MO-44-27297
B-29-36-MO-44-27298
B-29-36-MO-44-27299
B-29-36-MO-44-27300
B-29-36-MO-44-27301
B-29-36-MO-44-27302
B-29-36-MO-44-27303
B-29-36-MO-44-27304
B-29-40-MO-44-27353
B-29-40-MO-44-27354
B-29-45-MO-44-86291
B-29-45-MO-44-86292
B-29-50-MO-44-86346
B-29-50-MO-44-86347

The fifteen Silverplate B-29s assigned to the 393rd were delivered in increments to the Army Air Forces from the Glenn L. Martin Aircraft Plant in Omaha in the spring of 1945. Four were delivered in March, seven in April, two in May, and two in June. Crews from the 393rd flew the first nine of these aircraft from Omaha to Wendover in April. Two more were flown to Wendover in May and the last four went in June. It is believed that the crew to which a particular aircraft was assigned ferried that B-29 from the Martin Omaha plant to Wendover once it had been accepted by the Army Air Forces.

The crews then flew their assigned aircraft to Tinian, all but two of them departing Wendover during the month of June. The last two, 44-86346 and 44-86347, did not leave Wendover until 26 July because of their use in transporting Fat Man bomb components from Kirtland Army Air Field to Tinian.

Figure 6 shows the northwest end of Tinian as it looked during 509th operations in the summer of 1945. The tip of the island of Saipan can be seen in the upper

2. Development and Production 17

6. Tinian North Field in 1945. (Leon D. Smith)

right hand corner. The parking revetments for the 393rd B-29s are located in the upper portion of the picture. The two pits for loading the atomic and pumpkin bombs into the B-29 bomb bays are in the dark, heart-shaped area above the B-29 revetments. The Project Alberta facilities (see Appendix E for more information on Project Alberta) are to the left of the B-29 parking areas, and the bomb assembly buildings are to the north along the coast. Two of the four east-west runways at North Field are visible in the photograph.

The list below identifies the Silverplate B-29s that were assigned to the 393rd Bombardment (Very Heavy) Squadron of the 509th Composite Group during operations from North Field on Tinian Island from June to November 1945. The combinations of aircraft with crew and Airplane Commander shown in the list were the normal arrangements during operations on Tinian, but variations often occurred. Detailed information concerning each aircraft is contained in the individual Silverplate B-29 histories in Appendix G. Different combinations of airplane and crew on specific missions are shown in Appendix B.

B-29 Aircraft Serial Number	Victor No. Orig	Victor No. Final	Aircraft Name	Crew No.	Airplane Commander
44-27296	4	84	*Some Punkins*	B-7	James N. Price
44-27297	7	77	*Bockscar*	C-13	Frederick C. Bock
44-27298	13	83	*Full House*	A-1	Ralph R. Taylor
44-27299	6	86	*Next Objective*	A-3	Ralph N. Devore
44-27300	3	73	*Strange Cargo*	A-4	Joseph E. Westover
44-27301	5	85	*Straight Flush*	C-11	Claude R. Eatherly
44-27302	2	72	*Top Secret*	B-8	Charles F. McKnight
44-27303	1	71	*Jabit III*	B-6	John A. Wilson
44-27304	8	88	*Up An' Atom*	B-10	George W. Marquardt
44-27353	9	89	*The Great Artiste*	C-15	Charles D. Albury
44-27354	10	90	*Big Stink*	A-5	Thomas J. Classen
44-86291	11	91	*Necessary Evil*	C-14	Norman W. Ray
44-86292	12	82	*Enola Gay*	B-9	Robert A. Lewis
44-86346	-	94	(see below)	C-12	Herman S. Zahn
44-86347	-	95	*Laggin' Dragon*	A-2	Edward M. Costello

The first 13 Silverplate B-29s to arrive on Tinian were assigned Victor call numbers that ran from 1 to 13. The Victor numbers were changed in early August 1945 as shown in the list above. The last two aircraft to deploy to Tinian (44-86346 and 44-86347) arrived after the Victor numbering system was changed. For the Hiroshima mission, the call sign was changed from Victor to Dimples to hide the identity of the unit flying the mission.

Classen and crew A-5 were assigned 44-27354 when it was delivered from the Martin plant in Omaha. They used this B-29 at Wendover, flew it to Tinian, and flew training and combat missions in it during Tinian operations. When Classen and his crew were selected (with Wilson, crew B-6, and 44-27303) to return to Wendover on 9 August to be ready to transport components of the third atomic bomb to Tinian, 44-86346 was selected for their use. Aircraft 44-27354 was then reassigned to Zahn and crew C-12, who had flown 44-86346 to Tinian. The list above reflects the original crew/aircraft assignments and not those that existed after 9 August.

Except for 44-86292 (*Enola Gay*), names were not given and nose art not applied to 509th B-29s until after 9 August 1945. The name *Enola Gay* was painted on 44-86292 on 5 August 1945 (the day before the Hiroshima mission). In addition, 44-27303 and 44-86346 left Tinian on 9 August 1945 and did not receive names and nose art while the 509th was on Tinian. After the 509th returned to Roswell Army Air Field (NM), and probably in 1946, 44-86346 was given nose art and named *Luke The Spook*. It is not known if nose art was ever painted on 44-27303, although it is generally accepted that it was called *Jabit III*.

Serial number 44-27354 (*Big Stink*) was renamed *Dave's Dream* and was the B-29 that dropped a Fat Man atomic bomb on 1 July 1946 in Test Able of Operation Crossroads. It was given the new name in honor of Dave Semple, the bombardier for most of the early Manhattan Project drop testing of bomb prototypes and test models. Semple was scheduled to be the bombardier for Test Able but was killed in a B-29 crash in March 1946.

When the Commanding Officer of the 509th Composite Group, Paul W. Tibbets, flew missions, he usually used 44-86292 (*Enola Gay*) and members of crew B-9. The normal Airplane Commander for this aircraft, Robert A. Lewis, became the pilot and other crew members were replaced according to the mission being flown. The bombardier on the Hiroshima mission was Thomas W. Ferebee and the navigator was Theodore J. Van Kirk. The remaining crew positions were filled by members of crew B-9.

When the Commanding Officer of the 393rd Bombardment Squadron, Charles W. Sweeney, flew missions, he took the position of Airplane Commander on 44-27353 (*The Great Artiste*) with crew C-15. The usual Airplane Commander, Charles D. Albury, became the pilot on such missions. An exception to this routine occurred on the Nagasaki mission when Sweeney and crew C-15 used 44-27297 (*Bockscar*) to carry the Fat Man atomic bomb used at Nagasaki. For this mission, Frederick C. Bock and crew C-13 flew 44-27353 as the instrumentation aircraft.

Other individuals who served as an Airplane Commander on missions during Tinian operations included James I. Hopkins, Jr., the Group Operations Officer, who flew with crew C-14; and Elbert B. Smith who flew with crew A-5 before they returned to the United States on 9 August 1945.

B-29s used in the Pacific in World War II had a unit designator marking painted on the vertical stabilizer/rudder surface. The Silverplate B-29s of the 509th Composite Group used a forward-facing arrow in a circle as their designator until the atomic bombing missions were flown. For the Hiroshima and Nagasaki missions, the tail designators of 509th aircraft were changed to those of other Bombardment Groups operating from Tinian, Saipan, and Guam in order to confuse the Japanese. The changes were:

- Victor numbers 71, 72, 73, and 84 used a plain letter A.
- Victor numbers 77, 85, 86, and 88 used the letter N in a triangle.
- Victor numbers 83, 94, and 95 used the letter P in a square.
- Victor numbers 82, 89, 90, and 91 used the letter R in a circle.

As soon as the 393rd crews arrived on Tinian, they went through a ground indoctrination program to become familiar with 20th Air Force procedures for operations from bases in the Marianas Islands. Beginning on the last day of June and continuing through 18 July, the Silverplate B-29s of the 393rd were used on seven training and orientation missions. There were 27 sorties flown in these missions. Appendix B provides information on the training and orientation missions.

During the period 1 July through 2 August 1945, the B-29s of the 393rd were used on 15 practice bombing missions in which various combinations of 500- and 1,000-pound general purpose (GP) high-explosive bombs were dropped on nearby islands still held by Japanese forces. The islands of Rota, Truk, Guguan, and Marcus were the targets for these 89 bombing sorties. More information on the practice bombing missions is included in chapter 3 and Appendix B.

On 20 July 1945, the 509th began a series of missions in which 10,000-pound, high-explosive bombs known as pumpkins were dropped on Japanese targets. The pumpkin bomb was a Fat Man outer casing filled with 6,300 pounds of a high-explosive mixture known as Composition B. They were fitted with three contact fuses. There were no provisions for radar-operated air burst detonations.

In the sixteen pumpkin missions flown, there were 51 sorties by Silverplate B-29s of the 393rd. Because of two aborts, only 49 of the pumpkin bombs were dropped. In one of the aborted missions, the pumpkin bomb was jettisoned near Iwo Jima. In the second case, the pumpkin bomb was returned to Tinian without mishap. More details of the pumpkin missions are provided in chapter 3 and Appendix B. Additional information on the pumpkin bombs is included in chapter 7.

Five different aircraft of the 393rd were used for tests in which Little Boy and Fat Man models were dropped near Tinian. Four missions were flown to drop Little Boy test units and one mission was flown to transport a Little Boy model to Iwo Jima to test the unloading and loading facility at Iwo Jima. Three Fat Man test articles were dropped prior to the Nagasaki mission. These Little Boy and Fat Man test missions also served as rehearsals for the crews that would fly the Hiroshima and Nagasaki missions. For more information on the Tinian tests, see chapter 4.

The 509th carried out the two missions for which it was organized, trained, and equipped on 6 and 9 August 1945. The Hiroshima mission on 6 August in which *Enola Gay* dropped the Little Boy atomic bomb also involved six other Silverplate B-29s' of the 509th in supporting roles. On 9 August, *Bockscar* was used to drop the Fat Man atomic bomb on Nagasaki with support from five other 509th Silverplate B-29s. A more detailed account of the two atomic missions is provided in chapter 3.

On the day of the Nagasaki mission, two of the Silverplate B-29s from the 509th left Tinian for Wendover Air Field. Classen and crew A-5 flew 44-86346 and Wilson and crew B-6 flew 44-27303. Their mission was to proceed to Wendover and be prepared to transport components of a second Fat Man bomb to Tinian if the need arose. At the time of the two B-29s' departure from Tinian, Los Alamos scientists estimated that the next Fat Man components would be ready for shipment from Kirtland Air Field on about 12 August 1945. The day after the Nagasaki bombing, the Japanese indicated they would surrender and General Groves halted any further shipments of material to Tinian.

44-86346 remained at Wendover with Classen and his crew until November 1945, when they flew it to Roswell Air Field to rejoin the aircraft and crews of the 393rd arriving from Tinian at about the same time. The fate of 44-27303, however, was a somewhat different story. While awaiting further orders at Wendover after returning from Tinian, Wilson and his crew flew 44-27303 on a cross-country training mission. On 29 September 1945, a mishap during a landing at the Chicago Municipal Airport resulted in damage to 44-27303 so severe that the aircraft was scrapped at that location (see chapter 5).

The 13 Silverplate B-29s of the 393rd that remained on Tinian after the war ended were finally flown back to Roswell in November 1945. At Roswell during this period, they were joined by 44-86346 from Wendover and seven of the eight Silverplate B-29s covered in Phase Four.

Of the 15 aircraft delivered to the 509th in this phase, four were ultimately lost to accidents, two were transferred to museums (*Enola Gay* and *Bockscar*), three were transferred to the U.S. Navy for use as gunnery and bombing targets at China Lake, and six were eventually declared surplus and scrapped.

Phase Four — Final Production

The eight aircraft included in this phase were delivered to Wendover Army Air Field after the last of the 509th B-29s had departed for Tinian. They were built at the Martin Omaha plant in the standard Silverplate configuration established for the group of 28 aircraft produced during 1945 under Project 98228-S.

Two of the aircraft in this phase were first delivered in August 1945 to Wright Army Air Field in Ohio for additional Silverplate modifications. They were then assigned to the Test section of the 216th Base Unit at Wendover in October for use in further Los Alamos drop tests of atomic bomb models. In November 1945, they were both reassigned to the 509th Composite Group and flown to Roswell Army Air Field. The serial numbers of these two Silverplate B-29s were:

B-29-60-MO-44-86430   B-29-60-MO-44-86432

Both of the above aircraft were assigned to Task Force 1.5 in March 1946 for use in Test Able of Operation Crossroads, then reassigned to the 509th in August 1946. They were both involved in additional assignments to other units and locations and were eventually declared surplus and scrapped many years later.

Four of the remaining six B-29s in this phase were delivered to Wendover in August 1945. The last two of the six were delivered to Wendover in October of that year. All six were assigned to the 509th Composite Group as reserve aircraft in case replacements were needed on Tinian. All were flown to Roswell in November 1945 to supplement the 509th aircraft flown back from Tinian at the same time. The serial numbers of these six Silverplate B-29s were:

| B-29-55-MO-44-86382 | B-29-55-MO-44-86384 | B-29-60-MO-44-86472 |
| B-29-55-MO-44-86383 | B-29-60-MO-44-86431 | B-29-60-MO-44-86473 |

Records show that 44-86472 and 44-86473 were among the last B-29s produced at the Glenn L. Martin Aircraft plant in Omaha, Nebraska. The plant ceased production and closed within 30 days of V-J Day as the U.S. began to close war production plants and demobilize immediately after the end of World War II.

As a sad footnote to the story of these six aircraft, five were lost to accidents within a few years of their delivery. Serial number 44-86384 was the only one to serve in several assignments and eventually be declared surplus and scrapped.

Phase Five — Additional Requirements

As 1945 came to a close, a total of 46 Silverplate B-29s had been produced. This total included the prototype, 17 delivered in the first group in late 1944, and 28 produced in 1945. There were 22 Silverplate B-29s assigned to the 509th Composite Group at Roswell Army Air Field and seven B-29s in the Silverplate configuration at Wendover and Kirtland involved in Los Alamos bomb tests. The remaining 17 aircraft had been placed in storage.

On 21 March 1946, the 509th became the nuclear strike element of the newly established Strategic Air Command, and on 6 May 1946 two additional bombardment squadrons, the 715th and the 830th, joined the 393rd as combat elements of the 509th. The B-29s assigned to the 509th were distributed among the three squadrons. The parent organization of the 509th was the 58th Bombardment Wing.

In December 1945, the B-29s of the 509th started cycling through the Oklahoma City Air Materiel Area depot at Tinker Air Field in Oklahoma for installation of the MX-344 radar computer, more easily removed engine cowlings, winterization for Arctic operations, and other miscellaneous modifications to improve performance. Then in January 1946, ten of the recycled aircraft were assigned to Task Force 1.5 of Operation Crossroads for use in the Pacific atomic bomb tests. The nine Silverplate B-29s actually deployed for Operation Crossroads all returned to Roswell Air Field in early July 1946.

In accordance with decisions in Washington for an expanded and improved atomic strike force in the Strategic Air Command, the Air Materiel Command issued orders on 26 July 1946 for the modification of 19 additional B-29s to the Silverplate configuration.[16] The aircraft were removed from storage locations in mid–1946 and flown to the Sacramento Air Materiel Area depot facility at McClellan Air Field in California, which had been selected as the location for the modification effort under Project DOM-515C. Twelve of the B-29s had been originally produced at the Martin Omaha plant, while seven had been built at the Boeing Wichita plant in Kansas.

All of the Silverplate B-29s listed below were delivered from the McClellan depot facility during 1947, with the last aircraft completed in December. Three of the 19 aircraft were later involved in accidents and were salvaged, but nine served in various assignments before being eventually declared surplus and scrapped. Four were transferred to the U.S. Army for tests at the Aberdeen Proving Ground in Maryland, two were turned over to the U.S. Navy for use as targets at the China Lake facility in California, and one was tested to destruction by the U.S. Air Force.

The serial numbers of the three modified Silverplate B-29s assigned to Kirtland Air Field in mid–1947 for use in atomic bomb development tests were:

B-29-60-MO-44-86444   B-29-60-MO-44-86447   B-29-90-BW-45-21818

The serial numbers of the 16 aircraft assigned to the 509th at Roswell after completion of the Silverplate modifications at McClellan were:

B-29-40-MO-44-86263   B-29-60-MO-44-86443   B-29-90-BW-44-87771
B-29-55-MO-44-86394   B-29-60-MO-44-86445   B-29-90-BW-44-87774
B-29-55-MO-44-86401   B-29-60-MO-44-86448   B-29-90-BW-45-21707
B-29-60-MO-44-86437   B-29-60-MO-44-86451   B-29-90-BW-45-21736
B-29-60-MO-44-86439   B-29-90-BW-44-87752   B-29-90-BW-45-21739
B-29-60-MO-44-86440

During the period in which the 19 aircraft in this phase were being modified to the Silverplate configuration, the use of the Silverplate code word came to an abrupt end. In a letter from Army Air Forces headquarters to the Air Materiel Command on 12 May 1947, further use of the code name Silverplate was prohibited because the security of its meaning had been compromised.[17] A second letter on the same date directed the use of the term Saddletree as the new code word for "The overall modification of the B-29 aircraft necessary for the transport of Atomic Bombs." The code word change had no effect on the modification of the 19 aircraft at the McClellan depot. Although 12 of the 19 aircraft included in this phase were not delivered out of the McClellan modification facility until after the code name was changed to Saddletree, they are still classified as Silverplate B-29s in this narrative since they entered into the modification process under the Silverplate code name.

Phase Six — Saddletree

The basic purpose of the Saddletree project remained the same as that of Silverplate, which was to equip U.S. bomber aircraft to carry the atomic bomb. However, the scope of the project was expanded to include additional types of bombers and to incorporate further improvements in aircraft capabilities.

After a number of planning studies during the latter half of 1947, the Joint Chiefs of Staff issued a directive in January 1948 for the Saddletree modification of 225 bombers. The program was to include 80 B-29s plus quantities of B-50 and B-36 aircraft, and was to be completed by December 1948. Air Materiel Command Project DOM-595C was established on 15 March 1948 for the B-29 modification effort.[18]

On 16 April 1948, Air Force Headquarters directed the use of the code word GEM for the overall program of modifications and improvements designed to provide the U.S. with an atomic strike capability. The Saddletree project, as it applied to the next group of B-29s to be modified was part of Program GEM. Other projects beside Saddletree involved B-50 and B-36 bombers, enhanced communications and radar systems, capabilities for air-to-air refueling (Ruralist and Superman), and winterization for operations in the far northern latitudes.

The B-29 segment of GEM included winterization modifications for 36 of the 80 aircraft as part of Project DOM-595C. It also included the addition of Ruralist capabilities for receiving air-to-air refueling for 36 of the 80 aircraft under Project DOM-599C. Exact serial numbers for the B-29s modified to carry atomic bombs under the Saddletree project have not been identified; however the list provided by Lloyd states that the ranges for GEM/Saddletree aircraft were 44-61910 through 44-62329 and 44-87634 and subsequent numbers.

Without an exact identification of the Saddletree serial numbers, it is not possible to describe the delivery schedule. Given that the last Silverplate B-29 was completed at the Sacramento facility in December 1947, it is highly probable that the production of Saddletree B-29s continued through 1948 and possibly into 1949. It should also be noted that there is some confusion as to the total number of B-29s included in the Saddletree project, with Fenwick's history of Saddletree referencing both 80 and 82 as the number of aircraft involved. The quantity of 80 seems more likely and that is the number used in this story.

Summary

With 65 Silverplate B-29s and 80 Saddletree B-29s, the fleet of B-29s capable of carrying atomic bombs totaled 145 over the period from early 1944 on into the 1950s. Of this total, 28 were assigned to test and training activities and 117 were involved in operational assignments.

The totals shown for test purposes in the table below were assigned to either the 216th Base Unit at Wendover or the 428th Base Unit at Kirtland. It should be noted that four of the 14 aircraft initially assigned to the 509th at Wendover in phase 2 were later reassigned to the 216th Base Unit at Wendover in early 1945. In addition, the two aircraft shown as being assigned for test purposes at Wendover in phase 4 were subsequently reassigned to the 509th at Roswell Army Air Field in late 1946.

The totals for initial assignments of the Silverplate B-29s for each of the five phases described earlier in this chapter are shown in the table below.

Phase	Total	509th	Test
1	1	-	1
2	17	14	3
3	20	15	5
4	8	6	2
5	19	16	3
Totals	65	51	14

The final disposition of the 65 Silverplate B-29s is covered in chapter 9.

3 Combat Operations

Silverplate B-29s deserve historical note by virtue of their use in atomic bombings in August 1945, but a lesser known fact is that they were also used for other combat missions over Japanese territory before and after the Hiroshima and Nagasaki flights. The purpose of this chapter is to provide details of both the atomic and non-atomic combat operations.

The fifteen Silverplate B-29s that operated from North Field on Tinian were assigned to the 509th Composite Group, a unit with a somewhat unusual organizational structure. Because of security concerns and the need for self-contained capabilities, the 509th was equipped with most of the resources needed for combat and required little assistance from other units on Tinian. Within the 509th organization were elements to provide air operations, maintenance, supply, ordnance, airlift, administration, security, and support from the Manhattan Project.

The 509th Composite Group was attached to the 313th Bombardment Wing of the 20th Air Force for administrative purposes while it was stationed on Tinian. Operational control was maintained by 20th Air Force Headquarters in Washington, DC, and to a great extent, by General Groves of the Manhattan Project. The Manhattan Project support was provided by Project Alberta personnel, known officially as the 1st Technical Services Detachment. The detachment of Manhattan Project personnel, mostly from Los Alamos, was attached to the 509th for administrative and logistic support (see Appendix E).

The authorized strength of the 509th was 225 officers and 1,542 enlisted men for a total of 1,767 personnel. In addition, there were 51 Project Alberta officials, scientists, engineers, and technicians from Los Alamos assigned to the 1st Technical Services Detachment to perform assembly and other functions associated with the atomic bombs. The roster of 509th and Project Alberta personnel on Tinian included in Appendix D is considered to be quite accurate. It lists 1,768 men in the 509th, 51 individuals in Project Alberta, and two representatives from Washington for a total of 1,821 people.

As a matter of historical accuracy, the 320th Troop Carrier Squadron did not officially transfer from Wendover Army Air Field to Tinian. Although the C-54 aircraft of the 320th constantly shuttled back and forth between locations in the United States and Tinian, the base of operations of the 320th remained at Wendover.

The combat element of the Group, the 393rd Bombardment (VH) Squadron, was organized with a headquarters section and three flights of crews, designated A, B, and C. The headquarters staff included the Commanding Officer and personnel responsible for operations planning, engineering, armament, radar, and communications. The flight crews, primary Airplane Commanders, normally assigned aircraft, Tinian arrival date, and number of practice bombing and combat missions flown by the crews are listed below. The date of arrival is an estimate based on the known date of departure from Wendover Army Air Field. For more information regarding alternate Airplane Commanders, see the listing and information included in chapter 2.

Crew	Primary Airplane Commander	Aircraft	Arr Date	Practice Bombings	Combat Missions Pumpkin	Atomic
A-1	Ralph R. Taylor, Jr.	44-27298	16 June	8	4	2
A-2	Edward M. Costello	44-86347	2 August	0	0	0
A-3	Ralph N. Devore	44-27299	16 June	10	5	0
A-4	Joseph E. Westover	44-27300	10 June	8	4	0
A-5	Thomas J. Classen	44-27354	24 June	2	3	0
B-6	John A. Wilson	44-27303	10 June	10	3	1
B-7	James N. Price, Jr.	44-27296	13 June	9	5	0
B-8	Charles F. McKnight	44-27302	10 June	9	4	2
B-9	Robert A. Lewis	44-86292	6 July	2	4	1
B-10	George W. Marquardt	44-27304	16 June	7	2	2
C-11	Claude R. Eatherly	44-27301	13 June	8	5	1
C-12	Herman S. Zahn, Jr.	44-86346	2 August	0	0	0
C-13	Frederick C. Bock	44-27297	16 June	11	4	1
C-14	Norman W. Ray	44-86291	2 July	2	4	1
C-15	Charles D. Albury	44-27353	27 June	3	4	2

After arrival on Tinian, each crew went through ground indoctrination to become familiar with 20th Air Force and Tinian air operations procedures. The ground training was followed by several training and orientation flights in the vicinity of Tinian and a number of practice bombing missions to nearby islands still held by Japanese forces.

In the practice bombing missions, the Silverplate B-29s dropped 500- or 1,000-pound general purpose, high-explosive bombs on the islands of Rota, Truk, Guguan, and Marcus. No credit for a combat mission was given on these practice bombing runs. The listing above shows the number of these type missions flown by each crew.[1] More information on the practice bombing missions is provided in chapter 7 and Appendix B.

The 509th flew a total of 64 combat sorties in 18 missions over Japanese targets during July and August 1945 (a sortie is defined as one aircraft as part of an overall mission). Bombs were dropped on targets in 51 of these sorties, including the two atomic bombs dropped on Hiroshima and Nagasaki. The sorties were:

- 51 sorties with pumpkin bombs. Two of these sorties were aborted.
- Two sorties with atomic bombs (Little Boy and Fat Man).
- Eleven sorties in support of the atomic bombing missions (photography, instrumentation, weather reconnaissance, and standby aircraft on Iwo Jima).

Pumpkin Missions

The pumpkin bombs carried on 51 sorties were Fat Man shapes filled with 6,300 pounds of high explosives. The overall weight of the pumpkin bomb was about 10,000 pounds. The most noticeable differences in the pumpkins from the atomic Fat Man bomb were the use of three contact fuzes on the nose instead of four, a welded mid-section joint instead of eight bolt/nut assemblies, and the absence of radar antennas. Additional information on the pumpkin bombs is included in chapter 7.

The 509th record of pumpkin missions in 1945 included:

- Four missions with ten sorties on 20 July (with one abort).
- Three missions with ten sorties on 24 July.
- Two missions with ten sorties on 26 July.
- Three missions with eight sorties on 29 July.
- Two missions with six sorties on 8 August (with one abort).
- Two missions with seven sorties on 14 August.

Two of the 15 Silverplate B-29s assigned to the 509th did not fly any pumpkin missions due to their late arrival on Tinian (44-86346 and 44-86347). The crews that flew the 13 aircraft used on the pumpkin missions sometimes flew B-29s other than the aircraft shown as normally assigned in the listing on the previous page.

The listing that follows provides information on the pumpkin missions on which each Silverplate B-29 was used in July and August 1945. The material for this listing was extracted from 20th Air Force mission planning documentation, 509th Operations Orders, a 20th Air Force Tactical Mission Report, and 509th Mission Reports. A complete listing of all missions (orientation, training, practice bombing, and combat) is shown in Appendix B.

The notation "Tgt of Opp" under the Target Category column in the list means a target of opportunity (i.e., a target other than the primary or secondary). The bombing altitude for all of the pumpkin missions was about 30,000 feet. The entries in the Results column were taken from the 509th mission reports.[2]

Date	Crew	Airplane Commander	Target Category	Bombing Method	Results	Target Area
44-27296 (*Some Punkins*)						
20 Jul	B-7	Price	Primary	Radar	Unobserved	Toyama
24 Jul	B-7	Price	Primary	Radar	Unobserved	Ogaki
26 Jul	B-7	Price	Secondary	Visual	Very Poor	Shimoda
8 Aug	B-7	Price	Primary	Visual	Poor	Yokkaichi
14 Aug	B-7	Price	Primary	Visual	Poor	Nagoya
44-27297 (*Bockscar*)						
24 Jul	C-13	Bock	Primary	Visual	Excellent	Fukushima
26 Jul	C-15	Albury	Secondary	Radar	Unobserved	Toyama
29 Jul	C-13	Bock	Secondary	Visual	Poor	Mushashino

Date	Crew	Airplane Commander	Target Category	Bombing Method	Results	Target Area
44-27298 (*Full House*)						
20 Jul	A-1	Taylor	Primary	Visual	Poor	Toyama
24 Jul	A-1	Taylor	Primary	Visual	Excellent	Niihama
26 Jul	A-1	Taylor	Tgt of Opp	Radar	Poor	Yaizu
29 Jul	A-1	Taylor	Primary	Visual	Poor	Ube
14 Aug	C-13	Bock	Primary	Visual	Excellent	Koroma
44-27299 (*Next Objective*)						
20 Jul	A-3	Devore	Primary	Visual	Very Poor	Toyama
24 Jul	A-3	Devore	Secondary	Visual	Excellent	Niihama
8 Aug	A-3	Devore	Mission aborted[3]			
14 Aug	A-3	Devore	Primary	Visual	Poor	Nagoya
44-27300 (*Strange Cargo*)						
20 Jul	C-13	Bock	Primary	Radar	Unobserved	Fukushima
24 Jul	A-4	Westover	Primary	Visual	Excellent	Kobe
8 Aug	A-4	Westover	Secondary	Visual	Excellent	Tsuruga
14 Aug	A-4	Westover	Tgt of Opp	Visual	Excellent	Nagoya
44-27301 (*Straight Flush*)						
20 Jul	C-11	Eatherly	Tgt of Opp	Radar	Unobserved	Tokyo
24 Jul	C-11	Eatherly	Secondary	Visual	Excellent	Otsu
26 Jul	C-11	Eatherly	Tgt of Opp	Visual	Poor	Tsugawa
29 Jul	C-11	Eatherly	Secondary	Visual	Excellent	Maizuru
14 Aug	C-15	Albury	Primary	Visual	Poor	Koroma
44-27302 (*Top Secret*)						
20 Jul	B-8	McKnight	Secondary	Radar	Unobserved	Otsu
24 Jul	B-8	McKnight	Secondary	Visual	Excellent	Yokkaichi
26 Jul	A-4	Westover	Tgt of Opp	Visual	Poor	Taira
29 Jul	B-8	McKnight	Primary	Visual	Excellent	Ube
8 Aug	C-11	Eatherly	Primary	Visual	Poor	Yokkaichi
14 Aug	B-8	McKnight	Primary	Visual	Poor	Koroma
44-27303 (*Jabit III*)						
20 Jul	B-6	Wilson	Secondary	Radar	Unobserved	Taira
26 Jul	A-3	Devore	Secondary	Visual	Good	Osaka
29 Jul	B-6	Wilson	Primary	Visual	Poor	Ube
8 Aug	B-6	Wilson	Secondary	Visual	Good	Uwajima
44-27304 (*Up an' Atom*)						
20 Jul	B-10	Marquardt	Secondary	Radar	Unobserved	Taira
26 Jul	B-10	Marquardt	Secondary	Radar	Unobserved	Hamamatsu
29 Jul	A-5	Smith	Secondary	Visual	Unobserved	Wakayama
8 Aug	B-9	Lewis	Tgt of Opp	Visual	Poor	Tokushima
14 Aug	C-14	Hopkins	Primary	Visual	Poor	Nagoya
44-27353 (*The Great Artiste*)						
20 Jul	C-15	Albury	Mission aborted[4]			
24 Jul	C-15	Albury	Primary	Visual	Excellent	Kobe
29 Jul	B-9	Lewis	Primary	Visual	Excellent	Koriyama
44-27354 (*Big Stink*)						
20 Jul	A-5	Classen	Primary	Radar	Unobserved	Nagaoka
26 Jul	A-5	Classen	Tgt of Opp	Visual	Good	Hitachi

Date	Crew	Airplane Commander	Target Category	Bombing Method	Results	Target Area
44-86291 (Necessary Evil)						
24 Jul	C-14	Ray	Primary	Visual	Excellent	Kobe
26 Jul	C-14	Ray	Secondary	Radar	Unobserved	Kashiwazaki
29 Jul	C-14	Ray	Primary	Visual	Poor	Koriyama
44-86292 (Enola Gay)						
24 Jul	B-9	Lewis	Primary	Visual	Unobserved	Kobe
26 Jul	B-9	Lewis	Secondary	Radar	Unobserved	Koriyama

44-86346 (Luke the Spook)
No pumpkin missions were flown in this aircraft.

44-86347 (Laggin' Dragon)
No pumpkin missions were flown in this aircraft.

As a note of explanation, Silverplate B-29s 44-86346 and 44-86347 did not arrive on Tinian until 2 August 1945, which was after the majority of the pumpkin missions had been flown. In the case of 44-86346, it departed Tinian on 9 August on a mission back to the United States (see individual history in Appendix G). 44-86347 was used for the weather reconnaissance mission over Nagasaki on 9 August.

One of the most unusual pumpkin missions was the one flown by Claude Eatherly and crew C-11 in 44-27301 on 20 July. With cloud cover obscuring their primary and secondary targets, Eatherly and his crew decided to drop their pumpkin bomb on a target of opportunity, the Imperial Palace in Tokyo. Because of clouds over Tokyo, the bomb run was made using radar. The bomb missed the Emperor's palace and hit a railway station. Had the bomb hit the palace, Eatherly would undoubtedly have been in trouble.[5]

The United States Strategic Bombing Survey was established by the U.S. Secretary of War in November 1944 to assess the effectiveness of the bombing campaign on Germany in World War II. In August 1945, the Survey team was directed to conduct a similar study of the effects of the air attack on Japan. Because of their unusual weight, a special survey of the damage caused by the pumpkin bombs was completed and a report issued in May 1947.

The Survey team examined the damage caused by pumpkins in nine incidents. The general conclusion of the Survey was that the pumpkin bomb's biggest damage agent was blast, and that it was a reasonably effective weapon against Japanese factories when a direct hit was scored in a vital area.

Hiroshima Mission

On 6 August 1945, the Little Boy atomic bomb was dropped on Hiroshima. The mission plan included the use of seven Silverplate B-29s. Three aircraft were used for weather reconnaissance over the three potential targets one hour in advance of the strike force, one B-29 carried blast measurement instrumentation packages that were dropped simultaneously with the bomb, and one aircraft was equipped with cameras to photograph the detonation. The *Enola Gay* was the bomb carrier and one aircraft was pre-positioned at Iwo Jima as a backup in case of an emergency.

The aircraft, crews, Airplane Commanders, and their functions on the Hiroshima atomic bombing mission on 6 August 1945 were[6]:

44-86292	*Enola Gay*	B-9	Tibbets	Carried Little Boy atomic bomb
44-27353	*The Great Artiste*	C-15	Sweeney	Blast measurement instrumentation
44-86291	*Necessary Evil*	B-10	Marquardt	Photographic equipment
44-27301	*Straight Flush*	C-11	Eatherly	Advanced weather at Hiroshima
44-27303	*Jabit III*	B-6	Wilson	Advanced weather at Kokura
44-27298	*Full House*	A-1	Taylor	Advanced weather at Nagasaki
44-27354	*Big Stink*	B-8	McKnight	Backup at Iwo Jima

7. Personnel on *Enola Gay* on Hiroshima Mission. ***Bottom row (left to right):*** Jacob Beser (electronic counter-measures), Morris Jeppson (electronics test officer), Dutch Van Kirk (navigator), Tom Ferebee (bombardier), William "Deak" Parsons (bomb commander), Paul W. Tibbets (airplane commander), Robert Lewis (pilot). ***Standing in the back (left to right):*** Robert Shumard (assistant engineer), Richard Nelson (radio operator), Joseph Stiborik (radar operator), Wyatt Duzenbury (flight engineer), George Caron (tail gunner). (Robert W. Krauss)

3. Combat Operations

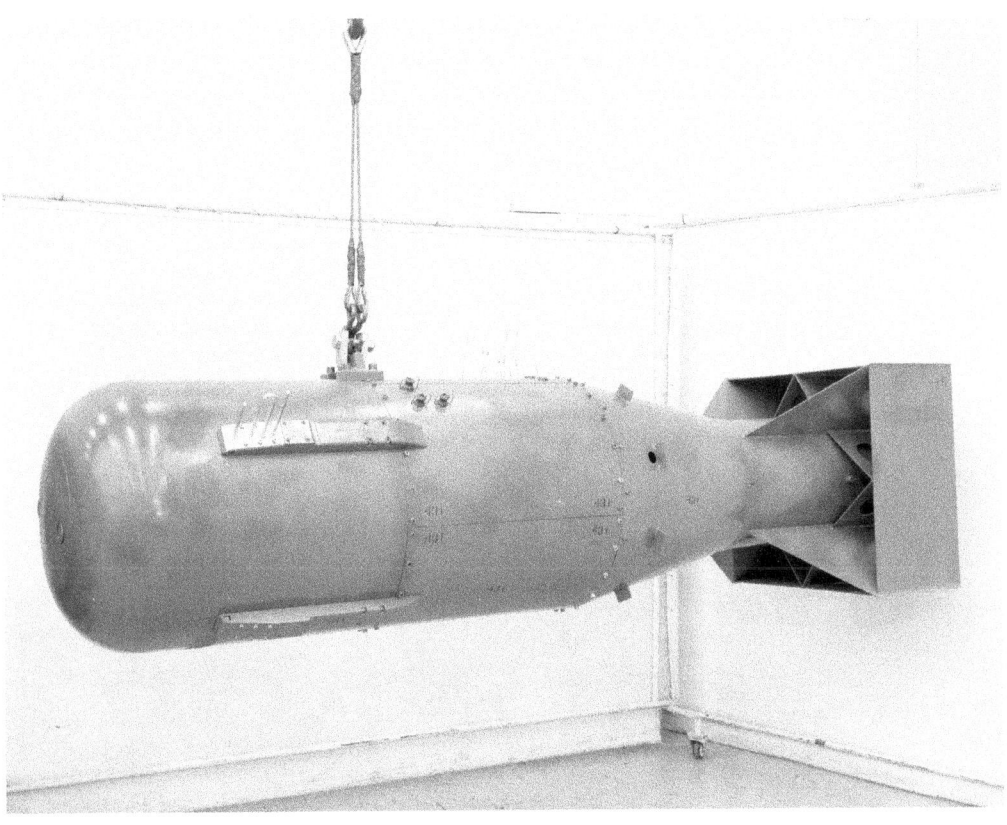

8. Little Boy Casing. (National Atomic Museum)

The Hiroshima mission was scheduled as 20th Air Force Special Bombing Mission Number 13 under Field Order Number 13, dated 2 August 1945. 509th Operations Order number 35 was issued for the mission in accordance with the 20th Air Force tasking. Takeoff was at 2:45 A.M., the Little Boy bomb was released over the target at 9:15 A.M., and *Enola Gay* landed back at Tinian at 2:58 P.M. (times are Tinian time). The total elapsed time for the mission was 12 hours and 13 minutes. Figure 7 shows all of the individuals that were on *Enola Gay* for the mission,[7] including those persons not normally included in a Silverplate crew.[8]

Figure 8 shows a Little Boy casing that was photographed many years ago in the National Atomic Museum in Albuquerque, New Mexico. Information on the design and operation of the Little Boy atomic bomb is included in chapter 7.

Nagasaki Mission

The Nagasaki mission in which the Fat Man atomic bomb was dropped was carried out on 9 August 1945. The primary target was Kokura, but haze conditions prevented visual release of the bomb and the strike force proceeded to the secondary target, which was Nagasaki. The six 509th B-29s involved in the mission included two aircraft for advance weather reconnaissance over the two potential targets, one B-29 with the blast measurement instrumentation, and one aircraft equipped with special cameras. *Bockscar* carried the Fat Man bomb and one aircraft was pre-positioned at Iwo Jima in case of an emergency. The aircraft, crews, Airplane Commanders, and their functions on the Nagasaki mission were:

44-27297	*Bockscar*	C-15	Sweeney	Carried Fat Man atomic bomb
44-27353	*The Great Artiste*	C-13	Bock	Blast measurement instrumentation
44-27354	*Big Stink*	C-14	Hopkins	Photographic equipment
44-86292	*Enola Gay*	B-10	Marquardt	Advanced weather at Kokura
44-86347	*Laggin' Dragon*	B-8	McKnight	Advanced weather at Nagasaki
44-27298	*Full House*	A-1	Taylor	Backup at Iwo Jima

Figure 9 shows the entire complement of personnel on **Bockscar** for the Nagasaki mission, including individuals not normally assigned to a Silverplate crew.[9]

9. Personnel on *Bockscar* on Nagasaki Mission. *Bottom row (left to right):* **Philip Barnes** (electronics test officer), Jacob Beser (electronic counter-measures), Fred Olivi (co-pilot), Kermit Beahan (bombardier), Don Albury (pilot), James Van Pelt (navigator), Charles Sweeney (airplane commander), Frederick Ashworth (bomb commander). *Standing in the back row (left to right):* **John Kuharek** (flight engineer), Abe Spitzer (radio operator), Ray Gallagher (assistant engineer), Ed Buckley (radar operator), Al Dehart (tail gunner). (Robert W. Krauss)

3. Combat Operations

10. Fat Man Dropped on Nagasaki. (Robert W. Krauss)

The Nagasaki mission was flown as 20th Air Force Special Bombing Mission Number 16 under Field Order Number 17, dated 8 August 1945. 509th Operations Order number 39 was issued for the mission in accordance with 20th Air Force tasking. Takeoff was at 3:49 A.M. on 9 August, but the Fat Man bomb was not released over Nagasaki until 11:58 A.M. that morning because of two difficulties. Figure 10 shows the actual Fat Man bomb used on the mission.

The first unplanned situation was a delay at the rendezvous point while Sweeney in *Bockscar* and Bock in *The Great Artiste* waited for the photo aircraft (Hopkins in *Big Stink*) to arrive. The photo aircraft never did find the rendezvous point and, after waiting 45 minutes, Sweeney and Ashworth finally decided (mutually, it is believed) to proceed with the mission.

The second problem was that the primary target (Kokura) was obscured by clouds, and even though three bomb runs were attempted the bomb could not be released. Under orders to drop the bomb only under visual conditions, Sweeney was forced to move on to the secondary target (Nagasaki). With fuel running low, a bomb run using radar was initiated, but at the very end of the run a break in the clouds enabled the bombardier to sight the ground and release the bomb visually.

Due to the fuel shortage caused by the delay at the rendezvous point, *Bockscar* made an emergency landing on Okinawa at 2:00 P.M., and after three hours at Yontan Air Base, it finally made it back to Tinian at 11:06 P.M.[10] The total mission time was 19 hours and 17 minutes, including the three hours on the ground on Okinawa.[11]

Additional information on the design and operation of the Fat Man atomic bomb is included in chapter 7.

Preparing and Loading the Bombs

The pumpkin bombs arrived on Tinian from the Navy storage facility in the San Francisco bay area by boat and were placed in a bomb storage area (see chapter 7 for more details on the manufacture of the pumpkin bombs). The components for the atomic bombs were transported to Tinian by air (see the latter part of this chapter for more details).

There was little preparation required for the pumpkin bombs before they were moved to the loading pit area for mounting in the Silverplate B-29s. The atomic bombs (test models and live units) were assembled and tested in one of the assembly buildings located a short distance from the loading pits before they were transported to one of the loading pits.

The two loading pits constructed on Tinian were essentially the same as those built at Wendover and Kirtland. The pits were concrete lined and were about 20 feet long, 10 feet wide, and 8 feet deep. A hydraulic lift (similar to those found in auto

11. Atomic Bomb Assembly Building on Tinian. (Air Force Historical Research Agency)

12. Bomb Trailer over Loading Pit. (National Archives and Records Administration)

service facilities) was installed in the center of the bottom of the pit. Controls for operating the hydraulic lift were mounted on one wall.

The process for loading a pumpkin or atomic bomb unit into a Silverplate B-29 was the same for such an operation on Tinian as it was at Wendover and Kirtland Army Air Fields. The first step was to transport the unit from the storage or assembly area to the loading pit. This was accomplished by loading the bomb on a cradle which was mounted on a transport trailer. The cradle was attached to the trailer with four large pins, which could be removed when the bomb and cradle were to be lifted off the trailer.

The loaded trailer was then towed to the loading pit and positioned across the loading pit on rails as shown in the photograph in Figure 12. This photograph shows the loading operation on Tinian for the Fat Man bomb used on the Nagasaki mission.

The next step in the loading process was to raise the trailer a foot or so and then remove the rails. The trailer was then rotated so that it was aligned with the long dimension of the pit. The photograph in Figure 13 shows the trailer with the Fat Man bomb used on the Nagasaki mission in this position.

The trailer, with the bomb mounted on the cradle, was then lowered to the bottom of the pit. The pins holding the cradle to the frame of the trailer were then removed so that the bomb and cradle were ready to be lifted up into the front bomb

13. Ready to Lower Fat Man Bomb into Loading Pit. (National Archives and Records Administration)

bay of the Silverplate B-29 with the transport trailer remaining at the bottom of the pit.

The next step in the loading process was to position the aircraft over the loading pit. On Tinian this was accomplished by backing the aircraft over the pit with the left and right main landing gears straddling the pit.

Enola Gay was moved into position for loading the Little Boy bomb by a ground service vehicle using a tow bar connected to the front landing gear structure. *Bockscar* moved back over the loading pit for receiving the Fat Man bomb by using reverse pitch on its propellers for thrust and its main landing gear brakes for steering. The photograph in Figure 14 shows *Enola Gay* being backed over the loading pit.

Once the aircraft was correctly positioned over the loading pit, the cradle and bomb were raised up into the bomb bay by the hydraulic lift. The photograph in Figure 15 shows the cradle and bomb entering the front bomb bay with the piston of the lift almost fully extended. With the bomb in position, the bomb bay shackle was attached to the lug on the bomb and sway braces were installed to keep the bomb firmly mounted. The final step in the loading process was to add any final pieces of equipment to the bomb (such as contact fuses and radar antennas) and to attach the various cables from points in the bomb bay to the bomb. As described in chapter 7, these cables provided aircraft power to the bomb and established circuits for monitoring the condition of the bomb and controlling equipment inside the bomb.

14. *Enola Gay* and a Loading Pit on Tinian. (Air Force Historical Research Agency)

As a final note on the loading process for the pumpkin and atomic bombs, the reason for the use of loading pits was that the bombs were too big to be simply wheeled under the aircraft and lifted into the bomb bay. As future versions of nuclear bombs became smaller, loading pits were no longer needed. The loading pits on Tinian and at Kirtland have been filled in, but at least one of the three pits at Wendover has been excavated and can be viewed by visitors.

Special Topics

Three aspects of the atomic bombing phase of the combat operations on Tinian deserve special mention as a result of confusion and controversy that has developed since 1945. The first item concerns the matter of where the atomic bombs were assembled and how the bomb materials got to Tinian. The second area of confusion relates to a third (second Fat Man) bomb that might have been used if the war had not ended when it did. The third subject concerns the directive for the atomic missions.

With regard to the transportation and assembly of the atomic bombs, the eyewitness accounts of Ramsey and Russ should be sufficient to convince anyone that the final assembly of the bombs took place on Tinian. Yet, Rowe in his book, *Project W-47*, makes the claim that the bombs were assembled at Wendover and then flown to Tinian. His assertion is not true, and others who have made similar statements based on his book are equally in error.

15. Hydraulic Lift Piston Extended. (Los Alamos National Library)

The best description of the transportation of the bomb materials from the United States to Tinian is found in a memorandum dated 17 August 1945 from Major J.A. Derry to Admiral W.S. De Lany. Major Derry was an Army Corps of Engineers officer in General Groves' office in Washington. Admiral De Lany is believed to have been in a U.S. Navy position in Washington responsible for liaison with the Manhattan Project. The memorandum is one of two documents replicated at the end of this chapter.

The three B-29s mentioned in the last paragraph of the memorandum were 42-65386, 44-86346, and 44-86347. For more details on these three Silverplate B-29s, refer to their individual histories in Appendix G. Several documents found in the Los Alamos archives record the fact that a loading pit was constructed on a remote part of Kirtland Army Air Field for the specific purpose of installing the Fat Man units in these three aircraft.

The "3 HE preassemblies of the implosion type bomb encased in the outer shell" referenced in Derry's memorandum were Fat Man units designated as F31, F32, and F33. None of the three units contained a plutonium core during the transportation to Tinian. Assembly F33 (without the core) was dropped near Tinian on 8 August 1945 in a rehearsal for what turned out to be the Nagasaki mission. Sweeney and crew C-15, using Silverplate B-29 44-27297, conducted this test. They also conducted two earlier drop tests of Fat Man test units near Tinian on 1 and 5 August 1945, using 44-27297.

The Fat Man assembly designated F31 was used in the Nagasaki mission on 9 August 1945. After arrival on 2 August, it was partially disassembled in order to check the high explosive lenses for damage and to prepare the inner components for final assembly. These preparations included insertion of the initiator in the center of the plutonium core, installation of the core in the insertion capsule, and emplacement of the capsule into the sphere assembly (see chapter 7 for details on the Fat Man assembly).

The plutonium core (mounted in its insertion capsule) for Fat Man unit F31 arrived on Tinian on 28 July 1945 after leaving Kirtland on 26 July 1945. It was the only cargo on a C-54 of the 320th Troop Carrier Squadron, the transportation arm of the 509th. There were actually two C-54s of the 320th that made the trip, with one serving as a backup in case of problems with the primary aircraft. Military intelligence officer Lieutenant Colonel Peer de Silva was the official courier of the pit for the trip to Tinian.

The second subject of some debate over the years is whether or not there was a third bomb (a second Fat Man unit), and if there was, where was it and what happened to it. There have been stories that a completely assembled Fat Man was ready at Wendover for transport to Tinian. There have even been claims that this Fat Man unit was loaded into an airplane sometime after 9 August and was somewhere over California en route to Tinian when it was recalled. Neither story is true.

The truth of the matter is that the non-nuclear components for a second Fat Man bomb were available on Tinian immediately after the Nagasaki mission on 9 August 1945. Fat Man assembly F32 was one of the three units referenced in the last paragraph of the Derry memorandum as arriving on Tinian on 2 August 1945. The various arming and firing components required for a second Fat Man bomb were available to the Los Alamos assembly team by 9 August. The only piece missing, and it was the most critical element of the bomb, was the plutonium capsule.

On 13 August 1945, the plutonium core and initiator for the third bomb were ready to ship from Los Alamos to Kirtland Army Air Field in Albuquerque, New Mexico. From there, they probably would have been flown to Tinian the next day by either a C-54 of the 320th Troop Carrier Squadron or one of the 509th Silverplate B-29s positioned at Wendover for just such a mission. The core and initiator never left Los Alamos.

As related by Lawren, General Groves made a decision on 13 August 1945 that further shipments of material from Los Alamos should be halted in view of the possibility of a Japanese surrender in the next few days.[12] Lawren continues, "Returning to his office, Groves immediately phoned Los Alamos and told them to hold the third bomb. He was just in time. Bacher had just signed the official receipt for the bomb, and its components were already loaded in a waiting car." Robert F. Bacher was a Los Alamos scientist who would have accompanied the pit to Tinian with a security escort.

With respect to the directive to proceed with the atomic bombing missions, Rhodes quite clearly describes the situation on page 691 in *The Making of the Atomic*

Bomb. Groves drafted the document and had it forwarded for approval to Secretary of the Army Stimson and Army Chief of Staff General Marshall who were attending the conference in Potsdam. As Rhodes states, "Marshall and Stimson approved the directive at Potsdam and presumably showed it to Truman, though it does not record his formal authorization; it went out the next morning to the new commander of the Strategic Air Forces in the Pacific." The directive is the second document replicated at the end of this chapter.

Based on the various accounts in published literature, there is no doubt that the atomic bombings of Hiroshima and Nagasaki were carried out with the approval of the highest levels of the government of the United States.

WAR DEPARTMENT
P.O. Box 2610
WASHINGTON, D.C.

17 August 1945

MEMORANDUM FOR: Admiral W.S. De Lany

Subject: Transportation of Critical Shipments

The U.S.S. Indianapolis departed from San Francisco on 16 July 1945 after picking up the following project cargo at Hunters Point:

a. 1 box, wt. about 300 lbs, containing projectile assembly of active material for the gun type bomb.

b. 1 box, wt. about 300 lbs, containing special tools and scientific instruments.

c. 1 box, wt. about 10,000 lbs, containing the inert parts for a complete gun type bomb.

The Indianapolis arrived at Tinian Harbor, Marianas on 28 July and discharged the project cargo without mishap.

3 ATC C-54 airplanes departed from Kirtland Field, Albuquerque, New Mexico, at 1510Z 26 July, with each airplane carrying equal segments of the target assembly of active material for the gun type bomb. The airplanes arrived at Tinian on 28 July (about 48 hours lapsed time) and discharged project cargo without mishap.

2 ATC C-54 airplanes also departed from Kirtland Field at 1510Z 26 July and carried the sphere of active material and initiator for the implosion type bomb. The airplanes arrived at Tinian on 28 July and discharged project cargo safely.

3 B-29 specially modified bombers departed from Kirtland Field at 1250Z 28 July and carried 3 HE preassemblies of the implosion type bomb encased in the outer shell. All 3 B-29s arrived at Tinian at 0230Z 2 August and discharged project cargo safely.

J.A. DERRY
Major, C.E..xnt

3. Combat Operations

WAR DEPARTMENT
OFFICE OF THE CHIEF OF STAFF
WASHINGTON 25, D.C.

25 July 1945

TO: General Carl Spaatz
     Commanding General
     United States Army Strategic Air Forces

The 509 Composite Group, 20th Air Force will deliver its first special bomb as soon as weather will permit visual bombing after about 3 August 1945 on one of the targets: Hiroshima, Kokura, Niigata and Nagasaki. To carry military and civilian scientific personnel from the War Department to observe and record the effects of the explosion of the bomb, additional aircraft will accompany the airplane carrying the bomb. The observing planes will stay several miles distant from the point of impact of the bomb.

Additional bombs will be delivered on the above targets as soon as made ready by the project staff. Further instructions will be issued concerning targets other than those listed above.

Dissemination of any and all information concerning the use of the weapon against Japan is reserved to the Secretary of War and the President of the United States. No communiques on the subject or releases of information will be issued by Commanders in the field without specific prior authority. Any news stories will be sent to the War Department for special clearance.

The foregoing directive is issued to you by direction and with the approval of the Secretary of War and of the Chief of Staff, USA. It is desired that you personally deliver one copy of this directive to General MacArthur and one copy to Admiral Nimitz for their information.

/s/ Thos T. Handy
THOS. T. HANDY
General, G.S.C.
Acting Chief of Staff

(retyped for clarity)

4 THE LOS ALAMOS TEST PROGRAM

With the concept for an atomic device beginning to materialize at Los Alamos in the summer of 1943, attention was focused on the integration of the nuclear component into the design of a bomb and on the development of an aircraft delivery system. An Ordnance Division, with Navy Captain William S. "Deak" Parsons as the director, was established at the laboratory in June 1943 to manage bomb design and aircraft integration efforts.[1]

Responsibility within the Ordnance Division for integration of bomb designs with an appropriate airplane was assigned to the Delivery Group, headed by Norman F. Ramsey, Jr. One of his first tasks was to organize a program to test the flight characteristics of the bomb design then under consideration, which was a gun assembly model using plutonium as the active material, called Thin Man. On 13 August 1943, the first drop test of a prototype scale model was conducted at the Dahlgren Naval Proving Ground in Virginia. The aircraft used for the test was a Grumman TBF Avenger torpedo bomber.[2]

Although drop test activities using scale models continued at Dahlgren until December 1943, a decision had been made two months earlier that a program of full scale tests should be initiated as soon as possible. The B-29 Superfortress was selected as the aircraft to use in the tests and modification work on the prototype Silverplate B-29 began at Wright Army Air Field at the end of November 1943. The aircraft modified was serial number 42-6259. The prototype Silverplate B-29 is described in chapter 2.

The two bomb types on which the modification of the prototype was based represented the two concepts for achieving a nuclear explosion under consideration in the fall of 1944. The plutonium gun–type bomb, given the nickname Thin Man, was estimated to be 204 inches long with a maximum diameter of 23 inches. The plutonium implosion version, known as Fat Man, was estimated to be 111 inches long with a diameter of 59 inches. The weight of each version was estimated to be around 8,000 pounds. The length of the Thin Man model necessitated the joining of the two bomb bays in the prototype and installation of long bomb bay doors.

After completion of the modifications at Wright Field, 42-6259 was flown to Muroc Army Air Field (later Edwards Air Force Base) in California, arriving there on 20 February 1944. Two trial runs were made on 28 February using standard inert practice bombs to allow ground camera crews practice in tracking the bomb during its fall to earth. The first drop test using an actual prototype bomb was conducted on 3 March, but completion of this series of tests was delayed four weeks by rain and aircraft problems.

On what became the last mission of this series on 16 March 1944, the test bomb released prematurely and fell onto the bomb bay doors. The crew was able to get the doors open and jettison the bomb, but the doors were badly damaged. After temporary repairs at San Bernadino Air Depot in California, 42-6259 was flown back to Wright Field where the doors were completely repaired, the bomb release mechanisms modified, and three new engines installed.

The second series of tests using 42-6259 was conducted at Muroc in June 1944. These tests were generally satisfactory and the prototype Silverplate B-29 returned to Wright Field for further modifications. At about the time the second series of Muroc tests was completed, Los Alamos scientists concluded that a gun-type bomb using plutonium would not work and the Thin Man concept was abandoned.

Using uranium in the gun-type bomb called Little Boy resulted in a much shorter casing, thus eliminating the need for the long bomb bay in the B-29. The prototype was therefore modified back to the standard configuration with front and rear bomb bay doors. It was also realized at this time that the Fat Man implosion bomb would be heavier than previously thought, thus requiring a new suspension system and structural changes in the front bomb bay of the B-29.

Another significant development occurred on 11 August 1944. On this date, the Army Air Forces officers working with Los Alamos recommended that steps be taken to activate, equip, and train the Army Air Forces unit that would drop the bomb should a decision be made to use it. Action was soon taken on this recommendation and Wendover Army Air Field was selected as the location where this unit, the 509th Composite Group, would organize and train.

It was also decided at this time that an expanded Los Alamos test program would be undertaken and based at Wendover, using new Silverplate B-29s produced in conjunction with the aircraft to be provided the 509th. Chapter 2 describes this phase of the Silverplate B-29 history. The prototype was flown from Wright Field to Wendover in September 1944 and drop tests using it resumed in October, first at a remote area of Wendover and later at new locations in California.

There were several objectives in the Los Alamos drop test program, one of which was to test different shapes of bomb casings for their ballistic characteristics. As the testing program progressed and the outer shapes of the Fat Man and Little Boy casings were set, repeated drop tests were necessary to determine the ballistic coefficients of the two types of bombs for use by the bombardiers in the Norden bombsight.

Another objective of the tests was to gather data on the performance of arming, fuzing, and firing components of the bombs. Tests for this purpose was critical to the development of the equipment that would arm the bombs after they left the bomb bay and trigger the detonation at the desired altitude. Testing and refining the configuration of the bomb bay release mechanism was an additional important objective throughout the test program. The tests also provided a means to develop and refine a system for monitoring the condition of the bombs once they were loaded into the bomb bay. Monitoring of the bombs was particularly crucial during the long flight of the B-29 from Tinian to the target area.

The organizational arrangements for the Los Alamos test program at Wendover were somewhat unusual. A Test Section in the 216th Base Unit at Wendover was activated by the Army Air Forces and given responsibility for test operations. The air crews and aircraft used in the tests were assigned by the Army Air Forces to this Test Section, which was headed by Major Clyde S. Shields, the original Wright Field pilot assigned to the Silverplate project at its inception.

Although the Test Section, its personnel, and its assigned aircraft were Army Air Forces assets, management of the test program at Wendover was exercised by the Ordnance Division at Los Alamos. There were no Los Alamos personnel assigned to Wendover, but representatives from Los Alamos made the trip to the Utah base frequently to coordinate test schedules and procedures and to review test results. A special ordnance section of the 216th did the assembly and preparation of the bomb models to be tested, and a maintenance section of the 216th kept the assigned test aircraft in commission.

An interesting account of the test activity at Wendover in 1945 can be found in Rowe's *Project W-47*. Although there are errors in Rowe's book, specifically regarding the assembly of the bombs dropped on Hiroshima and Nagasaki, he does provide a good description of the hectic pace of the test program and the near total absence of Los Alamos personnel from Wendover.[3]

In addition to the prototype 42-6259, the Army Air Forces initially supplied three Silverplate B-29s for the Los Alamos drop test program at Wendover. The serial numbers of these three aircraft were 42-65234, 42-65235, and 42-65258. They were flown to Wendover in November 1944. The prototype aircraft was damaged in a landing accident in late 1944 and was never used again in the test program. It was eventually repaired and transferred to Davis-Monthan Army Air Field for storage.[4]

On 21 February 1945, an in-flight engine fire on 42-65235 caused a test mission to be aborted. The pilot made a safe landing at Wendover and as soon as the aircraft came to a stop on the runway, the crew abandoned it as the fire spread to other sections of the aircraft. This B-29 was also never used again in the test program, although it was repaired sufficiently to be later reassigned to Davis-Monthan for storage.[5]

With the loss of two test program aircraft and increasing requirements for test drops, there was a dire need in the 216th Test Section for additional Silverplate B-29s. To solve the aircraft shortage problem, four B-29s were reassigned from the 509th to the 216th Test Section. The four aircraft transferred to the 216th in the latter part of February 1945 included serial numbers 42-65236, 42-65259, 42-65260, and 42-65262.

With the addition of these aircraft, the 216th now had six B-29s with which to conduct drop tests. One of these aircraft was usually based at the Navy Ordnance Test Station airfield near Inyokern, California, to support drop tests conducted by the California Institute of Technology, which was supporting Los Alamos on the development of the Fat Man bomb.

The next change in the inventory of aircraft used in the Los Alamos drop test program occurred as a result of the decision in January 1945 to equip the 393rd and the test program with improved aircraft (see chapter 2). Five improved Silverplate B-29s, identical to the improved airplanes provided the 509th at this time, were delivered to the 216th at Wendover in April 1945. The serial numbers of these aircraft were 42-65384, 42-65385, 42-65386, 42-65387, and 44-27295.

Of the six older aircraft assigned to the 216th when the new models arrived, three were soon reassigned to other locations for storage. The serial numbers of the transferred aircraft were 42-65236, 42-65259, and 42-65260. Thus, from the end of April 1945 until after the end of World War II, eight Silverplate B-29s were involved in the Los Alamos drop test program. It should be noted that aircraft and crews assigned to the 393rd were occasionally used on drop test missions.

As mentioned earlier, the first and second drop test series with the prototype were conducted at the Muroc dry lakebed, using a target area in a remote part of the base. The targets for the drop tests based at Wendover included a remote section of Wendover Army Air Field, two locations at the Salton Sea Naval Auxiliary Air Station in California, and the bombing range at the Naval Ordnance Test Station near Inyokern, California.

One of the target locations at the Salton Sea facility was situated in shallow water. The other target, given the name Sandy Beach, was positioned inland about eight tenths of a mile from the shoreline. The Sandy Beach target was established so that the bomb prototypes dropped there could be recovered. The aircraft using the Inyokern location were based at the airfield at the Navy Test Station.

One of the most unusual mishaps that occurred in the drop test program happened to a 393rd crew flying a test mission on 22 March 1945. As the aircraft was on the final approach to the target at the Sandy Beach location with the bomb bay doors open, the Little Boy model released prematurely. The test unit impacted in a field approximately three miles south and east of the town of Calipatria, California. After locating the impact crater, a recovery team probed to a depth of eight feet without detecting any piece of the unit. The report on the incident included an estimate that the Little Boy test unit probably penetrated to a depth of 35 feet or more. The hole was filled and there is no record that the unit was ever recovered.

The pace of drop test missions began at a low level in late 1944 and increased considerably in the spring and early summer of 1945, particularly after most of the crews and aircraft of the 393rd departed Wendover for Tinian in June 1945. The tests conducted in late July and early August 1945 at Wendover were particularly important with respect to the Fat Man bomb because they served as final proof tests of critical components of that model.

As an example, the Fat Man firing unit, known as the X-Unit, was not qualified in a drop test at Wendover until 4 August, just five days before it was used in the bomb dropped on Nagasaki on 9 August. A final confirmation test of the X-Unit was successfully conducted on 8 August when a Fat Man test bomb was dropped in the ocean off Tinian, as described below.

Several Little Boy and Fat Man test units were dropped by 509th crews and aircraft near Tinian in late July and early August 1945. These tests were conducted for the Los Alamos contingent deployed to Tinian to support the atomic bomb missions.

They also served as crew and procedural rehearsals for the atomic missions about to be flown. The tests are described below (the "L" and "F" numbers refer to the designation numbers assigned by Los Alamos).

The first Little Boy (L1 unit) drop test from Tinian was conducted on 23 July 1945. The Silverplate B-29 used in this test was 44-27354 (later to be named *Big Stink*) and the Airplane Commander was Tibbets. The dummy Little Boy was fired in the air by a signal from the bomb's radar system. The test took place over the ocean near Tinian.

The second and third Little Boy tests took place on 24 and 25 July, using L2 and L5 units. The aircraft used in both tests was 44-27303 (known later as *Jabit III*) and Tibbets was the Airplane Commander on both missions. In both cases, the dummy bomb was dropped in the ocean near Tinian to confirm the operation of all components.

On 29 July, test unit L6 was used in a test of facilities at Iwo Jima for emergency reloading of the bomb into a standby aircraft. Sweeney was the Airplane Commander in aircraft 44-27299 (later named *Next Objective*). The test unit was returned to Tinian.

The fourth and last test of the Little Boy before the Hiroshima mission was conducted on 31 July with test unit L6 loaded into aircraft 44-86292 (known later as *Enola Gay*) and with Tibbets as the Airplane Commander. In this dress rehearsal for the live mission to be run a few days later, the bomb-carrying aircraft flew with two accompanying observation Silverplate B-29s of the 509th to Iwo Jima where a rendezvous was made. The three aircraft then returned to the vicinity of Tinian where the test unit was dropped and observed to function properly.

The first Fat Man test out of Tinian was conducted on 1 August with test unit F13 and aircraft 44-27297 (later named *Bockscar*). Sweeney was the Aircraft Commander on this test. Two additional drop tests of Fat Man units, F18 and F33, were conducted on 5 and 8 August using aircraft 44-27297 in both cases. The second of these tests was similar to the last Little Boy test in that it was a dress rehearsal for the live mission conducted on 9 August.

The successful development and use of the atomic bomb in World War II would not have been possible without the Los Alamos drop test program. The scientists demonstrated that an atomic device would work in the Trinity test on 16 July 1945, but it was in the drop tests that workable bomb designs and components were proven. The 155 test drops at Wendover, Sandy Beach, and Inyokern, as well as the seven test drops near Tinian, were the essential steps from theory and design to the bombs that ended World War II.

5 Silverplate Accidents

Most Silverplate B-29s served for many years in operational assignments before being declared surplus and consigned to the scrap heap. After being used in an atomic bomb-carrying role, many had their Silverplate features removed and were converted to other configurations for continued active duty. However, 16 out of the 65 aircraft were involved in confirmed or suspected accidents that resulted in either total destruction or damage so severe that they were later scrapped or put to other uses.[1]

42-6259

The incident that brought an end to the prototype's use in the Los Alamos test program at Wendover Army Air Field is included in this listing of accidents even though it was later used in a non-flying role. In late 1944, with Charles Sweeney as the pilot, 42-6259 was damaged in a landing accident at Wendover and was never used again in test missions.

After repairs it was flown to Davis-Monthan Army Air Field in January 1945 for storage. Removed from storage in August 1946, it was assigned to Fort Worth Army Air Field as a ground instructional aircraft. It was declared surplus in May 1948 and scrapped. Information on this accident was taken from Dike's report and the Aircraft Record Card.

42-65235

While being used on a mission in the Los Alamos drop test program at Wendover Army Air Field in February 1945, 42-65235 had an engine fire. George W. Marquardt was the pilot. The crew made an emergency landing at Wendover and evacuated the aircraft immediately after coming to a stop on the runway.

Fire damage to the airplane was considerable and it was never used again in tests at Wendover. It was eventually repaired sufficiently for flight and was flown to Davis-Monthan Army Air Field in January 1946 for storage. 42-65235 was declared surplus in May 1954 and scrapped. Information on this accident was found in the daily activity reports prepared during 1945 by Major Clyde S. Shields, head of the Test Section of the 216th Base Unit at Wendover.

42-65385

One of the aircraft assigned to the Los Alamos drop test program at Wendover Army Air Field in early 1945, 42-65385 was reassigned to Kirtland Army Air Field in October 1945 for continued use in the same capacity. On 27 January 1947, it lost altitude and crashed immediately after take-off from runway 21 at Kirtland on a routine maintenance test flight. All twelve men on board were killed. Although a specific cause for the accident was not documented, it is believed that a fire in one engine immediately after liftoff and the pilot's failure to compensate for the loss of power caused the crash.

Information on this accident was taken from an article in the 26 January 1997 edition of the *Albuquerque Journal* and the Aircraft Record Card. The accident report for this incident has not been found.[2]

42-65387

Another of the Silverplate B-29s assigned to the 216th Base Unit at Wendover Army Air Field in early 1945 to support the Los Alamos bomb testing program, 42-65385 was reassigned to Kirtland Army Air Field in January 1946. On 7 March 1946, it was used on a practice bombing mission from Kirtland to the Los Lunas bombing range southwest of Albuquerque.

After dropping a 10,150 pound Fat Man shape, it disintegrated for reasons unknown and spun in from about 32,000 feet. The main piece of wreckage, including the four engines, was located half buried 48 miles southwest of Albuquerque. Other wreckage, including major segments of the wings and empennage, were strewn up to a distance of 16 miles from the main segment. All ten men on board died, including the bombardier, David Semple.

Semple was the original bombardier for the prototype Silverplate B-29 tests and was involved in many of the drop test missions conducted for Los Alamos at Muroc, Salton Sea, and Wendover in 1944 and 1945. He was also responsible for refining the design of the tail fin assembly of the Fat Man shape to improve its ballistic characteristics. The Silverplate B-29 (44-27354) that dropped the atomic bomb on 1 July 1946 in Test Able of Operation Crossroads in the Pacific was given the name *Dave's Dream* in his honor.

Information on this accident was taken from Army Air Forces Report of Major Accident number 46-3-7-6 and the Aircraft Record Card.[3]

44-27296

After returning to the 509th Composite Group at Roswell Army Air Field from Tinian in November 1945, 44-27296 was involved in a taxiing accident while deployed to Kirtland Army Air Field on 1 March 1946.

Although there are references to Roswell as the site of the accident in some doc-

16. Damage to 44-27296 (*Some Punkins*). (Air Force Historical Research Agency)

uments, the circumstances of the incident and the assignment histories shown in both aircraft record cards for the aircraft involved lead to the conclusion that it happened at Kirtland.

According to James N. Price, Jr., the Airplane Commander of 44-27296 on Tinian, someone (alleged to be Major Clyde S. Shields) undertook to taxi another 509th Silverplate B-29 deployed to Kirtland (44-86473) on the Kirtland tarmac without energizing the hydraulic system for the landing gear brakes. Once in motion, 44-86473 could be stopped only by running into another object. That object happened to be the parked *Some Punkins* (44-27296).

The accident resulted in considerable structural damage to both aircraft. Figure 16 shows the condition of 44-27296 shortly after the incident.

After being reassigned to the 428th Base Unit at Kirtland Army Air Field in April 1946, it was declared surplus and in August of that year was set on fire and destroyed in a fire-fighting demonstration, as shown in Figure 17.

Information on this incident and its aftermath was taken from the applicable Aircraft Record Cards, documents and photographs supplied by the Air Force Historical Research Agency. Oral statements by James N. Price, Jr., the Airplane Commander of *Some Punkins* at Wendover and on Tinian, added details to the history of this accident.

17. The Burning of *Some Punkins*. (Air Force Historical Research Agency)

44-27299

In April 1949 44-27299 was reassigned from the 509th Bombardment Group at Walker Air Force Base in New Mexico (formerly Roswell Army Air Field) to the 97th Bombardment Group at Biggs Air Force Base in Texas. Shortly after takeoff on a navigation and radar training mission on 25 May 1949, a fire broke out in the right outboard engine. When the fire could not be extinguished, the crew bailed out.

One crew member, the navigator, died when his parachute did not open (believed to be the result of the navigator striking his head on the nose-gear operating assembly as he exited the aircraft through the nose-gear opening).[4] The abandoned aircraft made a two-mile circle after the crew bailed out and struck the ground 35 miles northeast of El Paso, Texas, exploding on impact. Following the explosion, pieces of the aircraft were scattered over a three-quarter mile area. It was dropped from inventory as salvage in July 1949. Information on this accident was taken from Report of Major Accident number 49-5-25-3 and the Aircraft Record Card.

44-27300

One of the 15 Silverplate B-29s used by the 509th Composite Group on Tinian in 1945, the case of 44-27300 (*Strange Cargo*) is one in which an accident is suspected as being the cause of its removal from inventory. After its conversion to a WB-29 configuration in 1949, it was used in North Africa as a tow-target aircraft and in other roles before being assigned to the 3920th Base Unit at RAF Brize Norton in July 1957. While no aircraft accident report or other confirming evidence has been found, it was suddenly dropped from inventory in August 1957 as salvage. An accident of some sort is believed to be the cause of the salvage action. The information for this suspected accident was taken from the Aircraft Record Card.

44-27303

This aircraft (*Jabit III*) was one of two flown back from Tinian to Wendover Army Air Field in August 1945 to be in position for the transportation of additional atomic bomb components to Tinian. On 29 September 1945, while awaiting further orders, John A. Wilson and his crew flew 44-27303 on a cross-country training mission.

While landing at Chicago Municipal Airport that afternoon, the aircraft struck several objects at the approach end of the runway and suffered damage so severe that it was never repaired and flown again. It was dropped from inventory as salvage in April 1946 as a result of the accident.[5] Information on this accident was taken from Army Air Forces Report of Major Accident number 46-9-29-1 and the Aircraft Record Card.

44-27353

As the only Silverplate B-29 to have been part of the strike force on both atomic bombing missions in August 1945, *The Great Artiste* was a prime candidate for preservation in a museum after its operational usefulness ended. In fact, because of the confusion over the identity of the B-29 that actually carried the Fat Man bomb on the Nagasaki mission, the Aircraft Record Card for 44-27353 included a hand-written notation that this aircraft was the B-29 that dropped the bomb on Nagasaki. However, a future in some museum was not to be the case.

In September 1948 it was deployed with several other B-29s of the 509th Composite Group to Goose Bay Air Field in Labrador for polar navigation training. During a routine navigation training flight on 3 September 1948, an engine problem after takeoff resulted in the mission being aborted.

The pilot made a high approach downwind and touched down half way down the runway. The pilot was unable to stop the aircraft and it left the runway onto an unfinished runway extension where it ground looped to avoid a tractor.

Damage to the aircraft was so severe that it was never repaired and never flew again. It was reassigned from the 509th to one of the units at Goose Bay immediately after the accident. Despite its historical importance, it was scrapped at Goose Bay in September 1949. The photograph shown in Figure 18, taken just three weeks after the accident on 24 September 1948, is believed to be one of the last photographs taken of 44-27353.

Information on this accident was taken from Army Air Forces Report of Major

18. *The Great Artiste* at Goose Bay. (Air Force Historical Research Agency)

Accident number 48-C-9-3-4, records of the 538th Air Base Group at Goose Bay, and the Aircraft Record Card.

44-86382

While assigned to the 509th Bombardment Group at Roswell Army Air Field, 44-86382 was involved in a landing accident at Mitchel Field in New York on 18 April 1947. The damage was minor and the aircraft was repaired and returned to operational status. After additional assignments and conversion to a TB-29 configuration, it suffered a far worse fate in another accident nearly seven years later.

Assigned to the 7th Radar Calibration Squadron at Sioux City Air Force Base in Iowa, it was involved in a landing accident at Ogden Municipal Airport in Utah on 19 December 1953. The aircraft was almost totally destroyed by the fire resulting from the accident. The pilot and co-pilot mistook the Ogden airport runway for a runway at nearby Hill Air Force Base (where they intended to land), and with a much shorter runway at the Ogden airport and excess landing speed, they could not get the B-29 stopped in time.

It ran off the end of the runway, crossed a deep ditch and a 10-foot-wide canal, bounced over a highway, and came to a stop in pieces 527 feet from the end of the runway. Fire broke out immediately. There was one fatality and two other members of the crew were injured. The aircraft was removed from inventory in December 1953 as lost to crash.

The information regarding this major accident was taken from Report of Aircraft Accident number 53-12-18-1 and the Aircraft Record Card.

44-86383

As part of a group of 509th Bombardment Group B-29s deploying to Goose Bay in Labrador for polar navigation training, 44-86383 departed Walker Air Force Base (formerly Roswell Army Air Field) on 12 August 1948 with 21 crew members and passengers on board. Immediately after liftoff from the runway it lost altitude and impacted the ground. After bouncing back into the air momentarily, it crashed six tenths of a mile from the point of first contact with the ground. The aircraft disintegrated and burned. There were seven fatalities and major injuries to other members of the crew and to the passengers. The aircraft was removed from inventory in August 1948.

The information regarding this accident was taken from Report of Major Accident number 48-C-8-12-7 and the Aircraft Record Card.

44-86431

As one of the Silverplate B-29s of the 509th Composite Group selected to participate in Operation Crossroads, 44-86431 was flown to the depot at Tinker Army Air Field for modifications in January 1946. Although no report of an accident has been located, it is believed this aircraft was severely damaged in a fire while at the modification center. It was never repaired and was dropped from inventory as surplus in August 1947.

The information regarding this suspected accident was taken from the Aircraft Record Card and Chapter XII (The End of Project SILVERPLATE) of the report, "A History of the Air Force Atomic Energy Program, 1943–1953."

44-86472

Although confirming records have not been found, the early demise of 44-86472 makes it very likely that it was involved in an accident while assigned to the 509th Bombardment Group at Roswell Army Air Field. The Aircraft Record Card shows that this aircraft was dropped from inventory at Roswell in June 1947.

Other Silverplate B-29s produced at the same time and having similar assignments in 1945 and 1946 were not declared surplus until many years later, thus leading to the conclusion that this aircraft was involved in an accident with damages sufficient to result in a decision to not repair the aircraft.

The information on this suspected accident is limited to the Aircraft Record Card. A report of an accident has not been located.

44-86473

While assigned to the 509th Composite Group at Roswell Army Air Field and deployed to Kirtland Army Air Field for practice bombing missions, 44-86473 was involved in an accident on 1 March 1946 that ultimately resulted in the loss of two Silverplate B-29s. In fact, it was the cause of the accident, which occurred on the tarmac at Kirtland. Although there are references to Roswell as the site of the accident in some documents, the circumstances of the incident and the assignment histories shown in both aircraft record cards for the aircraft involved lead to the conclusion that the accident happened at Kirtland.

Someone (believed to be Major Clyde S. Shields, the pilot for most of the Los Alamos drop test missions) was taxiing it for some unknown reason without properly energizing the hydraulic system for the brakes.

Once in motion and without brakes and steering (nose steering was accomplished by applying brakes to one side or the other), it could only be stopped by an impact with another object. That object was 44-27296, another 509th Silverplate B-29 deployed to Kirtland for practice bombing missions. The damage resulting from the accident was so severe that 44-86473 was assigned to the 428th Base Unit at Kirtland for salvage and was dropped from inventory in April 1946.

Information regarding this accident was taken from the Aircraft Record Cards for both involved aircraft and from Chapter XII (The End of Project SILVERPLATE) of the report, "A History of the Air Force Atomic Energy Program, 1943–1953." An accident report on this incident has not been found.

45-21707

One of the 19 B-29s removed from storage and converted to the Silverplate configuration, 45-21707 was assigned to the 509th Bombardment Group at Roswell Air Force Base in December 1947. The Aircraft Record Card shows that it was assigned to the 509th Maintenance Support Group at Roswell in March 1949 for unknown reasons. It is believed that this aircraft was involved in an accident of some kind since it was subsequently dropped from inventory as salvage in August 1949.

The information on this probable accident was taken solely from the Aircraft Record Card. A confirming accident report has not yet been found.

45-21736

One of the 19 B-29s removed from storage and converted to the Silverplate configuration, 45-21736 was eventually assigned to the 509th Bombardment Group at Walker (formerly Roswell) Air Force Base in New Mexico in February 1949. The Aircraft Record Card indicates that at some time after its assignment to the 509th, it was used in a deployment to RAF Marham in the United Kingdom. Since it was dropped from inventory in August 1950, it is very probable that it was involved in an accident at Roswell or Marham in which it suffered damage sufficient to remove it from service.

A relevant accident report has not been found. The information on this probable accident is based solely on information contained in the Aircraft Record Card.

6 Places and Units

Silverplate B-29s flew into and out of many bases in the course of their operations as atomic bomb carriers, but there were very few places and organizations to which they were assigned for continuing operations.[1] It should be noted that many of these aircraft were eventually converted to other B-29 configurations and received assignments to numerous places and units around the world before being retired and scrapped.

The Army Air Fields and Air Force Bases from which these aircraft operated as Silverplate B-29s are described below. The units associated with these locations are also identified. As a matter of interest, the descriptions also include places and units involved in the storage of Silverplate B-29s prior to their further assignments or disposal.

By way of explanation, the U.S. Army Air Forces (the U.S. Air Corps) became the U.S. Air Force on 17 September 1947, and operating locations known as Army Air Fields became Air Force Bases soon thereafter. There are also a few locations involving Silverplate B-29 operations where the name of the base was changed. Such changes are noted in the descriptions.

Biggs Air Force Base

Located outside El Paso in the extreme western tip of Texas, Biggs Air Force Base was home to 28 Silverplate B-29s in the 1949–50 time period. The aircraft were assigned to the 97th Bomb Wing of the 8th Air Force. The 97th was the only combat unit other than the 509th Composite Group (later Bombardment Group and Bomb Wing) to have Silverplate B-29s assigned to it.

All but two of the Silverplate B-29s assigned to the 97th were transferred from the 509th at Walker Air Force Base (NM) in 1949. The two exceptions were 44-27295 and 42-65234, both of which was reassigned from Kirtland Air Force Base (NM). The 29 Silverplate B-29s that were assigned to the 97th Bomb Wing were:

42-65234	44-27302	44-86347	44-86432	44-86448
44-27295	44-27304	44-86382	44-86437	44-86451
44-27298	44-27354	44-86384	44-86439	44-87752
44-27299	44-86263	44-86394	44-86440	44-87774

44-27300	44-86291	44-86401	44-86443	45-21739
44-27301	44-86346	44-86430	44-86445	

Of the 29 Silverplate B-29s assigned to the 97th, one (44-27299) was lost in an accident, one (44-86451) was reassigned to the 8th Air Force at Carswell Air Force Base near Ft. Worth (TX), and one (44-27300) was transferred to the Sacramento Air Depot for conversion to a WB-29 configuration. By May 1950, the remaining 26 had been transferred to the Oklahoma City depot where they lost their Silverplate identity and were converted to a TB-29 configuration.

The forerunner of Biggs Air Force Base was an encampment at Fort Bliss for the 82nd Field Artillery that was established in 1915. It was used the next year as a stopping point for aircraft used in the action against Pancho Villa in Mexico and was referred to as Fort Bliss Aviation Field, but on 5 January 1925 it was officially named Biggs Field after Lieutenant James B. "Buster" Biggs. Lt. Biggs was a native of El Paso who was killed in action in France on 27 October 1918.

Between the two World Wars, Biggs Army Air Field served as a refueling stop for transient military aircraft. During World War II, it was used for training of bomber crews. On 1 February 1948, the installation was renamed Biggs Air Force Base, and in May 1948 the 97th Bomb Wing moved to Biggs from Smokey Hill Air Force Base in Kansas. The 97th left Biggs in 1959 and the base was deactivated as an Air Force installation in 1966. It is now operated by the U.S. Army as Biggs Army Air Field.

Davis-Monthan Army Air Field

Ten Silverplate B-29s were stored at Davis-Monthan Army Air Field on the southeastern edge of Tucson (AZ) after they had been used either in the training of 509th Composite Group crews or in the Los Alamos drop test program.

The prototype Silverplate B-29 (42-6259) was assigned to the 4105th Base Unit at Davis-Monthan after it was used at Wendover Army Air Field in support of Los Alamos tests. After storage at Davis-Monthan from January 1945 to August 1946, it was assigned to Fort Worth Army Air Field (TX) as a TB-29 instructional aircraft.

Seven of the original group of 14 Silverplate B-29s assigned to the 393rd Bombardment Squadron at Wendover in late–1944 were stored at Davis-Monthan after the 393rd began receiving improved airplanes in the spring of 1945. All of these aircraft were assigned to the 4105th Base Unit and were eventually declared surplus and scrapped. The seven airplanes were:

42-65209	42-65237	42-65239	42-65264
42-65235	42-65238	42-65260	

Two Silverplate B-29s were assigned to the 4105th Base Unit at Davis-Monthan for temporary storage before being transferred to museums. One of these aircraft was *Bockscar* (44-27297), which went into storage in August 1946. It was dropped from inventory in September 1946 by transfer of title to the Air Force Museum. While in storage it was displayed with the markings of *The Great Artiste* (44-27353) in the erroneous belief that 44-27353 was the airplane that had dropped the Fat Man bomb on the Nagasaki mission. It was not until 26 September 1961 that 44-27297 was flown to Wright-Patterson Air Force Base for display in the museum. The confusion in identity was eventually resolved and *Bockscar* is displayed in the museum with the correct markings.[2]

The other Silverplate B-29 stored temporarily at Davis-Monthan before being transferred to a museum was *Enola Gay* (44-86292). After being deployed to Kwajalein for Operation Crossroads in 1946, it was flown back to Davis-Monthan and assigned to the 4105th Base Unit for storage on 24 July 1946. It was dropped from inventory on 30 August 1946 when title to it was transferred to the Smithsonian Institution. After almost three years in storage at Davis-Monthan, 44-86292 was retrieved from storage and flown to Orchard Place Air Field near Chicago, Illinois, on 3 July 1949. On arrival, it was accepted by the Smithsonian Institution and began a long period of storage and neglect at several locations. The rest of the *Enola Gay* story is included in Appendix G.

Davis-Monthan Army Air Field began as a landing strip established in November 1925 on the outskirts of Tucson by the Air Service of the U.S. Army Signal Corps. It was named Davis-Monthan Landing Field in honor of two Tucsonans who died in separate military aircraft accidents. Lieutenant Samuel H. Davis died in an accident in Florida in 1921. Lieutenant Oscar Monthan was killed in the crash of a Martin bomber in Hawaii in 1924.

The Davis-Monthan Landing Field served as the Tucson Municipal Airport for many years. The field was selected for expansion and restriction to military operations in 1940 and became known as Davis-Monthan Army Air Field on 3 December 1941. During World War II it served as a training base for bomber crews.

Immediately after the war, Davis-Monthan was assigned to the San Antonio Air Technical Service Command (later Air Materiel Command) at Kelly Army Air Field in Texas for use as a storage base for military aircraft not kept in an operational status. The 4105th Base Unit was activated at the base in late–1945 to administer the storage activities. In May 1946, training and operation of aircraft of the new Strategic Air Command became the primary mission of the base, but the storage and disposition of excess aircraft remained under the auspices of the Air Materiel Command and the War Assets Administration.

Davis-Monthan Air Force Base became the official designation of the field in early 1948. The storage of aircraft from all military services is now managed at the base by the Aerospace Maintenance and Regeneration Center (AMARC).

Kirtland Army Air Field

Located on the southeastern edge of Albuquerque (NM), Kirtland Army Air Field served as a transportation transfer point during World War II for personnel and material going to and from the Los Alamos laboratory of the Manhattan Project. One of the more critical air shipments originating at Kirtland was the transportation of three Fat Man units (less the plutonium cores) to Tinian in late–July 1945. One of these units was the bomb used in the Nagasaki mission. Three Silverplate B-29s, 42-65386, 44-86346, and 44-86347, were flown from Wendover to Kirtland on 27 July 1945. Using a loading pit constructed in a remote section of the field, Los Alamos personnel loaded the three Fat Man units into the front bomb bays of the airplanes and they departed for Tinian the next morning.

In the fall of 1945, the test activities that had been conducted by the 216th Base Unit at Wendover were transferred to the 428th Base Unit (designated earlier as the 237th Base Unit) at Kirtland. Many of the personnel that had been responsible for the Wendover testing were also transferred to Kirtland. The Silverplate B-29s used in test operations at Kirtland included (dispositions from Kirtland are noted):

42-65234	To 97th BG (Oct 49)	42-65387	Lost in accident (Mar 46)
42-65258	To Castle AAF (Apr 46)	44-27295	To 97th BG (Sep 49)
42-65384	To Oklahoma City (Apr 50)	44-86444	To Oklahoma City (Apr 50)
42-65385	Lost in accident (Jan 47)	44-86447	To Oklahoma City (Apr 50)
42-65386	To Hanscom AFB (Jan 53)	45-21818	To Oklahoma City (Feb 53)

Kirtland was also used by crews and aircraft of the 509th Composite Group (later Bomb Group) as a base of operations for training missions in which inert Fat Man models were dropped at a bombing range south of Albuquerque. Kirtland was used for these missions because of the availability of the loading pit mentioned above.

The field began operations in April 1941 when Albuquerque Army Air Field was activated just east of Albuquerque's new municipal airport. The name was changed to Kirtland Army Air Field in February 1942 in honor of Colonel Roy C. Kirtland, one of the Army's oldest pilots who had died a year earlier. Kirtland was primarily used during World War II as a training base for pilots, bombardiers, and entire bomber crews. Its name was changed to Kirtland Air Force Base in late–1947.

Muroc Army Air Field

The first drop tests of Thin Man and Fat Man shapes with the prototype Silverplate B-29 (serial number 42-6259) were conducted at the Muroc Bombing and Gunnery Range in March 1944. A second series of tests was accomplished in June 1944. Additional drop tests of bomb prototypes were conducted at Muroc late in 1944 and early in 1945 by Silverplate B-29s of the 216th Base Unit at Wendover Army Air Field.

The bombing and gunnery range was established in September 1933 on a portion of Rogers Dry Lake about 100 miles northeast of Los Angeles. When the initial tests in early 1944 were conducted, 42-6259 and its crew, ground support personnel, and a test group from Los Alamos were based at Muroc Army Air Field, which was established along the edge of the dry lake bed in 1942.

In 1910, the Corum family settled at the edge of Rogers Dry Lake. They opened a general store and a post office, and attempted to have the post office called by the family name. Their request was denied because of a similar name at a nearby location. The Corums simply reversed the spelling of their name and "Muroc" was approved for their post office. This name came to be associated with the dry lake bed and was used to designate the range and the air field.

In 1949, Muroc Army Air Field was renamed Edwards Air Force Base in honor of Captain Glen W. Edwards, who was killed in the crash of an experimental YB-49 "Flying Wing" in June 1948. The Air Force Flight Test Center and the Air Force Test Pilot School are two of the major units based at Edwards.

Pyote Army Air Field

Established in 1942 adjacent to the town of Pyote in southwestern Texas, Pyote Army Air Field was used to train bomber crews during World War II. After the war, the field served as a storage and disposal facility for fighter and bomber aircraft. There are reports that more than 4,000 military aircraft were sent to the Pyote facility for melting into scrap metal and that as many as 2,000 airplanes were stored there at one point in time.

The town of Pyote, originally called Pyote Tank, is about 50 miles southwest of Odessa, Texas, along what is now Interstate 20. The name for the town may have come from the pronunciation of the word coyote by Chinese railroad workers in the 1880s, or it may be taken from the peyote cactus common to the region.

Storage of aircraft at Pyote Army Air Field (later known as Pyote Air Force Station) was under the jurisdiction of the Aircraft Distribution Office of the Air Technical Service Command at Wright Field, Ohio. Once the USAAF (or USAF) determined that an airplane was surplus, final disposal was managed by the War Assets Administration, and later the General Services Agency. Private companies under contract with the government conducted the actual salvage and smelter operations.

Silverplate B-29s stored and scrapped at Pyote were from the initial group of 17 aircraft delivered to the 393rd Bombardment Squadron at Wendover in the fall of 1944 (see Chapter 3). There were eight Silverplate B-29s assigned to the 236th Base Unit and the 4141st Base Unit at Pyote for storage. The serial numbers were:

42-65216	42-65258
42-65217	42-65259
42-65236	42-65261
42-65240	42-65263

All eight Silverplate B-29s assigned to Pyote for storage and disposal were scrapped by mid–1954. Pyote Air Force Station was closed in 1966.

Robins Army Air Field

The final destination for one Silverplate B-29 was Robins Army Air Field (GA). After service with the 509th Composite Group and the 216th Base Unit at Wendover,

42-65262 was assigned to the 4000th Base Unit at Wright Army Air Field (OH) in April 1945. In April 1946, it was reassigned to the 4117th Base Unit at Robins for storage. It was declared surplus and scrapped at Robins in April 1953.

Located 16 miles south of Macon (GA), Robins Army Air Field came into existence in January 1942 as the base of air operations for what was then known as the Wellston Air Depot. The field was named in honor of Brigadier General Augustine Warner Robins, an early leader in the development of air logistics. General Robins died suddenly of a heart attack on 16 June 1940. The depot experienced several name changes during World War II and was known as Warner Robins Air Materiel Area for many years after the end of the war. The name of the field was changed to Robins Air Force Base in early–1948 and the name of the depot was changed to Warner Robins Air Logistics Center in April 1974.

Roswell Army Air Field

Roswell Army Air Field (later Roswell Air Force Base and then Walker Air Force Base) was the home of the 509th Composite Group when it returned from Tinian in November 1945 and for many of the Silverplate B-29s for several years.

Thirteen of the fifteen Silverplate B-29s used by the 509th on Tinian were flown back to Roswell in November 1945. The other two (44-27303 and 44-86346) had been flown back to Wendover in August to be in position to transport components for the next Fat Man bombs to Tinian had the bombs been needed (see chapter 3 for details). One of the two flown back to Wendover (44-27303) was involved in a landing accident at an airport in Chicago during a training mission in September 1945 and was eventually scrapped at that location. The second of the two flown to Wendover was flown to Roswell in November 1945.

The eight Silverplate B-29s delivered to Wendover in 1945 after the 509th had deployed to Tinian were also flown to Roswell in November 1945. Six of these airplanes had been assigned to the 509th at Wendover as reserve aircraft and two were assigned to the 216th Base Unit for the Los Alamos test program.

Thus, on 1 January 1946, there were 22 Silverplate B-29s assigned to the 509th at Roswell. During 1946, many of the personnel of the 509th and several of its aircraft were deployed from Roswell to Kwajalein in the Pacific to participate in the atomic bomb tests in Operation Crossroads. Also in 1946, as shown in the list that follows, the 509th lost five of its Silverplate B-29s. Two were placed in storage to await transfer to museums, two were lost in accidents (44-27296 and 44-86473), and one (44-86431) was assigned to the Oklahoma City depot for modifications and was lost when a fire at the depot destroyed it. *Enola Gay* (44-86292) was stored at Davis-Monthan Army Air Field before being transferred to the Smithsonian Institution. *Bockscar* was also stored at Davis-Monthan before being eventually transferred to the Air Force Museum near Dayton, Ohio.

Starting with 22 Silverplate B-29s at the beginning of 1946 and losing five during the year, the 509th at Roswell ended 1946 with 17 Silverplate B-29s. The 22 aircraft and their ultimate dispositions were as follows:

44-27296	Accident (Mar 46)	44-86292	To storage (Jul 46)
44-27297	To storage (Aug 46)	44-86346	To 97th BG (Jun 49)
44-27298	To 97th BG (Jun 49)	44-86347	To 97th BG (Aug 49)
44-27299	To 97th BG (Apr 49)	44-86382	To 97th BG (Jul 49)
44-27300	To 97th BG (Jun 49)	44-86383	Accident (Aug 48)
44-27301	To 97th BG (Jun 49)	44-86384	To 97th BG (Jun 49)
44-27302	To 97th BG (Jun 49)	44-86430	To 97th BG (Jun 49)
44-27304	To 97th BG (Aug 49)	44-86431	To Ok City (Jan 46)
44-27353	Accident (Sep 48)	44-86432	To 97th BG (Mar 49)
44-27354	To 97th BG (Jun 49)	44-86472	Accident (Jun 47)
44-86291	To 97th BG (Jun 49)	44-86473	Accident (Mar 46)

Several events at Roswell in 1946 involving the 509th are worth mentioning. In a leadership change, Colonel William H. Blanchard replaced Colonel Paul W. Tibbets as the Commanding Officer of the 509th on 22 January 1946. Colonel Tibbets was named as technical advisor to Operation Crossroads. On 17 May 1946, two additional bombardment squadrons, the 715th and 830th, were assigned to the 509th in addition to the already existing 393rd. Finally, the 509th was redesignated as the 509th Bombardment Group (Very Heavy) on 10 July 1946.[3]

Starting with 17 Silverplate B-29s at the beginning of 1947, the 509th gained 16 additional aircraft during the next 12 months from the Silverplate modification program at the Sacramento Air Depot at McClellan Air Force Base. One aircraft (44-86472) was lost in 1947 due to an accident. The net result was that there were 32 Silverplate B-29s assigned to the 509th at Roswell at the end of 1947. The 16 aircraft gained by the 509th in 1947 are listed below. As noted, all but three of these Silverplate B-29s were transferred to the 97th Bombardment Group at Biggs Air Force Base in the summer of 1949.

44-86263 (97th)	44-86439 (97th)	44-86448 (97th)	44-87774 (97th)
44-86394 (97th)	44-86440 (97th)	44-86451 (97th)	45-21707 (see below)
44-86401 (97th)	44-86443 (97th)	44-87752 (97th)	45-21736 (see below)
44-86437 (97th)	44-86445 (97th)	44-87771 (see below)	45-21739 (97th)

With regard to the three Silverplate B-29s noted in the list immediately above as not being transferred to the 97th Bombardment Group, two were lost in accidents or situations not fully explained in the Aircraft Record Cards. 45-21707 was removed from operational service in the 509th at Walker Air Force Base (formerly Roswell Army Air Field) in March 1949 and assigned to the 509th Maintenance Support Group. Without ever being returned to operational status, it was dropped from inventory as salvage in August 1949. The situation with 45-21736 is also unclear. It was used in a deployment to RAF Marham in the United Kingdom sometime after February 1949, but the next entry in the records shows it being dropped from inventory as salvage at Walker in August 1950.

The third aircraft in the list above that did not go to the 97th was 44-87771. After deployments to locations in the United Kingdom for periods of time after August 1947, it was transferred to the 9th Bombardment Wing at Travis Air Force Base in California in November 1951.

19. Silverplate B-29's of the 509th in Formation. (Milford L. Foley)

Figure 19 shows several of the Silverplate B-29s assigned to the 509th Bombardment Group at Roswell Army Air Field flying in formation near Roswell in 1947. Markings for 44-27300 (upper) and 44-86291 (lower) can be seen. Two of the aircraft appear to have the lower fuselage painted black.

By August 1949, all but two of the Silverplate B-29s of the 509th had either been transferred to the 97th Bombardment Group at Biggs Air Force Base in Texas or had been lost to accidents. One of the last two was removed from assignment to the 509th in August 1950. The last Silverplate B-29 was reassigned from the 509th in November 1951. In June 1950, the 509th began receiving B-50D bombers as its replacement aircraft.

Roswell/Walker was the base of operations for 38 Silverplate B-29s at one time or another, with 22 coming from Wendover and Tinian in November 1945 and 16 from the modification program at the Sacramento Air Depot in 1947. An accounting of the 38 Silverplate B-29s at Roswell/Walker from late–1946 to 1951 shows the following:

Quantity	Disposition
2	To storage for transfer to museums
7	Lost in accidents
1	To Oklahoma City depot and not returned
1	To 9th Bomb Wing at Castle AFB
27	To 97th Bomb Group at Biggs AFB

Located 8 miles south of the city of Roswell in the southeast section of New Mexico, Roswell Army Air Field was activated in 1942 as a facility for training bomber crews. At the end of World War II, it was selected as the location for basing the 509th Composite Group.[4]

Known briefly as Roswell Air Force Base after the establishment of the U.S. Air Force as a separate military service in September 1947, it was renamed Walker Air Force Base on 1 August 1948 in honor of Brigadier General Kenneth Newton Walker. General Walker was killed in a B-17 mission over Rabaul, New Britain in the south Pacific on 5 January 1943. A Medal of Honor winner, General Walker was born in Cerrillos, New Mexico. The base was deactivated on 1 July 1967.

Tinian North Field

Tinian North Field was the base for combat operations for the 509th Composite Group in the Pacific from June to November 1945. The 509th was administratively assigned to the 313th Bombardment Wing while it was stationed on Tinian; however, operational control of its activities was actually retained in Washington. The 15 Silverplate B-29s that were based on North Field are listed below. Details of these aircraft and their missions are included in chapter 3 and in appendices B and G.

44-27296	44-27299	44-27302	44-27353	44-86292
44-27297	44-27300	44-27303	44-27354	44-86346
44-27298	44-27301	44-27304	44-85291	44-86347

One additional Silverplate B-29 was on Tinian for a brief period of time. As one of the three aircraft that transported Fat Man units from Kirtland Army Air Field to Tinian in late–July 1945, 42-65386 from the 216th Base Unit at Wendover arrived on Tinian with 44-86346 and 44-86347 on 2 August 1945. It is believed that 42-65386 departed Tinian to return to Wendover within one or two days.

Two of the Silverplate B-29s (44-27303 and 44-86346) departed Tinian on 9 August 1945 to return to Wendover. Their mission was to be ready to transport additional Fat Man bomb components to Tinian should the need arise (which it didn't due to the Japanese surrender on 14 August 1945). The remaining 13 Silverplate B-29s were flown back to Roswell Army Air Field in November 1945.

Tinian was one of the Marianas Islands purchased from Spain by Germany in 1899. It was one of the islands mandated to Japan in 1919 after the defeat of Germany in World War I. The Japanese used the island mainly to grow sugar cane, with Korean slaves providing the labor. Elements of the 2nd and 4th U. S. Marine Divisions invaded the island on 24 July 1944 and gained total control by 1 August. Compared to the seizure of other islands in the Pacific, the Marine losses were light: 317 killed, 1,550 wounded, and 27 missing. Construction of the four, 8,000-foot runways on the north end of the island began immediately thereafter.

Tinian is about 38 square miles in area and is about the same size and shape as Manhattan Island in New York.[5] It is about 10 miles long from north to south. The

20. Tinian North Field Runway. (Leon D. Smith)

strategic importance of Tinian in World War II was that it was only 1,500 miles from Tokyo, which was within the range of the hundreds of B-29 bombers based at five fields on Tinian, Saipan, and Guam in the Marianas.

Tinker Air Force Base

The Air Materiel Command depot at Tinker Air Force Base in Oklahoma City, Oklahoma, was the last destination for one Silverplate B-29 and the location where 31 of these special configuration B-29s lost their capabilities for carrying atomic bombs.

The one Silverplate B-29 that never left Tinker after being transferred to the Oklahoma City depot was 44-86431. It was sent to the 4136th Base Unit at Tinker from the 509th for depot modifications in January 1946 in preparation for Operation Crossroads, but an accident of some unknown nature led to its demise. It was removed from inventory as being surplus in August 1947.

All but one of the 31 Silverplate B-29s transferred to Tinker for modifications that removed their capabilities to carry atomic bombs came from the 97th Bombardment Group at Biggs Air Force Base and the test organizations at Kirtland Air Force Base. The one exception was 44-87771. It was transferred from the 509th at Walker Air Force Base to the 9th Bombardment Wing at Travis Air Force Base in California in November 1951, then placed in temporary storage at Davis-Monthan Air Force Base in August 1954. It was removed from storage in September 1955 and assigned to the Oklahoma City Air Materiel Area depot at Tinker where it was converted to a TB-29 configuration. 44-87771 was eventually transferred to the U.S. Army and flown to the Army Aberdeen Proving Ground where it was used for tests that resulted in its destruction.

The thirty Silverplate B-29s from Biggs and Kirtland that were converted to TB-29s are listed below. Biggs supplied 26 of the aircraft and four came from test activities for Los Alamos and the military at Kirtland. The four that were from Kirtland are marked with an asterisk.

42-65234	44-27304	44-86382	44-86437	44-86447*
42-65384*	44-27354	44-85384	44-86439	44-86448
44-27295	44-86263	44-86394	44-86440	44-87752
44-27298	44-86291	44-86401	44-86443	44-87774
44-27301	44-86346	44-86430	44-86444*	45-21739
44-27302	44-86347	44-86432	44-86445	45-21818*

Located 8.5 miles southeast of downtown Oklahoma City, Oklahoma, Tinker Army Air Field was constructed in 1943 along with a modification center operated by Douglas Aircraft Company. The installation was first known as the Midwest Air Depot but was later called the Oklahoma City Air Depot. A large maintenance and supply facility was added to the modification center in 1945. The field was named in honor of Major General Clarence L. Tinker of Pawhuska, Oklahoma, who lost his life while leading a flight of LB-30 bombers on a raid against Japanese forces on Wake Island early in 1942. The base was renamed Tinker Air Force Base in 1948.

Wendover Army Air Field

Located on the south edge of the small town of Wendover at the very western edge of Utah, Wendover Army Air Field was the base of operations at one time or another of 46 Silverplate B-29s.

The 393rd Bombardment Squadron was detached from the 504th Bombardment Group at Fairmont Army Air Field in Nebraska in September 1944 and assigned to Wendover for continued training. When the 509th Composite Group was activated at Wendover on 17 December 1944, the 393rd became the combat element of the 509th. As described below, 35 Silverplate B-29s were assigned to the 509th at Wendover in three separate phases over the 11-month period from October 1944 to August 1945.

When Wendover was selected as the location for organizing and training the 509th, a decision was made to use the same base for Los Alamos test operations. To support the Los Alamos test program, the field's 216th Base Unit was augmented with personnel and equipment. Special weapon assembly facilities and bomb loading pits were constructed in early 1945 when the pace of test activities increased. The bombing and gunnery range south and east of the field was used for some of the Los Alamos drop test missions.

A Test Section established as part of the 216th Base Unit conducted the test operations using Silverplate B-29s assigned for that purpose. The first Silverplate B-29 used for tests at Wendover was the prototype (42-6259) that had been used for drop tests at the Muroc Bombing and Gunnery Range in California in early 1944 (see chapter 2).

The first contingent of Silverplate B-29s delivered from the Martin Omaha plant to Wendover for test activities by the 216th Base Unit and training by the 509th included 17 aircraft. They were delivered during the months of October and November 1944. The 509th aircraft were actually assigned to the 393rd Bombardment Squadron since the 509th had not yet been activated. Chapter 2 provides details of this group of Silverplate B-29s.

Three of this first group of 17 aircraft were assigned to the 216th Base Unit to support the Los Alamos drop test program. The other 14 Silverplate B-29s were initially assigned to the 393rd Bombardment Squadron for crew training, but four of these aircraft were reassigned to the 216th when the pace of the test program was significantly increased. The 17 Silverplate B-29s in this group are listed below. Aircraft assigned to the 216th are noted with a single asterisk and those that were reassigned from the 393rd to the 216th are shown with a double asterisk.

42-65209	42-65236**	42-65258*	42-65263
42-65216	42-65237	42-65259**	42-65264
42-65217	42-65238	42-65260**	
42-65234*	42-65239	42-65261	
42-65235*	42-65240	42-65262**	

The second group of Silverplate B-29s delivered to Wendover included 28 airplanes, 20 of which are described in chapter 2. The other 8 aircraft, delivered after the 509th deployed to Tinian, are also covered in chapter 2. Seven of the airplanes in this group of 28 were assigned to the 216th Base Unit for use in the Los Alamos test program. The remaining 21 Silverplate B-29s were assigned to the 509th, 15 of which were flown to Tinian for combat operations.

The 28 aircraft in this group are listed on the next page. A single asterisk indicates those that did not go to Tinian; a double asterisk denotes those assigned to the 216th.

42-65384**	44-27298	44-27353	44-86383*
42-65385**	44-27299	44-27354	44-86384*
42-65386**	44-27300	44-86291	44-86430**
42-65387**	44-27301	44-86292	44-86431*
44-27295**	44-27302	44-86346	44-86432**
44-27296	44-27303	44-86347	44-86472*
44-27297	44-27304	44-86382*	44-86473*

Located 110 miles west of Salt Lake City, Utah, on the border with Nevada, Wendover's history goes back to 1920 when an enterprising man named Bill Smith decided to build a gas station at a desolate spot between Salt Lake City and Reno along what was then U.S. Highway 40. The location he selected was actually on the Nevada side of the border. His business prospered since it provided much needed services to motorists crossing the barren Bonneville Salt Flats. He later added a restaurant, hotel, and gambling hall that was initially known as the Stateline Club. It is now called the State Line Nugget Hotel and Casino.

Wendover Army Air Field was activated on 28 March 1942 on land that was on the Utah side of the border between the two states. For the next two years it was used as a training base for bomber crews. In April 1944, the mission of the base changed when training of P-47 fighter pilots began. The P-47 training ended abruptly in September 1944 when Wendover was selected as the base for organizing and training the unit that would carry out the atomic bombing missions. The security advantage realized in the isolation of Wendover was a major factor in its selection as the home of the 509th.

Renamed Wendover Air Force Base in 1947, the facility was declared surplus and turned over to the town of Wendover, Utah, for a municipal airport in June 1976. The population of Wendover today is about 1,500. The Nevada side of the Wendover area was incorporated as the town of West Wendover in 1991. It has a population today of about 7,000 residents.

Wright Army Air Field

The Engineering Division of the Air Materiel Command at Wright Field produced the prototype Silverplate B-29 by modifying a standard configuration B-29 during the period from December 1943 to the end of January 1944. The 58th Bombardment Wing, in training at Smoky Hill Army Air Field at the time, delivered serial number B-29-5-BW-42-6259 to Wright Field for the modification process. More information on the prototype is included in chapter 2.

The predecessor to Wright Field was McCook Field, located on 254 acres of leased land just north of downtown Dayton. McCook Field opened on 4 December 1917 and became the home of the Airplane Engineering Division of the U.S. Army Signal Corps. A companion facility established at about the same time was Wilbur Wright Field, which was situated several miles northeast of Dayton on leased land that eventually became part of Wright Field. The Signal Corps Aviation School was the primary tenant of Wilbur Wright Field.

As activities and facilities at McCook Field expanded in the 1920s, the safety of operations deteriorated and it became apparent that a new facility with more room was needed. Construction of facilities at Wright Field began on 16 April 1926 on land donated to the federal government by the city of Dayton, Ohio. The transfer of equipment and operations from McCook Field to Wright Field was accomplished from March through June 1927. The formal dedication of Wright Field, named to honor both Wilbur and Orville Wright, was held on 12 October 1927 with Orville Wright raising the first flag over the new engineering center.

The Fairfield Aviation General Supply Depot was established on 40 acres of land adjacent to Wilbur Wright Field at the same time as McCook Field was established in 1917. The mission of the depot was to provide logistics support to Wilbur Wright Field and three other Signal Corps aviation schools in the Midwest.

The area that included the Fairfield Air Depot was named Patterson Field on 1 July 1931 in honor of Lieutenant John H. Patterson. Lieutenant Patterson was the son of Frank J. Patterson and nephew of John H. Patterson, co-founders of Dayton's National Cash Register Company. Lt. Patterson was killed on 19 June 1918 during a test flight at Wilbur Wright Field. On 13 January 1948, Wright Field and Patterson Field were officially merged into a single installation and redesignated Wright-Patterson Air Force Base.

7 THE BOMBS

No history of the Silverplate B-29s would be complete without a discussion of the various types of bombs they carried for test purposes and in combat. Although they were modified specifically to carry atomic bombs, the Silverplate and Saddletree versions of the B-29 were still able to carry standard general-purpose, high explosive bombs in both the front and rear bomb bays. As described in chapter 3, the aircraft of the 509th Composite Group on Tinian did carry out a number of missions in which non-atomic bombs were dropped, both general purpose and pumpkin.

The nicknames for the original atomic bomb concepts, Thin Man and Fat Man, aptly described the bomb shapes. One was long and thin; the other was an elongated sphere with fins. In his *History of Project A*, Ramsey credits Army Air Forces personnel with devising the names "Thin Man" and "Fat Man" in 1943 as they "…tried to make their phone conversations sound as if they were modifying a plane to carry President Franklin D. Roosevelt (the Thin Man) and British Prime Minister Winston Churchill (the Fat Man)." The aircraft in these conversations was the prototype Silverplate B-29 being modified at Wright Army Air Field near Dayton, Ohio.

Bowen provides a slightly different version of the use of the names at Wright Field. In his history of the Air Force atomic energy program, he relates that the project name of Pullman was assigned to the Wright Field effort to modify the first Silverplate B-29. As a cover story for communications on the highly classified project, Thin Man was supposed to refer to Roosevelt and Fat Man to Churchill, who together would be involved in a secret tour of the United States in a Pullman railroad car.[1]

Much of the material on the Little Boy and Fat Man atomic bombs was taken from *Atom Bombs: The Top Secret Inside Story of Little Boy and Fat Man* by John Coster-Mullen. Although the accuracy of the information on the bombs included in his book has not been confirmed by any government agency, it is believed the bomb data he has collected and published is near enough to the truth to merit use as a source in this chapter. Coster-Mullen's permission to use material from his book is appreciated.[2]

General Purpose High-Explosive Bombs

The bombs used by the 509th Composite Group in the practice bombing missions in July and August 1945 were the AN-M64A1 500-pound general-purpose

(GP) high-explosive bomb and the AN-M65A1 1,000-pound GP high-explosive bomb.³

In 15 practice bombing missions involving 90 B-29 sorties, 108 of the 500-pound GP bombs and 50 of the 1,000-pound GP bombs were dropped on the islands of Rota, Truk, Marcus, and Guguan. These particular islands were still held by Japanese forces but were bypassed as the United States concentrated on islands closer to Japan. The fifty tons of bombs dropped by the 509th in these practice missions was small when compared with the enormous number and tonnage of similar bombs dropped by other 20th Air Force units in the first half of 1945, but the 509th missions using the GP bombs represented valuable training for its crews.

The AN-M64A1 500-pound general purpose bomb was a little over 59 inches long with the tail fin assembly attached and actually weighed 560 pounds as released. The body of the bomb minus the fins was 47.5 inches long, had a diameter of 14.2 inches, and weighed 535 pounds. It contained 278.3 pounds of either Composition B, TNT, or amatol high explosive material.

The AN-M65A1 1,000-pound general purpose bomb was 69.5 inches long with the tail fin assembly attached and actually weighed 1,080 pounds as released. The

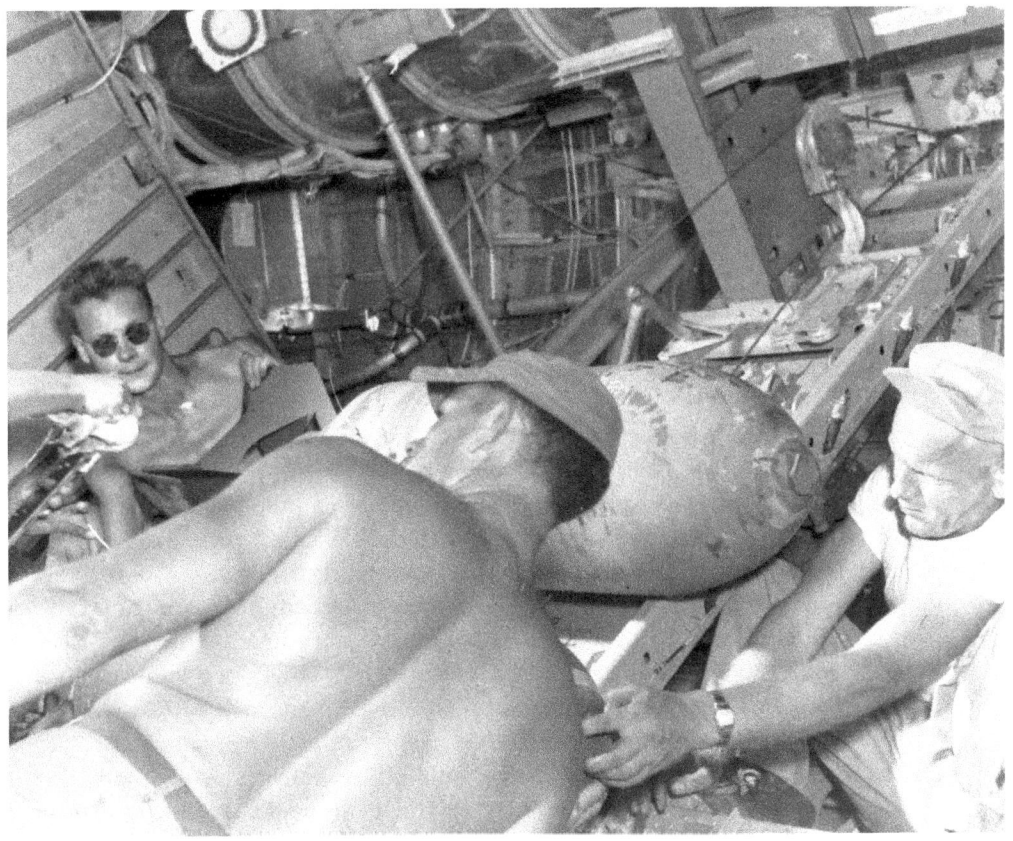

21. Loading a 500-lb General Purpose Bomb. (Air Force Museum)

body of the bomb minus the fins was 54 inches long, had a diameter of 18.8 inches, weighed 1,042 pounds. It contained a little over 572 pounds of either tritinal, Composition B, TNT, or amatol high explosive material.

The GP bombs dropped in the 509th practice missions were fitted with nose fuses and, in some missions, with tail fuses. Most missions were flown with the GP bombs mounted in the front bomb bay, but there were a few sorties in which the bombs were carried in the rear bomb bay.

The mission listing in Appendix B includes the practice bombing missions for each Silverplate B-29 on Tinian.[4]

Pumpkin Bomb

The term "Pumpkin" was used to denote three versions of Fat Man ellipsoidal shapes developed for test and development activities by Los Alamos Laboratory and for training and combat rehearsal missions by the 509th Composite Group. Los Alamos personnel also called the high explosive Pumpkin bombs that were developed for combat missions "blockbuster" bombs.

According to Los Alamos teletype TA-522, dated 4 March 1945, the Pumpkin name was suggested by Navy Captain William S. "Deak" Parsons of Los Alamos and Dr. Charles C. Lauritsen, head of the support effort at California Institute of Technology (Cal Tech or CIT).[5]

The three types of Pumpkin bombs were externally similar to the Fat Man atomic bomb, particularly with respect to dimensions and weight. One major difference was that the Pumpkins with a full load of high explosives used three contact fuses on the nose while the Fat Man atomic bomb employed four.

Some of the Pumpkins also differed from the Fat Man bombs in that the front and rear ellipsoidal outer casings for the Pumpkins were joined together with a weld around the major circumference. The Fat Man front and rear sections were bolted together with the outer lugs of the inner sphere. A fairing covered each of the eight bolt fittings.

The Fat Man bombs also had four radar antenna mounting pads around the circumference of the forward ellipsoidal casing as part of the arming and firing system whereas the Pumpkin units had none. Pumpkin bombs and the Fat Man units both used the same tail assembly, which was bolted in eight places to the rear section.

The front and rear Pumpkin shells were each fabricated by welding together four ellipsoidal segments formed from $3/8$" mild steel sheets. Los Alamos records indicate that a few ellipsoidal front and rear sections were fabricated out of armor steel, but the reason for this difference is not documented. The length of a Pumpkin unit was 128 inches with a maximum diameter of 60 inches.

Although different Pumpkin weights are given in several Los Alamos historical files, the weight most often quoted for the Pumpkins used during tests and missions in 1945 was 10,525 pounds. The steel parts for the ellipsoidal shape accounted for 3,800 pounds, the tail assembly weighed 425 pounds, and the high explosive or concrete filler weighed 6,300 pounds.

22. Pumpkin Bomb Used in Combat Missions. (Los Alamos National Laboratory)

The Pumpkin bomb shown in Figure 22 shows the three contact fuse housings, looking like headlights, used on the Pumpkin bombs dropped on Japanese targets. The large size of the Pumpkin bomb can be appreciated when it is compared to the size of the flatbed trailer on which it rests. Noticeable in the photograph is the single attachment lug on top of the bomb for mounting in the bomb bay in the same manner as the Fat Man atomic bomb.

In order to duplicate the center of gravity and moment of inertia of the Fat Man atomic bomb, the high explosive mixture and the concrete filler in test, training, and combat Pumpkin units had approximately the same weight as the inner sphere and pieces of equipment of the Fat Man bomb. This matching of the inner weight and distribution gave the Pumpkin shapes the same ballistic and handling characteristics as the Fat Man units.

The California Institute of Technology (Cal Tech or CIT) managed the development of the Pumpkin bombs under the terms of a support arrangement with Los Alamos. The ellipsoidal shells were initially manufactured by Consolidated Steel Co. and Western Pipe and Steel Co., both of Los Angeles, California, under a contract with CIT. Centerline Company of Detroit, Michigan, manufactured the tail assemblies.

In May 1945, procurement of the Pumpkin shells was transferred from CIT to the Navy's Bureau of Ordnance (BuOrd), using the same manufacturers. At the end of August 1945, 261 Pumpkins of all types had been produced and 225 additional units were in the production process. Out of a total order of 1,000 Pumpkins, 486 units were eventually delivered. The estimated cost of the Pumpkin shells in May 1945 was $1,500 to $2,000 each.

Pumpkins were produced as either "live" or "inert" units. The live Pumpkins contained a charge of high explosives, while the inert shapes contained an inner mass of concrete or plaster. The inert units were delivered by rail from Consolidated Steel and Western Pipe to Wendover Army Air Field, where they were prepared for either test or training missions by the ordnance section of the 216th Base Unit. Most of the inert test Pumpkins were dropped by the test section of the 216th Base Unit, although some drop test missions were flown by 509th crews as training exercises and to reduce the 216th workload.

The concrete mixture for the sphere used in dummy Fat Man drops was one bag of cement, one bag of plaster of paris, 240 pounds of sand, and enough water to result in a final concrete density of 1.67 to 1.68 (the density of the Composition B high explosive with which the live Pumpkins were loaded).

Navy Captain "Deak" Parsons and Colonel Paul Tibbets originated the idea of the high explosive Pumpkin bomb in December 1944. Specifications for the combat Pumpkin bomb required that they could be carried in the forward bomb bay of the Silverplate B-29, that they would make as effective use as possible of the carrying capacity of the plane, and that they would be fused in such a way that they would be effective against the enemy. In a meeting at Los Alamos on 13 December 1944, J. Robert Oppenheimer assured Tibbets that Los Alamos would do everything possible to provide the type and quantity of blockbuster (high explosive Pumpkin) bombs desired by Tibbets.

The primary motivation for having and using the high explosive Pumpkin bombs was to continue and enhance the training of 509th crews once they arrived on Tinian. The mission profile for the combat Pumpkin sorties was very similar to that planned for the atomic missions, and the targets selected for the Pumpkin missions were in the same area as the targets chosen for the atomic strikes.[6] Thus, the 509th crews were rehearsing the atomic missions and, as a bonus, inflicting damage on Japanese facilities when they flew the Pumpkin missions.

The live Pumpkin bombs used by the 509th Composite Group in a few training missions at Wendover and in 51 combat sorties from Tinian used the standard ellipsoidal shells produced in Los Angeles and the tail assemblies manufactured in Detroit. The ellipsoidal shells and tail assemblies were shipped to the Naval Ammunition Depot at McAlester, Oklahoma, where the shells were filled with 6,300 pounds of Composition B high explosive material. Composition B is a mixture of RDX high explosive, TNT, and wax.

The ellipsoidal shells for the combat Pumpkins were shipped to McAlester with a 4" diameter hole at a point on the maximum diameter. The shells were placed on a cradle in a horizontal position and the Composition B mixture poured into the shell in a slurry form. The high explosive mixture was then cured for 36 hours in a drying facility. After the Composition B had set into a solid form, the filler hold was covered and the attachment lug added. The Pumpkin assembly was completed with the addition of the tail assembly. The nose contact fuses were not installed until mission preparation on Tinian.

With the high explosive filling process completed, each Pumpkin was placed into a shipping container designed specifically for these bombs. They were then shipped by rail car to the U.S. Naval Magazine at Port Chicago in the San Francisco Bay area. This area was also known as the Inland Storage Area at Cowell, California, and was given the code name Three Igloo Job by Los Alamos.

The combat Pumpkins were shipped from the Port Chicago facility to Tinian by ship. It is not known for certain how many Pumpkins were shipped to Tinian, but the total was certainly more than the 51 units used in missions to Japan. When the shipments of Pumpkin bombs arrived in the Tinian harbor, the bombs were uncrated, offloaded onto a dock, and then moved to a bomb storage area.

When a combat mission was scheduled, the Pumpkins bombs needed for the mission were moved from the storage area to the 509th loading pits. Using the loading pits constructed on Tinian for the atomic bombs, a Pumpkin bomb was then loaded into the front bomb bay of each Silverplate B-29 participating in the mission.

After each bomb was secured in the bomb bay, the three contact fuses were installed and safety pullout wires from the fuse arming vanes connected to attach points in the bomb bay structure. After fueling and other servicing, the aircraft was then ready for the mission later that day or the next day.

Pumpkin missions from Tinian were flown in a manner similar to the atomic missions. As soon as the Pumpkin bomb was released and cleared the bomb bay doors, the pilot put the B-29 into the sharp turn for the escape maneuver. The Pumpkin bombs were released at an altitude of about 30,000 feet.

Immediately after the end of the war, the U.S. Strategic Bombing Survey (USSBS) conducted an analysis of the effectiveness of the U.S. bombing campaign against Japan, including the atomic and Pumpkin missions. A special report was issued by the USSBS on the effect of the Pumpkin bomb dropped on nine selected targets. The report concluded that it "was a reasonably effective weapon against Japanese plants when direct hits were scored on vital areas, or when the near-miss hit was sufficiently close to important buildings to cause severe structural damage." The report went on to state that blast was the primary cause of damage with secondary fires occasionally contributing to the total effect of the bombs.

A listing of the 509th Composite Group Pumpkin missions for each Silverplate B-29 on Tinian is included in chapter 3. The mission listing in Appendix B also includes the Pumpkin missions.

Thin Man Atomic Bomb

The Thin Man model was one of the original two atomic bomb concepts envisioned by Los Alamos scientists early in 1943. The second of the initial proposals was the Fat Man bomb that used the implosion method for achieving a critical mass and detonation of the fissionable material. Both concepts used plutonium-239 as the active material. This isotope of plutonium was to be produced in the reactors at the Hanford site along the Colombia River in Washington.

The concept for the Thin Man bomb involved the use of one segment of pluto-

23. Thin Man Test Units. (Los Alamos National Laboratory)

nium-239 propelled down a gun tube to mate with a second segment of Pu-239. In theory, the resulting critical mass would produce an atomic explosion.

The first drop tests of the Thin Man model (also called the "high pressure gun") were conducted in August 1943 at Dahlgren Naval Proving Ground in Virginia using 14/23 scale models. Nicknamed the "sewer pipe bomb," the test units were constructed by cutting a 23-inch diameter (empty) 500-pound bomb casing in half and welding a 12-foot length of 14-inch diameter pipe between the two halves. The ballistics of the first test units were so bad that the units fell in a flat spin. Changes in the center of center of gravity and the configuration of the tail fins resulted in greatly improved ballistic characteristics. Testing of the Thin Man models continued until the end of 1943.

A number of full-scale test units were produced (minus the plutonium material) and several drop tests were conducted at Muroc Army Air Field in March 1944 using the prototype Silverplate B-29. The Thin Man model tested at Muroc was 17 feet long and had a nose section diameter of 38 inches and a diameter of 23 inches through the middle section. The tail fin assembly was 38 inches across from tip to tip. The weight of the bomb was about 8,000 pounds.

During a drop test at Muroc on 16 March 1944, a Thin Man test unit released prematurely and fell onto the not yet opened bomb bay doors. The crew was able to

7. The Bombs

24. **Thin Man Test Models at Muroc Range.** (Los Alamos National Laboratory)

jettison the bomb by opening the bomb bay doors, but there was considerable damage to the doors of the prototype Silverplate B-29 in the process. The test series was terminated and the aircraft returned to Wright Field for repairs and further modification.

During the summer of 1944, while the prototype aircraft was being repaired at Wright Field, Los Alamos scientists began receiving the first samples of plutonium-239 from the reactors at Oak Ridge and the Hanford site. Much to their chagrin, they discovered that the reactor plutonium-239, the desired isotope for the Thin Man bomb, contained significant amounts of plutonium-240. This isotope of plutonium is an emitter of fast neutrons and would therefore prevent a nuclear detonation in the gun-assembly method because it would cause a weak premature reaction.

Development work on the Thin Man bomb was terminated as soon as the plutonium-240 contamination problem was confirmed in July 1943. In its place, the Los Alamos scientists devised a scaled-down version that would use uranium-235 and be much shorter. The alternate gun-type bomb became known as Little Boy.

When the decision was made to abandon the Thin Man concept and adopt the Little Boy design, the prototype Silverplate B-29 undergoing repairs at Wright Field was modified to replace the single bomb bay needed for the Thin Man bomb with the original configuration of two separate bomb bays. In addition, the suspension

25. Thin Man Test Articles at Muroc. (Robert W. Krauss)

equipment for the Thin Man bomb was removed and new shackles and release mechanisms for mounting the Fat Man and Little Boy bomb shapes in the front bomb bay were installed.

Little Boy Atomic Bomb

The Little Boy atomic bomb used on the Hiroshima mission on 6 August 1945 was a gun-type weapon that used uranium. It was developed by Los Alamos personnel after they discovered that the gun-type, plutonium-fueled Thin Man concept would not work. In essence, the Little Boy bomb was a scaled-down version of Thin Man with the primary difference being the use of uranium instead of plutonium.

The Little Boy bomb was about the same diameter and weight as the Thin Man bomb, but at ten feet in length it was seven feet shorter than the Thin Man. With respect to the explosive power of the two types of bombs, it is not possible to compare them since no records have been found to indicate the calculated yield of the Thin Man concept. It is known that the Little Boy bomb dropped on Hiroshima exploded with a force equal to about 15,000 tons of TNT, and it is reasonable to

26. Little Boy Test Model. (Los Alamos National Laboratory)

believe that Los Alamos scientists envisioned a Thin Man bomb with similar or better characteristics.

The uranium material used in Little Boy was given the code name "Oralloy," which stood for Oak Ridge alloy and was named for the facilities at Oak Ridge in Tennessee that produced it. The uranium used in Little Boy was actually a mixture of two isotopes, U-235 and U-238. The U-235 isotope is fissionable but the amount found in naturally occurring uranium is extremely small. The U-238 isotope that is the major constituent of uranium is not fissionable. The Oralloy produced by Oak Ridge was known as "highly enriched uranium," which meant that it had been processed to increase the U-235 content from less than 1 percent to somewhere near 80 percent.

Combat-type Little Boy units used in tests and on the Hiroshima mission were given a numerical designation. Units L-1, L-2, L-5, and L-6 (all without the uranium projectile and target assemblies) were dropped near Tinian in late July to test bomb equipment and handling procedures. Unit L-11 was used in the Hiroshima mission. Figure 27 shows Francis Birch of the Project Alberta contingent inscribing the L-11 designation on the Hiroshima bomb. Norman Ramsey, the technical director of the Project Alberta contingent on Tinian, is observing at the right.

27. Little Boy Atomic Bomb Used on Hiroshima Mission. Project Alberta personnel are Francis Birch *(at left)* and Norman Ramsey *(observing at right)*. (National Archives and Records Administration)

7. The Bombs

28. Little Boy Test Model L-1 Dropped Near Tinian. (Los Alamos National Laboratory)

The Little Boy bomb was basically a naval gun barrel threaded into a heavy nose section, a uranium target assembly mounted in the nose section, a uranium projectile, arming and firing components, an outer casing, and a tail fin assembly. It measured 120 inches in length and 28 inches in diameter. It weighed about 9,700 pounds.

The heart of the Little Boy bomb was the nose section and gun barrel assembly that represented over half the total weight of the bomb. The nose section was the two-piece target case that had a diameter of 28 inches and was about 36 inches long. Weighing over 5,000 pounds, it was forged from heat-treated high-alloy steel. Consisting of an inner and outer portion, the inner section held the uranium target assembly surrounded by the tamper material.

An adapter screwed into the aft end of the inner section of the target case was fabricated with about 8 inches of square-type threads machined into the inner wall of the adapter. The front end of the gun barrel, with matching threads, was then screwed into the adapter. The tamper sleeve was 13 inches in diameter and 13 inches long, with a bore of 6.5 inches. It was fabricated of a material that was basically a tungsten-carbide powder compacted under high pressure and sintered at high temperature in a furnace with a controlled atmosphere. A 6.5 inch smooth bore gun, almost 72 inches long and weighing about 1,000 pounds, was screwed into the aft end of the target case adapter. Manufactured by the Naval Gun Factory in Washington (DC), the forward end of the barrel was machined with about 8 inches of square threads to match those in the target case adapter.

A two-piece breech plug was threaded into the aft end of the barrel. The inner portion of the plug, about 3 to 4 inches in diameter and weighing between 15 and 20 pounds, contained the three primers and firing leads used to ignite four powder bags of Cordite smokeless gun propellant. The explosion of the powder bags propelled the uranium projectile about 52 inches down the gun barrel into the uranium target assembly at a velocity of nearly 1,000 feet per second.

The two-piece breech plug was developed to minimize the possibility that a nuclear detonation would occur if the carrier B-29 crashed on take-off. When Little Boy was loaded into *Enola Gay* for the Hiroshima mission, the four powder bags and the tools for removing and replacing the inner section of the breech plug were stowed separately in the bomb bay. Captain Parsons went into the bomb bay after take-off, removed the inner section of the breech plug, inserted the powder bags, and then replaced the breech plug unit.

An additional safety feature in the design of the Little Boy bomb (also used on the Fat Man bomb) was the use of safe/arm plugs. Three plugs with green handles were inserted into connectors mounted on the top of the bomb when it was assembled. These plugs disabled certain electrical circuits necessary for the bomb to arm and detonate. After take-off and insertion of the powder bags, the electronics test officer (Morris "Dick" Jeppson) replaced the green plugs with red-handled plugs that completed these circuits. The bomb was then in a configuration that permitted the arming and firing units to work.

The total amount of uranium used in Little Boy was slightly more than 141 pounds. The projectile contained about 60 percent of the total (about 85 pounds). The target assembly included about 40 percent of the total (about 56 pounds).

The critical portion of the target assembly consisted of six Oralloy rings, each with an outer diameter of 4 inches and a one-inch diameter hole in the center. The assembly of target rings thus formed a rod 7 inches long with a diameter of 4 inches. A cylindrical piece of tamper material 6.5 inches in diameter and 3.25 inches thick was attached to the front of the Oralloy rod.

A cylindrical forging of ductile material, known as the anvil, was mounted in the front of the cavity in the target case and just forward of the tamper/target ring assembly. The purpose of the anvil was to absorb as much of the kinetic energy of the projectile as possible, thereby helping to keep the target material from being physically altered before critical assembly could take place.

Holding the anvil and tamper/target ring assembly in position and aligned within the target case cavity was a one-inch diameter steel rod. This rod went from the Oralloy target ring assembly through the tamper plug and anvil and through the center of the front target case plug.

Pressed into the target cavity just ahead of the front end of the gun barrel was a tamper sleeve that was 13 inches in diameter and 13 inches long. It had a bore of 6.5 inches. The tamper/target ring assembly was fitted inside this tamper sleeve and could slide forward into the anvil when struck by the projectile. The tamper material was basically a tungsten-carbide mixture with some metallic natural uranium mixed in with it. The tamper plug and tamper sleeve served to contain the rapidly expanding nuclear detonation as long as possible by physically holding the reaction together and reflecting escaping neutrons back into the chain reaction.

The projectile was an assembly of nine Oralloy rings at the front with a tamper disk 3.25 inches thick behind it. The Oralloy rings each had an outer diameter of 6.3 inches and a hole with a diameter of 4 inches. To the rear of the tamper disk was a steel section 6.0 inches thick. These components were mounted in a steel can that had a wall thickness of 1/16 of an inch. The assembled projectile was 16.25 inches long and weighed about 190 pounds.

To initiate the fission reaction when the projectile was fired down the gun tube and encased the target assembly, four polonium-beryllium initiators were secured to the front of the target case/tamper assembly. The initiators were about 0.5 inches in diameter and 0.5 inches long. The polonium was kept separate from the beryllium by a piece of gold foil that was punctured by the impact of the projectile. When impact occurred and the initiators were crushed, the polonium mixed with the beryllium thus releasing a flood of neutrons that started the fission reaction.

The arming and firing system in the Little Boy bomb consisted of one clock box, six barometric sensing boxes, four battery boxes, a radar system that included four antenna units and four circuitry boxes, three safe/arm plugs, and several interconnecting cables. There were also three pull out plugs to provide aircraft power and permit monitoring during flight by the electronics test officer.

The clock box served as the main junction box or control unit. Measuring about 18 inches by 10 inches by 9.75 inches, it contained several of the arming and firing components along with electrical connections to the other arming and firing boxes. It also included the output cable that went to the propellant igniters in the breech plug of the gun barrel. Mounted in the clock box were eight 15-second timers that were activated when the bomb was released by pull out wires attached to the bomb bay structure. The primary reason for the 15-second delay was to ensure a safe separation distance between the bomb and the airplane before the radar system was enabled.

Figure 29 shows a section of the interior of the Little Boy bomb with arming and firing components mounted around the gun barrel. The clock box mounted at the top is connected to a test unit at the left.

Each of the six barometric (baro) sensing boxes contained an aneroid pressure sensitive device which closed an electrical circuit at a predetermined pressure altitude. The baro switches were connected to eight ports on the surface of the outer casing of the bomb by metal tubing and standard AN fittings. The primary function of the baro sensors was to determine when the bomb was at approximately the right altitude for control of the firing signal to be exercised by the highly accurate radar system.

The four radar units were an adaptation of the RT-34/APS-13 tail warning radar set developed for fighter aircraft of the U.S. Army Air Forces.[7] Each radar case was 7.5 inches high, 8.5 inches deep, and 15 inches wide. The same radar units were used in the Fat Man bomb. Front panel connectors provided 24-volt DC input power, a connection to the associated antenna, and a 24-volt DC output firing signal that went to the primers in the breech plug.

29. Arming and Firing Components of Little Boy Bomb. (National Archives and Records Administration)

The antennas for the radar units used the Yagi design that consisted of three elements made from metal rods having a diameter of ⅜ of an inch. The first element was a straight rod 6⅜ inches long that was known as the "director." The middle segment was a U-shaped "driven" element that was slightly longer than the first rod. The third element was a straight rod eight inches long that was known as the "reflector." The director and reflector focused radar signals going out and being received so that a cone-shaped field of radio waves was projected toward the nose of the bomb.

Four antenna bases were attached around the forward end of the bomb's outer surface. The Yagi antennas were mounted to these bases and the leads from the antennas were inserted through holes in the cylindrical outer casing plates to the radar units.

The four battery boxes provided 24-volt DC power to the various components of the arming and firing system. Prior to release from the bomb bay, power was provided by a connection to the power of the airplane that disconnected when release occurred. The three pull-out plugs also provided connections to a bomb-monitoring console in the carrier airplane.

The outer casing of the Little Boy bomb aft of the nose section was an arrangement of bulkheads and shaped steel plates. A steel bulkhead 27.25 inches in diame-

7. The Bombs

30. Little Boy Unit L-11 in Loading Pit. (National Archives and Records Administration)

ter and 1 inch thick was fitted around the gun barrel about 63 inches back from the nose of the bomb. This bulkhead was secured in place with a locking collar attached behind the bulkhead. Four curved steel plates 28.5 inches long, together with the top plate described below, were bolted between this bulkhead and the nose section target case to form the central section of the outer bomb case. The steel plates were formed from armor steel that was ⅜ of an inch thick.

A top plate 9.75 inches wide and 28.5 inches long was attached along the top between the nose section and the aft bulkhead. The top plate provided a mounting base for connectors to receive the three pull out plugs and the three arm/safe plugs. Eleven small holes drilled in the top plate allowed the insertion of pull out wires that were attached to the bomb bay structure.

A two-piece conical section, 24 inches long, was mounted between the large bulkhead and the rear cylindrical tail section. This conical section reduced the outer diameter of the Little Boy bomb from 28 inches to 17 inches. The 17-inch diameter cylindrical tail section, made of steel plate, was 33 inches long. The box-type tail fin assembly, 30 inches on each side and with four diagonal fins, was mounted around the tail section.

The Little Boy bomb was loaded into the front bomb bay of *Enola Gay* on the afternoon of 5 August 1945 (Tinian time).[8] Figure 31 is a photograph of the actual loading of Little Boy L-11 that was dropped on Hiroshima. After it was fitted into the bomb bay shackle and the sway braces were snubbed against the outer surface, the pull-out wires were attached to the bomb bay structure and the pull-out plugs inserted into their matching connectors. A description of the process for loading the Little Boy and Fat Man bombs into the aircraft is included in chapter 3.

31. Little Boy L-11 Being Loaded Into Bomb Bay. (National Archives and Records Administration)

The arming sequence actually began early in the flight when the powder bags were inserted inside the breech plug by Captain Parsons. The next step in arming Little Boy occurred a little later in the flight when Lieutenant Morris Jeppson replaced the green-handled "safe" plugs with the red-handled "armed" plugs.

Little Boy was released over Hiroshima at 17 seconds after 8:15 A.M. (Japanese time). When the bomb fell from the bomb bay, the pull-out plugs disconnected and internal power was energized. In addition, the pull-out wires activated the timing clocks to begin the 15-second delay in radar operation. At an altitude greater than the desired detonation height, the barometric switches enabled the radar sets. After a fall of 45.5 seconds, the radar units triggered the detonation of Little Boy at an altitude of about 1,900 feet.

The Little Boy and Fat Man bombs were similar only in their use of a fissile material to produce an explosion and certain commonalities in their arming and firing components. The major differences in the two bombs were their shape, method of achieving a chain reaction (gun versus implosion), and the fissionable material used (uranium versus plutonium). One other noticeable difference was the use of four contact fuses on Fat Man and none on Little Boy. It has been said that the Los Alamos scientists had such great confidence in the design of Little Boy that there was no need for contact fuses.

Fat Man Atomic Bomb

The second of the two concepts for an atomic bomb developed by Los Alamos in the summer of 1943 was called Fat Man. Its large diameter was dictated by the size of the high explosives sphere used to produce the implosion force that crushed the inner plutonium ball into a critical mass. Whereas the gun-type Thin Man design resulted in a long, thin shape, the implosion method used in the Fat Man bomb mandated a large, fat shape.

The original Fat Man bomb dimensions provided Wright Field personnel in late–1943 for use in designing the modifications to the prototype Silverplate B-29 were a diameter of 59 inches and a length of 120 inches. Although the external shape, weight, and internal configuration changed somewhat over the next 15 months, the basic concept and the overall dimensions remained basically the same.

Figure 32 shows what is probably one of the first Fat Man shapes used in early drop tests at Muroc Dry Lake. This version was basically a sphere with a conical afterbody tapering to a circular tail fin assembly. Provisions for two attach points are visible in the photograph. Although the purpose for the protuberance welded to the nose is unknown, it may have been an attempt to improve the ballistics of the shape.

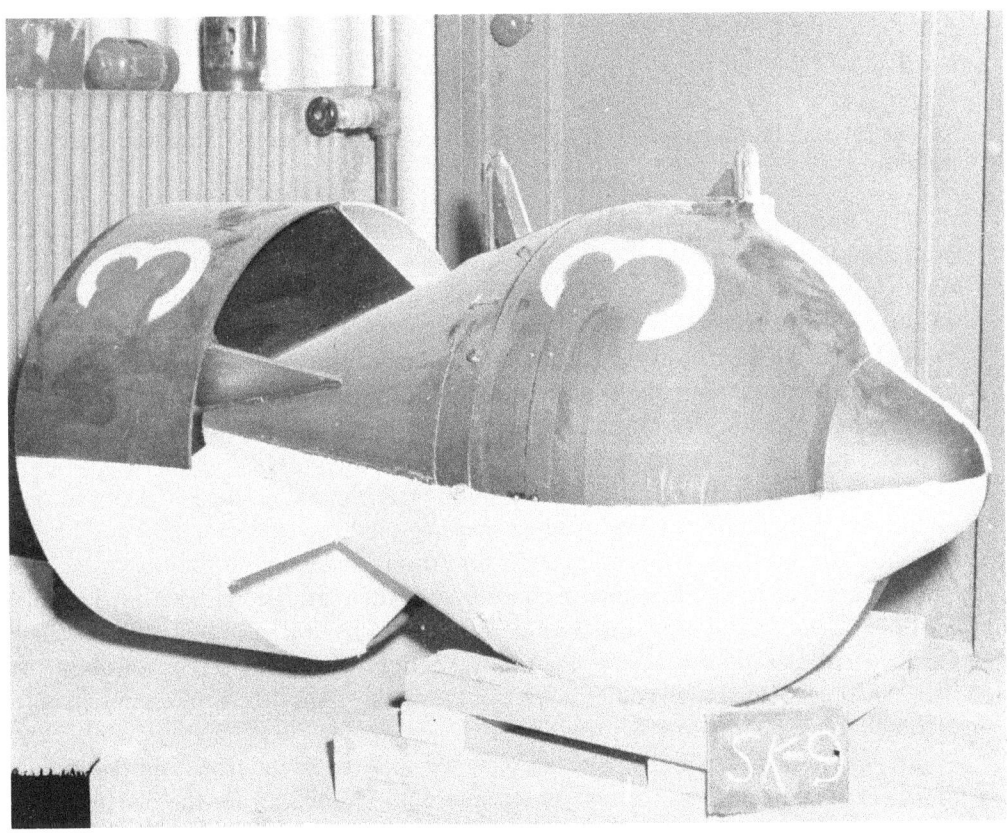

32. An Early Fat Man Shape. (Los Alamos National Laboratory)

33. The Fat Man Bomb Dropped on Nagasaki. (National Archives and Records Administration)

The final configuration of the Fat Man bomb (i.e., the Model 1561 version used in the Nagasaki mission) was 128.375 inches long, had a diameter of 60.25 inches, and weighed 10,265 pounds. The explosive force (yield) of the Fat Man bomb dropped on Nagasaki has been calculated to have been about 21 kilotons (the equivalent of 21,000 tons of TNT). The external shape of this model can be seen in Figure 33. The unit in the photograph is the actual Fat Man bomb used in the Nagasaki mission. The photograph shows the bomb undergoing final preparations prior to being taken to the loading pit.

The basic elements of the Fat Man bomb were the outer ellipsoidal casing, a square tail fin assembly, an inner sphere encasing the high-explosive shell and plutonium core, and the several components for arming and firing the bomb.

The front and rear ellipsoidal sections of the outer casing were fabricated from ⅜"-thick formed steel segments welded together. The two sections were bolted together with the inner sphere at eight points around the circumference, using U-shaped fittings welded to the outer surface of the casings. The descriptive name given to these pieces was "bathtub" fittings.

A shaped nose cap and a rear end plate were bolted to the front and rear sections. Circular steel plates were mounted internally as surfaces for the installation of arming and firing components. Holes of various diameters were drilled in the upper surfaces of both front and rear sections for safe/arm plugs, insertion of arm-

34. Fat Man Tail Fin Assembly Bolted to Rear Ballistics Case Section. (Los Alamos National Laboratory)

ing pullout wires, connectors for aircraft power and monitoring circuits, and openings for the barometric pressure sensing system. Mounting pads for the four radar antennas were welded at nearly equal points around the rear circumference of the front section. Four steel tube sections for installing contact fuses were also welded to the front end of the forward ballistic case section.

The tail fin assembly was 52" square and weighed about 500 pounds. It was constructed by riveting together sections of aluminum plate with a thickness of 0.20 inches. Baffles mounted around the rear of the assembly restricted the flow of air through the assembly, thereby improving its stability and ballistic characteristics. The assembly was mounted to the rear of the aft ellipsoidal casing at eight points using the same type U-shaped fittings that were used to connect the front and rear casing sections.

The duraluminum inner sphere consisted of two end caps and five equatorial segments joined together with 90 bolts to form an assembly that had an inner diameter of 55.25 inches and weighed 1,146 pounds without the inner components.

A layer of cork one-half inch thick separated the inner surface of the sphere from the next component, which was a shell of high explosives with an outer diameter of 54.25 inches and a total thickness of 18 inches.

35. Partial Explosive Sphere for Fat Man Bomb. (National Archives and Records Administration)

The high explosives shell was actually two layers, each composed of 32 cast lenses of a high explosive mixture known as Composition B. Each lens in the inner layer was cast with a Baratol inclusion to shape the shock wave inward when detonation occurred. Thin pieces of blotter paper were inserted between the outer and inner layers. Detonators wired to the firing unit were mounted in each lens in the outer layer. Coster-Mullen has calculated that each layer of high explosive lenses was nine inches thick and that the total weight of the high explosive shell was about 5,300 pounds.

The next inner shell was an aluminum hollow sphere called the pusher. Weighing 263 pounds, it had an outer diameter of 18 inches and a thickness of slightly more than 4.3 inches.

Thin pieces of blotter paper separated the pusher from the inner layer of high explosive lenses. The pusher served to transfer inward the shock wave from the exploding high explosive lenses to the next inner shell known as the tamper.

Made of natural uranium and coated with a layer of boron, the tamper had an outside diameter of nine inches and a thickness of about 2.7 inches. Its weight was 246 pounds.

The purpose of the tamper was to constrain the nuclear reaction in the core as long as possible in order to maximize the amount of energy developed before the

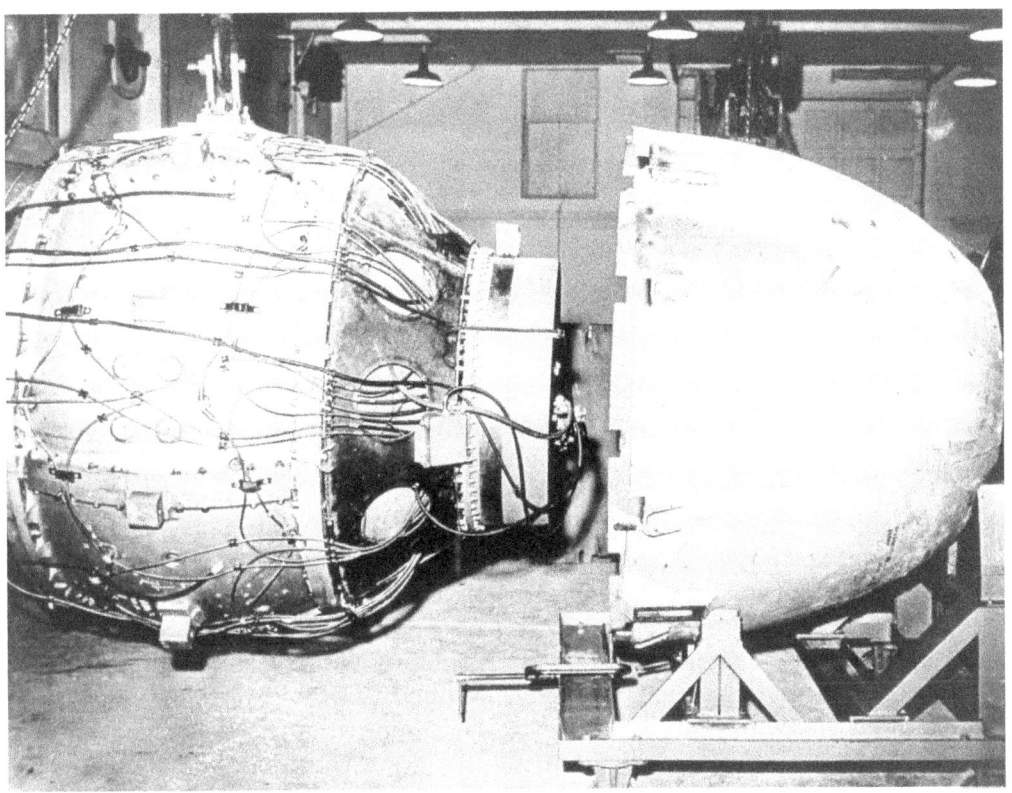

36. Fat Man Front Casing and Inner Sphere. (Los Alamos National Laboratory)

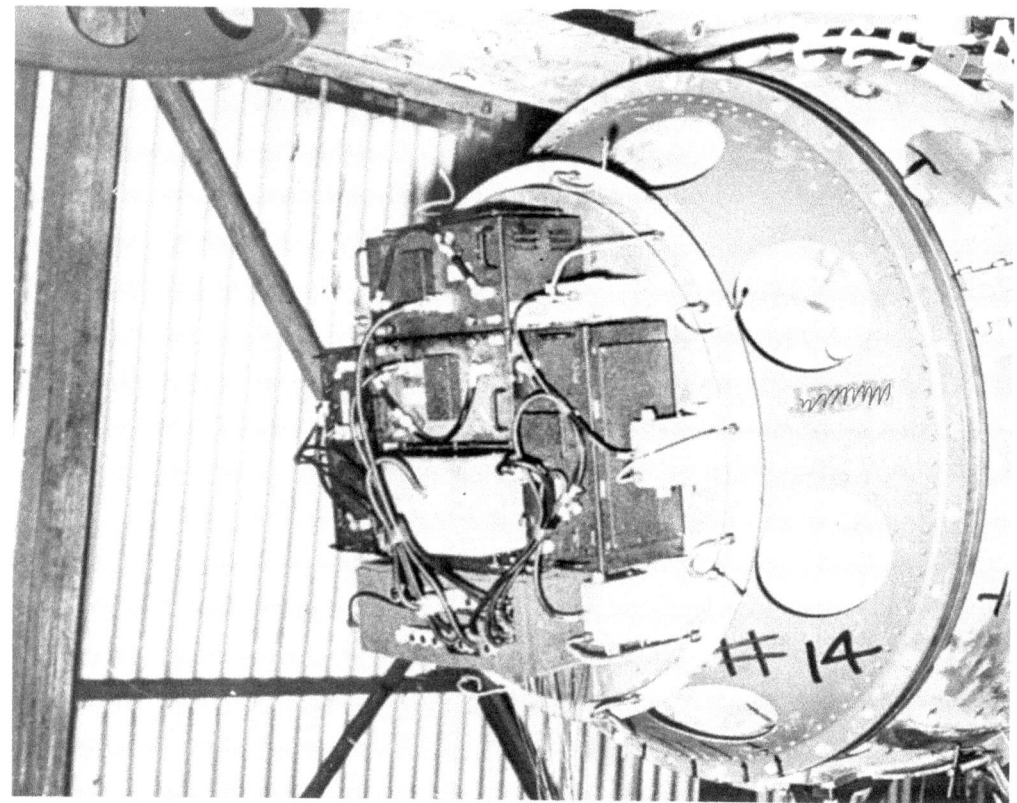

37. Fat Man Arming and Firing Components. (Los Alamos National Laboratory)

core was vaporized in the explosion. The boron coating served to reflect neutrons back into the core to enhance the fissioning process.

Nested inside the tamper was the Pu-239 core. Nickel plated, it weighed 13.6 pounds and had an outside diameter of 3.6 inches. At the center of the core was a spherical space for the polonium-beryllium initiator that provided a supply of neutrons when the core was crushed to a super-critical state.

The third major element of the Fat Man bomb was an arrangement of components and circuitry for arming and initiating the firing sequence to detonate the bomb at the right altitude. This arrangement also included safety provisions to keep the bomb from detonating until the correct moment and contact fuses that would destroy the bomb if the arming and firing mechanisms failed to operate properly.

The arming and firing components and the batteries to power the components during free fall were mounted to surfaces inside the ballistic casing and to conical frames bolted to the forward and rear ends of the inner sphere (see Figure 37).

After the Fat Man bomb was assembled on Tinian, all joints in the outer casing and tail assembly were sealed so that the barometric switches could sense true altitude pressures during the bomb's descent. The interior atmosphere of the casing was then evacuated to prevent freezing of components at altitude and two green-handled safety plugs were inserted into connectors mounted in the upper surface of the casing. The two green plugs contained internal wiring that disabled certain arming and firing circuits of the bomb. After takeoff, but before climbing to altitude, the electronics test officer (Philip Barnes) went into the bomb bay and replaced the green plugs with red-handled plugs that completed the circuits interrupted by the safety plugs.

After the bomb was loaded into the bomb bay of *Bockscar*, cables from the aircraft were connected to the bomb to provide power from the aircraft inverter and to monitor the status of internal components. Also installed after the bomb was securely mounted in the bomb bay were four contact fuses in the four sockets in the nose of the bomb and four radar antennas on the mounting pads around the circumference of the bomb casing. After the fuses were installed, pullout wires were attached to the fuses and bomb bay anchors. In addition, pullout wires from the bomb's internal clocks were attached to anchor points in the bomb bay.

When the bomb was released, the aircraft power and monitor cables disconnected and the fuse pullout wires allowed the four fuse arming propellers to spin off and arm the contact fuses. In addition, the clock pullout wires started the clocks, which in 15 seconds enabled the bomb's eight six-volt lead-acid batteries to provide power for the bomb's electrical arming and firing components.

When the barometric system sensed an atmospheric pressure equal to 8,000 feet altitude, it activated switches to close the circuits to the radar antennas. At an altitude of approximately 1,800 feet, the radar unit activated switches that closed the circuits from the firing unit (X-unit) to the 32 detonators. The detonators initiated the explosion of the high explosive lenses to create the shock wave that crushed the plutonium sphere to about one-half its original size. The reduction in size and density of the sphere resulted in an immediate state of criticality and the bomb detonated.

Mk-3 Atomic Bomb

The Mk-3 atomic bomb was the version of the Fat Man bomb stockpiled after the end of World War II. During the summer of 1945, a decision was made by General Groves and J. Robert Oppenheimer to establish a new division of the Los Alamos Laboratory and locate it on an area adjoining Kirtland Army Air Field known as Oxnard Field.

Given the designation of Z Division, the new organization was to be responsible for the assembly of a stockpile of existing Fat Man units, development of improved units, and testing of existing and improved models. The area occupied by the Z Division became known as Sandia Base, and later became the nucleus for Sandia National Laboratories. Sandia Base was later incorporated within the boundaries of Kirtland Air Force Base.

In the fall of 1945, all available Fat Man components were shipped to Sandia Base and stored in boxes and crates. These parts and components became the nuclear stockpile of the United States in the period immediately after the end of the war. In 1946, some minor changes were made in the design of the Fat Man and the improved version produced for the stockpile was designated as an Mk-3 bomb. Improved detonators and a more reliable arming and firing system were included in the Mk-3 bomb.

Production of about 120 of the Mk-3 bombs occurred between April 1947 and April 1949. Retirement of the Mk-3 began in April 1949 and was completed late in 1950. Although the Mk-3 was an improvement over the Fat Man unit dropped on Nagasaki, it still required a considerable amount of time and labor to assemble and was only available for use for about 48 hours before the batteries had to be replaced. The Mk-3 was no longer in the inventory by 1950, having been replaced by the M-4 bomb.

The estimated yield of the Mk-3 bomb was the same as the Fat Man bomb, about 21,000 tons of TNT. It was available for use in Silverplate B-29s assigned to both Walker Air Force Base in Roswell, New Mexico, and Biggs Air Force Base near El Paso, Texas.

Mk-4 Atomic Bomb

Development of components for a greatly improved version of the Fat Man bomb began at Los Alamos in 1945 before the end of World War II. The desired improvements included simpler production, greater dependability, increased safety, easier field handling, and better long-term storage characteristics and ballistic performance. The size would still be limited to the dimensions of the B-29 bomb bay in both Silverplate and Saddletree configurations.

Known as the Mk-4 bomb, development and testing of the weapon was carried out even as the Mk-3 was being produced and stockpiled. The Mk-4 was an implosion-type weapon based on the same plutonium fission concept as used in the Fat Man and Mk-3 bombs, but with significant changes in critical components. The overall dimensions were the same as the Fat Man and Mk-3 bombs, which were 128 inches long and 60 inches in diameter. The Mk-4 bomb weighed about 10,800 pounds (about 500 pounds more than the Fat Man and Mk-3).

The most significant improvements incorporated into the Mk-4 included a composite core that was levitated in the center of the high explosive shell and features that permitted insertion and extraction of the nuclear components after the carrier aircraft was airborne. The levitated composite core consisted of a solid ball of plutonium suspended at the center of a shell of uranium highly enriched with the U-235 isotope. The uranium sphere was mounted directly inside the tamper shell. The composite core used about 7 pounds of plutonium and 14.3 pounds of uranium. The plutonium center ball was suspended in the center of the uranium shell by thin wires strong enough to withstand handling of the assembled bomb. In comparison, the Fat Man and Mk-3 bombs used a core of plutonium that weighed about 13.6 pounds.

The most important change in the Mk-4 bomb, at least from a safety aspect, was the introduction of the capability to carry the nuclear capsule separate from the bomb on takeoff and landing. Once airborne, a crew member could then enter the bomb bay and insert or extract the nuclear components into or from the body of the

38. Mk-4 Bomb Being Loaded Into B-50 Bomber. (National Atomic Museum)

bomb through a door in the nose of the bomb. The benefits of this inflight insertion feature were evidenced in several accidents involving Saddletree B-29 and B-50D aircraft carrying one of the Mk-4 bombs. In these incidents, the high explosive components of the bomb exploded but the separated nuclear capsule did not detonate or result in a radioactive situation.

Other improvements in the Mk-4 bomb were better arming and firing components and circuitry, increased battery life, and the elimination of the four nose contact fuses. Eliminating joint fittings, external radar antennas, and the suspension lug as protuberances enhanced the ballistic characteristics. The suspension lug was recessed and the antennas were flush-mounted in the nose. The ballistic characteristics of the bomb were also improved by the replacement of the box fin used on Fat Man and the Mk-3 with four wedge-shaped fins having a span of 59 inches. The outer case was made of mild steel ⅜ inches thick.

The explosive power (yield) of the Mk-4 bomb was about the same as the Fat Man and Mk-3 bombs (about 21 KT). The first Mk-4 entered the stockpile in March 1949. About 550 Mk-4 bombs of all variations were produced between March 1949 and May 1951. All of these bombs were retired between July 1952 and May 1953.

8 THE 509TH COMPOSITE GROUP

The Silverplate B-29 was developed for the sole purpose of carrying the atomic bombs produced by the Manhattan Project. The 509th Composite Group was created with the specific mission of using these airplanes to deliver the atomic bombs on enemy targets. As a result of the East-West tensions that grew after World War II, the 509th inherited a new role. It became the nuclear deterrent force of the United States for several years.

Contrary to Einstein's belief in 1941 that an atomic bomb would be too heavy to be carried in an airplane,[1] Los Alamos scientists and engineers focused from the outset on a design for a bomb of a size and weight that could be delivered by a heavy bomber. Therefore, the need for trained crews to fly the bombers was implicit in the planning of the Manhattan Project.

The need for a tactical unit capable of dropping the atomic bomb was first broached with the military in a meeting in the spring of 1944 between General Groves, head of the Manhattan Project, and General Arnold, Commanding General of the U.S. Army Air Forces. At this meeting, Groves briefed Arnold on the progress being made in the development of the bomb and suggested that the time had come to think about forming and training a unit to deliver the bombs on enemy targets. Steps to create this combat unit were undertaken later in the summer of 1944 after Groves again met with Arnold and informed him that the first bomb would probably be ready by mid–1945.

One of the first actions taken was the selection of the airman who would organize and command this unit. After an interview with Captain William S. "Deak" Parsons, Norman Ramsey, and security officer John Lansdale at Colorado Springs (CO) on 1 September 1944, Lt. Colonel Paul W. Tibbets was informed that he was to assume command of an organization that might possibly shorten the war, even though it had not yet been activated.[2]

Three key decisions were made after Tibbets was picked to lead the new unit. The first was that the 393rd Bombardment Squadron, then in training at Fairmont Army Air Field in Nebraska, would be the combat element of the new organization. The second step was to select Wendover Army Air Field, an isolated base in western Utah, as the location for training the air crews. Finally, at the direction of General Arnold and with the wholehearted agreement of General Groves, the new unit would be a composite group with all necessary support elements contained within the unit.[3]

The 393rd was detached from its parent unit at Fairmont, the 504th Bombardment Group, in mid–September and placed on duty at Wendover without aircraft. Many of the support personnel of the 216th Base Unit at Wendover who had been supporting the previously resident training organizations were retained for the new unit that was being formed at the same base. After the 393rd was in position at Wendover, the first group of Silverplate B-29s began to arrive in October and November (as described in chapter 2). Thus, all of the basic ingredients for a combat organization began to coalesce at Wendover as December 1944 approached.

The first step to formalize the arrangements for the unit that was destined to play a key role in ending the war with Japan came on 9 December 1944 when the 509th Composite Group was constituted. This action meant that the organization was established on paper. Eight days later, on 17 December 1944, the 509th was activated at Wendover with Lt. Colonel Paul W. Tibbets commanding. It should be noted that Tibbets was promoted to Colonel early in 1945. The structure of the 509th at the time of its activation included the following:

- Headquarters, 509th Composite Group
- 393rd Bombardment (Very Heavy) Squadron
- 320th Troop Carrier Squadron
- 390th Air Service Group (including the Headquarters and Base Services Squadron)
- 603rd Air Engineering Squadron
- 1027th Air Materiel Squadron
- 1395th Military Police Company (Aviation)

An additional unit, the 1st Ordnance Squadron, Special (Aviation), was activated and added to the 509th on 6 March 1945.

Support to the 509th for the preparation of the atomic bombs on Tinian was provided by 51 Project Alberta (also called Project A) personnel from Los Alamos with Navy Captain William S. Parsons as the Officer-in-Charge. Attached to the 509th administratively, the War Department established the First Technical Services Detachment as the unit on Tinian to which Project A personnel were assigned. Additional information regarding Project Alberta is included in Appendix E.

The *Headquarters, 509th Composite Group* was the command element of the 509th that included the office of the Commanding Officer (Paul W. Tibbets) and the functions of operations (Operations Officer James I. Hopkins, Jr.), group navigator (Theodore J. VanKirk), group bombardier (Thomas W. Ferebee), intelligence, weather, and personnel. There were 98 men assigned to this organization on Tinian.

The *393rd Bombardment Squadron (Very Heavy)* was the combat arm of the 509th. It was actually activated on 11 March 1944 at Dalhart Army Air Field in Texas as one of the squadrons of the 504th Bombardment Group. The Group and its squadrons were reassigned to Fairmont Army Air Field in Nebraska on 12 March 1944. It was placed on detached duty at Wendover on 14 September 1944 and became an element of the 509th when the Composite Group was activated on 17 December 1944. The Commanding Officer of the 393rd when it was activated and when it became part of the 509th was Lt.Colonel Thomas J. Classen. He was replaced by Major Charles W. Sweeney on 2 May 1945 when Classen became Deputy Commanding Officer of the 509th.

The 393rd included 15 flight and ground crews for the Silverplate B-29s assigned to the 509th. The 393rd flew 16 combat missions in which 49 pumpkin bombs were dropped on Japanese targets (two pumpkin bomb sorties were aborted) and the two atomic bomb missions to Hiroshima and Nagasaki. Appendix C provides information on the 393rd crews and the combat missions that they flew. Other personnel assigned to the 393rd were engaged in operations, engineering, armament, communications, radar, ordnance, and personal equipment functions. This squadron had 535 men assigned to it on Tinian.

The *320th Troop Carrier Squadron*, known as the Green Hornet Line, was the air transportation asset of the 509th that supported both the 509th and the activities of the Manhattan Project. Originally assigned C-46 and C-47 cargo planes, the 320th received five new C-54 transport aircraft in the spring of 1945 in order to meet the requirements for moving cargo and personnel between Wendover and Tinian. Over 50 roundtrip missions from the United States to Tinian were flown by the 320th in 1945.

39. Green Hornet C-54 of the 320th Troop Carrier Squadron. (Leon D. Smith)

The original Commanding Officer of the 320th was Major Hubert J. Konopacki. He was replaced by Major Charles W. Sweeney on 6 January 1945. On 2 May 1945, Captain John W. Casey replaced Major Sweeney when Sweeney become Commanding Officer of the 393rd Bombardment Squadron. There were 149 men assigned to the 320th in August 1945.[4]

At the time of its activation on 17 December 1944, the *390th Air Service Group* was the parent organization of the Headquarters and Base Services Squadron, the 603rd Air Engineering Squadron, and the 1027th Air Materiel Squadron. In the months that followed activation, the 603rd and 1027th Squadrons operated more or less independently of the parent Group and their functions and personnel are described below.

The mission of the Headquarters and Base Services Squadron was to support the 509th command element and provide housekeeping functions such as finance, personnel, housing, administration, and food service. Not counting the 603rd and 1027th Squadrons, there were 189 men assigned to the 390th Air Service Group on Tinian. Lt. Colonel John W. Porter was the Commanding Officer.

The *603rd Air Engineering Squadron* was responsible for the maintenance and repair of 509th aircraft and all equipment, both airborne and ground support. The squadron was so organized that even a major overhaul could be accomplished with factory precision. In addition, it had the materials, equipment, and skilled personnel necessary to make almost any part or piece of equipment needed for the operations of the 509th. Approximately 60 percent of the personnel assigned to this squadron when it was activated were drawn from previous organizations stationed at Wendover at the time. There were 227 men assigned to the 603rd on Tinian. The Commanding Officer was Captain Earl O. Casey.

The mission of the *1027th Air Materiel Squadron* was to obtain, stock, and issue supplies and equipment for the 509th. Under the command of Major Guy Geller, there were 141 men assigned to the 1027th on Tinian.

An entirely new organizational concept was established with the assignment of the *1395th Military Police Company (Aviation)* to the 509th. An Army military police unit was not normally placed under the command of an Army Air Forces unit at the Group level. The 1395th was responsible for the security of 509th personnel and equipment, particularly the Silverplate B-29s and any activity associated with the atomic bombs. There were 133 men assigned to the 1395th on Tinian. The Commanding Officer was Captain Louis Schaffer.

Activated on 6 March 1945, almost three months after the 509th came into being, the *1st Ordnance Squadron, Special (Aviation)* was created to provide the men, skills, and equipment needed to support the assembly and handling of the atomic bombs. The men of the squadron worked closely with 1st Technical Services Detachment (Project Alberta) personnel from Los Alamos on all matters affecting the atomic bombs. In fact, two members of the squadron flew on the atomic bombing missions as electronics test officers. Lieutenant Morris Jeppson fulfilled this function on the Hiroshima mission and Lieutenant Philip Barnes did the same on the Nagasaki mission. A third member of the squadron, Leon Smith, later flew on *Dave's Dream* as the electronics test officer on Test Able in Operation Crossroads.

The Commanding Officer of the 1st Ordnance Squadron was Captain Charles F.H. Begg. There were 296 men assigned to his squadron on Tinian.[5]

Appendix D provides a roster of the 1,768 men assigned to the various units of the 509th during the time the 509th was stationed on Tinian in the summer of 1945. This roster also includes 51 Project Alberta personnel from Los Alamos and two Washington representatives. The two individuals from Washington were Brigadier General Thomas F. Farrell, deputy to General Groves, and Rear Admiral William R. Purnell, Navy member of the Military Policy Committee. Farrell and Purnell are shown in the photograph in Figure 40 along with Tibbets and Parsons. The photograph was taken on Tinian in the summer of 1945.

The 509th Composite Group was activated at Wendover in December 1944 and spent the next four months getting organized and training at this base. It then operated for about the next seven months on Tinian before returning to Roswell Army Air Field in New Mexico in November 1945.

Although it went through designation changes over the next few years, the 509th was stationed at Roswell for almost 13 years before moving to Pease Air Force Base in New Hampshire in August 1958. After spending 32 years at Pease, the 509th was

40. Key Officers on Tinian. *(Left to right):* Rear Admiral William R. Purnell, Brigadier General Thomas F. Farrell, Colonel Paul W. Tibbets, Navy Captain William S. Parsons.

reassigned to Whiteman Air Force Base in Missouri in September 1990. It is at present the 509th Bomb Wing at Whiteman with the mission of operating the B-2 *Spirit* stealth bomber. The 509th has been in existence for almost 60 years.[6]

Appendix A is a chronology of events associated with the 509th Composite Group, its successors, and World War II.

The 509th did not receive a unit commendation or award for its role in ending the war with Japan until 54 years after the atomic bombing missions. Colonel Tibbets was awarded the Distinguished Service Cross by General Spaatz immediately after returning from the Hiroshima mission, as shown in Figure 41. In addition, the crew members who participated in the atomic missions received medals after the missions.[7] As a result of the lobbying efforts of Fred Bock, the Air Force Association, and others, the Department of the Air Force awarded the Air Force Outstanding Unit Award (with Valor) to the 509th on 2 September 1999.[8] The award was officially presented to the 509th at its reunion in Washington, D.C., later that month. The citation that accompanied the award read as follows:

41. Colonel Tibbets Awarded Distinguished Service Cross by General Spaatz. *(Left to right)*: General Carl Spaatz, Commanding General of U.S. Army Strategic Air Forces, Pacific; Brigadier General John Davies, Commanding Officer of the 313th Bombardment Wing; Colonel Paul W. Tibbets, Commanding Officer of the 509th Composite Group.

The 509th Composite Group distinguished itself by exceptionally outstanding achievement in combat from 1 July 1945 to 14 August 1945. The 509th Composite Group was the first Army Air Force group to be trained, organized, and equipped, in adverse conditions for atomic warfare. Despite the awesome rigors of war, they carried out complex and highly secret missions without any breech of security and without losing a single plane or a single life. As President George Bush stated on 20 August 1990, "When elite, highly trained crews of the 509th Composite Group carried out their decisive atomic bombing missions of Hiroshima and Nagasaki during World War II, they ushered in a new era in military warfare. These historic missions helped to bring a swift end to the hostilities in the Pacific, saving countless American and Allied lives and reaffirming our determination to secure peace through strength." The distinctive accomplishments of the members of the 509th Composite Group reflect great credit upon themselves and the United States Air Force.

It is interesting to note the difference in the command structure for the unit that delivered the atomic bombs (the 509th Composite Group led by Colonel Tibbets) as compared to the group that prepared the bombs on Tinian and shared responsibility for the conduct of the missions (Project Alberta led by Navy Captain Parsons).

Chain of Command

President (Truman)
Secretary of War (Stimson)
U.S. Army Chief of Staff (General Marshall)

U.S. Army Air Forces CG (Gen Arnold)	Director, Manhattan Project
CG, USASTAF (Gen Spaatz)	(Maj Gen Groves)
CG, 20th Army Air Force (Lt Gen Twining)	
CO, 313th Bombardment Wing (Brig Gen Davies)	
CO, 509th Composite Group (Col Tibbets)	Director, Project Alberta (Capt Parsons)

Although USASTAF (U.S. Army Strategic Air Forces in the Pacific), the 20th Air Force, and the 315th Bombardment Wing were in the chain of command for the 509th for administrative control, operational control for the atomic missions was actually exercised by generals Arnold and Groves who both reported to General Marshall.

9 The End

In the beginning there was one Silverplate B-29. At the end of the Silverplate era almost eight years later, 65 of these special airplanes had been produced, they had flown 18 combat missions in World War II, they had brought the war with Japan to an end, and all were gone except for two placed in the custody of museums.

The Silverplate project officially began on 1 December 1943 when the directive to modify a B-29 Superfortress bomber to carry atomic bombs was sent from Army Air Forces Headquarters to Air Materiel Command at Wright Army Air Field. This prototype was completed in January 1944. The production and modification project ceased to be known as Silverplate on 12 May 1947 when the code name was changed to Saddletree, but many of these airplanes continued to serve as Silverplate versions in operational assignments for several more years.

The total of 65 Silverplate B-29s produced during the three and a half years of the project's official existence includes those in the process of conversion when the code name was changed. The last Silverplate B-29 in service as an atomic bomb carrier was reassigned from this role in November 1951, although it and many others remained in the inventory in different configurations. Thus, this special version of the B-29 existed from January 1944 to November 1951, a period of almost eight years.

Of the 65 Silverplate B-29s produced, 51 were initially assigned to the 509th Composite Group and 14 were initially allocated to support of the Los Alamos test program. Four of the first group of 509th airplanes were later transferred to the test program and two of the Los Alamos support aircraft were eventually reassigned to the 509th. Thus, six of these airplanes served both purposes.

Although the basic B-29 Superfortress was a significant improvement over the B-17 and B-24 bombers used in Europe and North Africa in terms of range, speed, and bomb load, the early versions of the B-29 were plagued with frequent engine problems. The initial Silverplate B-29s were no exception since they were fitted with basically the same Wright Cyclone R-3350 engine as the early production B-29s.[1]

However, the improved airplanes supplied the 509th in the spring of 1945 incorporated a much more reliable power plant and the excellent mission performance of the 509th on Tinian can to a great extent be credited to this change.[2]

The Statistical Control Unit of the 20th Air Force command element on Guam reported that out of 65 aircraft scheduled for the 16 Special Bombing Missions flown by the 509th, only one aircraft did not get airborne. Furthermore, out of the 64 aircraft airborne, only two airplanes aborted their combat sorties.

The one airplane that was scheduled for a mission but did not get airborne was *Strange Cargo* (44-27300) on 29 July 1945. For this mission, James I. Hopkins, Jr., was serving as Airplane Commander of crew A-4 (replacing the normal Airplane Commander, Joseph E. Westover, who was unavailable for medical reasons). This airplane did not get airborne because the pumpkin bomb it was carrying was inadvertently released on the taxiway prior to takeoff. The bomb went through the bomb bay doors and landed on the taxiway. It did not detonate but the resulting situation obviously caused the cancellation of this mission for 44-27300.

The pumpkin bomb incident related above was but one of several unusual occurrences that happened during Silverplate B-29 operations by the 509th and the Test Section of the 216th Base Unit at Wendover Army Air Field.

Two other unplanned bomb release incidents have already been described in previous sections of this book. In the first occurrence, during a test mission a Thin Man test unit was inadvertently released from its shackles while the bomb bay doors of the prototype were closed. The crew managed to jettison the bomb, but the doors sustained significant damage.[3]

In another test mission, a Little Boy test model was released prematurely while the bomb bay doors of one of the initial group of Silverplate B-29s were open. The Little Boy unit fell near the town of Calipatria, California, and buried itself at least 35 feet deep.[4]

There were several incidents in which an engine fire, a bad landing, or a ground mishap resulted in the premature demise of a Silverplate B-29. All of these occurrences are described in chapter 5. After a test mission, the damage to the prototype (42-6259) in a hard landing at Wendover was sufficient to eliminate it from further use in the Los Alamos test program. Major Clyde Shields noted in his activity report that Charles W. Sweeney was the pilot.

In another adverse situation at Wendover, an engine fire on 42-65235 while it was being flown on a test mission caused a rapid return to base and an emergency landing. The crew hastily abandoned the airplane and it sustained considerable damage. It was never used in the test program again.

A taxiing incident at Kirtland in 1946 resulted in the loss of two Silverplate B-29s. The two aircraft were *Some Punkins* (44-27296) and 44-86473. A bad landing at Goose Bay in 1948 was the cause of the premature scrapping of *The Great Artiste* (44-27353), and a similar situation at the Chicago Municipal Airport in 1945 resulted in the loss of *Jabit III* (44-27303).

In a different kind of unusual situation, one in which the consequences could have been much worse than what actually happened, a rapid loss of pressurization in a Silverplate B-29 on a training mission over San Francisco Bay in the spring of 1945 almost cost the lives of two crew members. As the story is related by Jacob Bontekoe (the pilot on the crew involved in the incident) in Krauss' outstanding book of 509th memories, a cover plate that replaced the front lower turret blew out and left a gaping hole in the floor of the front section of the airplane. The navigator and airplane commander had just moved forward in front of the area when the cover plate was lost. Had they been on the plate when it blew out, they would have been ejected from the plane without their parachutes.

As reported in area newspapers at the time, several pieces of equipment were sucked out of the airplane and found on the ground. The navigator[5] suffered an injury on his head when struck by a piece of his navigation equipment but he was later given medical attention and survives to this day.

An incident that might have been catastrophic but for the skill of the pilots occurred during the trip of *Laggin' Dragon* (44-86347) from Wendover to Tinian. Manned by crew A-2, it was in the company of two other Silverplate B-29s with similar missions. Each airplane had flown from Wendover to Kirtland where a Fat Man unit (minus the plutonium core and the arming and firing components) was loaded into the front bomb bay of each plane. The Fat Man units were to be delivered to Tinian for use in tests or in an actual bombing mission.

From Kirtland, the three aircraft flew to Mather Army Air Field for processing before departing for the Pacific. John Downey (the bombardier on crew A-2) recalls the situation in Krauss' 509th memories book, "...during takeoff, the storage area containing the seven man raft and all other survival gear, popped open and dumped its contents which hit the tail assembly and caused some exciting moments until we returned to the ground. Our load was sixteen people, all their gear, a bomb and a full load of fuel."[6]

What Downey didn't mention was that it was only the strength and skill of the pilots (Costello and Davis) that kept the airplane from crashing. The airplane was repaired and they left that night for Hawaii. It is believed that the Fat Man unit they carried was the one used in the Nagasaki mission.

The 509th existed as a Composite Group for only nineteen months. Most of the men in the organization at Wendover and on Tinian were in the group for no more than twelve months. Yet, the members of the 509th Composite Group have over the years maintained an identity with the unit, the mission they accomplished, and for the Silverplate B-29 they flew and supported.

Reunions of the men from the 393rd Bombardment Squadron began in 1962, 17 years after they served on Tinian. Reunions of the 509th began in 1975 and have continued ever since. As of the end of 2004, 18 reunions of members, families, and friends of the 509th Composite Group have been held.

The configuration of the Silverplate B-29 evolved as more and more airplanes were produced. As was the case in all military aircraft production in World War II, block numbers were included in the serial numbers to indicate incremental configuration changes in production. The number of Silverplate B-29s in each production block that included these special aircraft is shown below.

Block Number	Quantity
5	2
10	2
15	2
20	11
25	1
30	4

Block Number	Quantity
36	10
40	3
45	2
50	2
55	5
60	14
90	7

All of the airplanes included in the above list were assembled at the Glen L. Martin Aircraft Plant in Omaha, Nebraska, except for the prototype in Block 5 and the seven aircraft in Block 90. These eight Silverplate B-29s were the product of the Boeing plant in Wichita, Kansas.

There were only four locations where Silverplate B-29s were based. They called Wendover home for eleven months, Tinian was their base for only five months, Kirtland was the operational location for several of the test airplanes for about 6½ years, and Roswell was their assigned location for four years.

All but three of these special bombers lost their Silverplate identity by conversion to other configurations, by losses due to accidents, by being scrapped after being placed in storage, or by being stored and then placed in museums. The final dispositions of the 65 airplanes were as follows:

Converted to TB-29s	31
Converted to WB-29	1
Placed in storage and then scrapped	16
Lost in accidents	12
Placed in museums	2
Miscellaneous	3
Total	65

All of the conversions to TB-29s were accomplished at the Oklahoma City depot on Tinker Air Force Base in Oklahoma. More details on the operations at Tinker are provided in chapter 6. The lone conversion to a WB-29 configuration was accomplished at the Sacramento depot at McClellan Air Force Base. The storing and scrapping of Silverplate B-29s occurred at Davis-Monthan, Peyote, and Robins air bases. Those operations are also described in chapter 6.

Details of the 12 Silverplate B-29 accidents are provided in chapter 5. The stories of the two airplanes that were placed in temporary storage and then assigned to museums, *Bockscar* (44-27297) and *Enola Gay* (44-86292), can be found in their individual histories in Appendix G.

With respect to the disposition of the three aircraft listed above in the "miscellaneous" category, one (42-65386) was reassigned in June 1953 from Kirtland to Hanscom Field in Massachusetts for some unknown purpose.[7] A second (44-86451) was reassigned in April 1950 from the 97th Bombardment Group at Biggs Air Force Base to the 8th Air Force at Carswell Air Force Base in Texas where its configuration and usage are uncertain.[8] The third airplane in this category (44-87771) was reassigned in November 1951 from the 509th to the 9th Bombardment Wing at Travis Air Force Base in California where it may have been used as a trainer.[9]

Milestone dates for each Silverplate B-29 are shown in a summary listing included as Appendix F.

The efforts to produce the atomic bomb and the Silverplate B-29 were successful, but they were accomplished at considerable cost. Although estimates of the costs vary from one source to another, depending on what activities are included or omitted, some approximate numbers can be derived from basic information contained in several sources.

The cost figures that follow are provided in both 1945 and 2004 dollars,[10] but caution should be exercised in comparing the cost of something in 1945 with a similar item 60 years later. For example, although the B-29 bomber was a leap forward in aircraft technology in 1945, its technology and capabilities cannot be equated with those incorporated into the B-2 stealth bomber today. In other words, the purchasing power of the dollar in two different periods must be viewed in the context of what is being bought.

To put the atomic bomb and Silverplate B-29 costs into perspective, World War II cost the United States approximately $341 billion in 1945 dollars.[11] In terms of 2004 dollars, the cost was about $3.6 trillion.

The Manhattan Project expended about $1.9 billion in 1945 dollars, or $20.1 billion in 2004 dollars.[12] The total costs for development and production of the B-29 bomber was approximately $3.1 billion in 1945 dollars, or $32.6 billion in 2004 dollars.[13] While these cost figures may seem small compared to weapon costs in today's defense budgets, the funds spent in the 1940s to develop and produce the atomic bomb and the B-29 bomber were much greater than the amounts spent on other individual weapon systems of that era.

The method used to derive the cost of the Silverplate project deserves some explanation. To begin with, it should be understood that the development and production of the Silverplate B-29 bomber was just one part of the total Silverplate project. Other elements of the project included logistical support for the training and operations of the 509th Composite Group at Wendover and on Tinian and Silverplate support of Manhattan Project activities.

The cost of one Silverplate B-29 in 1945 dollars included the cost of the standard B-29 ($782,000) plus the cost to modify it to the Silverplate configuration ($32,700) for a total of $814,700.[14] Using the applicable inflation factor, the cost of one Silverplate B-29 in 2004 dollars would be about $8,562,000.[15]

The total cost of the Silverplate project in 1945 dollars was about $60 million.[16] This total includes $53 million for the aircraft and $7 million for logistical support of the 509th and its support of the Manhattan Project at Wendover and on Tinian. In terms of 2004 dollars, the total cost would be about $632 million. The various cost figures set forth above are summarized below.

Item	1945 dollars	2004 dollars
World War II	$341 billion	$3.6 trillion
Manhattan Project	$1.9 billion	$20.1 billion

Item	1945 dollars	2004 dollars
B-29 Program	$3.1 billion	$32.6 billion
Silverplate Project	$60 million	$632 million
One Silverplate B-29 Bomber	$815 thousand	$8.6 million
One B-2 Stealth Bomber	$128 million	$1.34 billion

And so the story of the Silverplate B-29 comes to an end. They were developed at first as a vehicle to end a war, but they ended their life as a force for deterring future wars. Amen.

APPENDIX A: CHRONOLOGY OF EVENTS

Events and actions directly related to the history of the Silverplate B-29 program, the Manhattan Project, and the 509th Composite Group are listed below. Other events having a direct bearing on this history, particularly those associated with World War II, are also listed.

Dec 38	Discovery of uranium fission by German scientists Lise Meitner and Otto Hahn.
2 Aug 39	Professor Albert Einstein signed letter to President Franklin D. Roosevelt regarding possible use of uranium in a bomb.
1 Sep 39	Germany invades Poland.
11 Oct 39	Einstein letter delivered to President Roosevelt by Dr. Alexander Sachs.
10 May 40	Germany invades France, Holland, and Belgium.
6 Sep 40	U.S. Army Air Forces contract with Boeing for first two XB-29s.
22 Jun 41	Germany invades Soviet Union.
21 Sep 41	First flight of Boeing XB-29.
7 Dec 41	Japanese attack Pearl Harbor.
9 Dec 41	United States declares war on Japan.
12 Dec 41	United States declares war on Germany and Italy.
17 Jun 42	Manhattan Engineer District established.
17 Sep 42	Colonel Leslie R. Groves, U.S. Army Corps of Engineers, put in charge of the Manhattan Project.
Nov 42	Los Alamos selected as location for laboratory to design and develop atomic bombs (it was known as Site Y).
8 Nov 42	Allied forces land in French North Africa.
2 Dec 42	First chain reaction in atomic pile (reactor) under direction of Enrico Fermi, Metallurgical Laboratory at University of Chicago.
Mar 43	Operations commence at Los Alamos laboratory.
13 Aug 43	First drop tests of prototype atomic bomb shape conducted at Dahlgren Naval Proving Ground in Virginia.
3 Sep 43	Allies land in Italy.

Appendix A

7 Oct 43	First production B-29 accepted by U.S. Army Air Forces.
1 Dec 43	U.S. Army Air Forces Headquarters directive to Air Force Materiel Command to modify one B-29 under "Silver Plated Project."
Feb 44	Modifications to prototype Silverplate B-29 completed; aircraft flown to Muroc Army Air Field (CA) for first series of drop tests of Thin Man and Fat Man shapes.
11 Mar 44	393rd BMS activated as part of the 504th Bombardment Group (BMG) at Dalhart Army Air Field (AAF), Texas.
12 Mar 44	504th BMG and 393rd BMS transferred to Fairmont AAF, Nebraska.
27 Apr 44	Lt. Colonel Thomas J. Classen named Commanding Officer (C.O.) of the 393rd BMS.
6 Jun 44	Allied forces land on Normandy beaches.
1 Aug 44	Tinian Island secured by U.S. Marines.
14 Sep 44	393rd placed on detached duty at Wendover AAF, Utah.
Oct 44	First Silverplate B-29s delivered to 393rd at Wendover.
20 Oct 44	U.S. invasion of Leyte in the Philippines.
25 Nov 44	393rd reassigned from 504th to Second Air Force.
9 Dec 44	509th Composite Group (CG) constituted (established on paper).
17 Dec 44	509th CG activated at Wendover AAF, Utah, with Lt. Colonel Paul W. Tibbets as C.O.
17 Dec 44	509th CG assigned to 315th Bombardment Group (BMG) under Second Air Force.
5 Jan 45	Major Charles W. Sweeney assigned as C.O. of the 320th Troop Carrier Squadron.
Jan 45	Lt. Colonel Paul W. Tibbets promoted to Colonel.
19 Feb 45	U.S. Marines invade Iwo Jima.
6 Mar 45	1st Ordnance Squadron, Special (Aviation) activated and assigned to the 509th Composite Group.
26 Mar 45	Iwo Jima secured.
Apr 45	First of improved Silverplate B-29s delivered to 509th.
1 Apr 45	U.S. forces invade Okinawa.
26 Apr 45	Main ground echelon of 509th departed Wendover for port of embarkation via troop train, arriving at Fort Lawton near Seattle, WA, on 28 Apr 45.
2 May 45	Lt. Colonel Classen reassigned from C.O. of the 393rd BMS to Deputy C.O. of the 509th.
2 May 45	Major Sweeney reassigned from C.O. of the 320th Troop Carrier Squadron to C.O. of the 393rd BMS.
6 May 45	Germany surrenders (V-E Day).
6 May 45	Main ground echelon of 509th departed Seattle for Tinian on the transport vessel Cape Victory, arriving Tinian on 29 May 45 after stopping in Hawaii 13–16 May.
15 May 45	Advanced air echelon departed Wendover for Tinian.
5 Jun 45	First three of 393rd BMS fifteen crews and B-29 aircraft depart Wendover for Tinian.

23 Jun 45	Okinawa secured.
16 Jul 45	United States Army Strategic Air Forces, Pacific (USASTAF-Pacific) established on Guam.
20 Jul 45	First series of Pumpkin bomb missions flown to Japan.
24 Jul 45	Second series of Pumpkin bomb missions flown to Japan.
26 Jul 45	Third series of Pumpkin bomb missions flown to Japan.
27 Jul 45	Last two of 393rd BMS crews and B-29 aircraft depart Wendover for Tinian, arriving Tinian on 2 Aug 45.
29 Jul 45	Fourth series of Pumpkin bomb missions flown to Japan.
6 Aug 45	Hiroshima atomic bombing mission (Little Boy).
8 Aug 45	Fifth series of Pumpkin bomb missions flown to Japan.
9 Aug 45	Nagasaki atomic bombing mission (Fat Man).
14 Aug 45	Sixth series of Pumpkin bomb missions flown to Japan.
14 Aug 45	Japanese indicate acceptance of Potsdam Declaration.
2 Sep 45	Japanese sign surrender documents on battleship Missouri.
17 Oct 45	Main ground echelon of the 509th departed Tinian for the United States on the transport ship SS Deuel.
5 Nov 45	Main ground echelon of the 509th arrived at Oakland (CA) and departed within a few hours for Roswell Army Air Field (NM).
5 Nov 45	The air echelon of the 509th departed Tinian for Roswell AAF, arriving there on 9 Nov 45.
7 Nov 45	509th CG reassigned to Roswell AAF, New Mexico.
22 Jan 46	Colonel William H. Blanchard replaces Colonel Paul W. Tibbets as C.O. of the 509th CG.
21 Mar 46	509th CG becomes part of newly established Strategic Air Command.
17 May 46	Two additional Bombardment Squadrons, the 715th and 830th, assigned to the 509th to join the 393rd.
May 46	509th CG assigned to Operation Crossroads in the Pacific.
1 Jul 46	Mk-3 Fat Man bomb dropped in Test Able of Operation Crossroads.
10 Jul 46	509th CG reassigned to Roswell AAF and redesignated as 509th Bombardment Group (Very Heavy).
3 Nov 47	509th Bombardment Wing (Very Heavy) established with 509th Bombardment Group as a subsidiary unit.
Jan 48	Roswell Army Air Field renamed Walker Air Force Base.
24 Jun 48	Soviet Union imposes Berlin blockade.
28 Jun 48	Berlin airlift begins.
2 Jul 48	509th redesignated as 509th Bombardment Wing (Medium).
19 Jul 48	509th Air Refueling Squadron established and assigned to 509th Bombardment Wing. The first tankers, the KB-29M, were received by the 509th in December 1948.
12 May 49	Berlin blockade lifted.
30 Sep 49	Berlin airlift ends.
Apr–Jun 50	Silverplate B-29s of the 509th transferred to 97th Bombardment Group at Biggs Air Force Base (TX).
23 Jun 50	509th received first B-50D bomber.

Appendix A

16 Jun 52	509th Bombardment Group deactivated with the bombardment squadrons reporting directly to the 509th Bombardment Wing.
Jan 54	509th began receiving KC-97 tankers to replace the KB-29M tankers.
10 Jun 55	509th began receiving B-47 bombers to replace the B-50D bombers.
Aug 58	The 509th Bombardment Wing moved from Walker AFB to Pease AFB in New Hampshire. The 509th retained its B-47 bombers and KC-97 tankers.
11 Jun 65	The last KC-97 tanker of the 509th departed Pease AFB.
23 Nov 65	The last of the B-47 bombers of the 509th departed Pease AFB.
23 Mar 66	The first B-52 bomber and the first KC-135 tanker assigned to the 509th arrived at Pease AFB.
2 Apr 66	The 509th was redesignated as the 509th Bombardment Wing (Heavy).
19 Nov 69	The last 509th B-52 departed Pease AFB.
16 Dec 70	The first FB-111A assigned to the 509th arrived at Pease AFB and the 509th was redesignated as the 509th Bombardment Wing (Medium).
5 Sep 90	The last of the FB-111As assigned to the 509th departed Pease AFB.
28 Sep 90	The last six KC-135 tankers of the 509th departed Pease AFB.
30 Sep 90	The 509th was transferred from Pease AFB to Whiteman Air Force Base in Missouri. The 509th was also redesignated as the 509th Bombardment Wing (Heavy).
1 Sep 91	The 509th was redesignated as the 509th Bomb Wing.
17 Dec 93	The first B-2 bomber for the 509th arrived at Whiteman AFB.

Appendix B: Silverplate B-29 Mission List (Tinian, 1945)

Serial Number	Opns Order	Combat Msn	1945 Date	Purpose of Mission	Airplane Commander	Crew
44-27296	*Some Punkins*		*Victor 84 (originally Victor 4)*			
	1	-	30 June	Calibration flight	Price	B-7
	2	-	1 July	Bomb Rota	Price	B-7
	4	-	2 July	Training—aborted	Price	B-7
	5	-	3 July	Bomb Rota	Price	B-7
	6	-	4 July	Bomb Rota	Price	B-7
	8	-	6 July	Bomb Rota	Price	B-7
	10	-	8 July	Practice bombing	Price	B-7
	20	4	20 July	Pumpkin bomb	Price	B-7
	22	-	22 July	Practice bombing	Price	B-7
	24	7	24 July	Pumpkin bomb	Price	B-7
	27	9	26 July	Pumpkin bomb	Price	B-7
	33	-	2 August	Bomb Guguan	Price	B-7
	38	15	8 August	Pumpkin bomb	Price	B-7
	44	17	14 August	Pumpkin bomb	Price	B-7
	46	-	18 August	Training	Price	B-7
	47	-	20 August	Training	Price	B-7
	48	-	22 August	Training	Price	B-7
44-27297	*Bockscar*		*Victor 77 (originally Victor 7)*			
	1	-	30 June	Calibration flight	Bock	C-13
	2	-	1 July	Bomb Rota	Bock	C-13
	4	-	2 July	Training	Bock	C-13
	5	-	3 July	Bomb Rota	Bock	C-13
	10	-	8 July	Practice bombing	Bock	C-13
	14	-	12 July	Bomb Rota	Bock	C-13
	15	-	14 July	Bomb Rota	Eatherly	C-11
	19	-	19 July	Bomb Guguan	Bock	C-13
	22	-	22 July	Practice bombing	Taylor	A-1
	24	5	24 July	Pumpkin bomb	Bock	C-13
	27	9	26 July	Pumpkin bomb	Albury	C-15
	30	11	29 July	Pumpkin bomb	Bock	C-13
	32	-	1 August	Fat Man F13 test drop	Sweeney	C-15

Appendix B

Serial Number	Opns Order	Combat Msn	1945 Date	Purpose of Mission	Airplane Commander	Crew
	34	-	5 August	Fat Man F18 test drop	Sweeney	C-15
	37	-	8 August	Fat Man F33 test drop	Sweeney	C-15
	38	16	9 August	Fat Man F31/Nagasaki	Sweeney	C-15
	45	-	15 August	Training	Marquardt	B-10
	46	-	18 August	Training	Bock	C-13
	47	-	20 August	Training	Bock	C-13
	48	-	22 August	Training	Bock	C-13
44-27298	*Full House*		*Victor 83 (originally Victor 13)*			
	1	-	30 June	Calibration flight	Taylor	A-1
	2	-	1 July	Bomb Rota	Taylor	A-1
	4	-	2 July	Training	Taylor	A-1
	5	-	3 July	Bomb Rota	Taylor	A-1
	6	-	4 July	Bomb Rota	Taylor	A-1
	8	-	6 July	Bomb Rota	Taylor	A-1
	11	-	9 July	Practice bombing	Taylor	A-1
	15	-	14 July	Bomb Rota	Taylor	A-1
	20	4	20 July	Pumpkin bomb	Taylor	A-1
	24	5	24 July	Pumpkin bomb	Taylor	A-1
	27	9	26 July	Pumpkin bomb	Taylor	A-1
	30	10	29 July	Pumpkin bomb	Taylor	A-1
	33	-	2 August	Bomb Guguan	Taylor	A-1
	35	13	6 August	Weather/Nagasaki	Taylor	A-1
	39	16	9 August	Backup at Iwo Jima	Taylor	A-1
	44	18	14 August	Pumpkin bomb	Bock	C-13
	46	-	18 August	Training	Taylor	A-1
	47	-	20 August	Training	Taylor	A-1
	48	-	22 August	Training	Bock	C-13
44-27299	*Next Objective*		*Victor 86 (originally Victor 6)*			
	1	-	30 June	Calibration flight	Devore	A-3
	2	-	1 July	Bomb Rota	Devore	A-3
	4	-	2 July	Training	Devore	A-3
	5	-	3 July	Bomb Rota	Devore	A-3
	6	-	4 July	Bomb Rota	Devore	A-3
	8	-	6 July	Bomb Rota	Devore	A-3
	11	-	9 July	Practice bombing	Devore	A-3
	15	-	14 July	Bomb Rota	Devore	A-3
	20	4	20 July	Pumpkin bomb	Devore	A-3
	22	-	22 July	Practice bombing	Devore	A-3
	24	5	24 July	Pumpkin bomb	Devore	A-3
	28	-	26 July	Little Boy L6 test	Sweeney	C-15
	29	-	29 July	Little Boy L6 test	Sweeney	C-15
	38	14	8 August	Pumpkin bomb — aborted	Devore	A-3
	44	17	14 August	Pumpkin bomb	Devore	A-3
	46	-	18 August	Training	Devore	A-3
	47	-	20 August	Training	Devore	A-3
	48	-	22 August	Training	Devore	A-3
44-27300	*Strange Cargo*		*Victor 73 (originally Victor 3)*			
	1	-	30 June	Calibration flight	Westover	A-4
	2	-	1 July	Bomb Rota	Westover	A-4
	4	-	2 July	Training	Westover	A-4

Silverplate B-29 Mission List (Tinian, 1945)

Serial Number	Opns Order	Combat Msn	1945 Date	Purpose of Mission	Airplane Commander	Crew
	5	-	3 July	Bomb Rota	Westover	A-4
	6	-	4 July	Bomb Rota	Westover	A-4
	7	-	5 July	Bomb Truk	Westover	A-4
	9	-	7 July	Bomb Marcus	Westover	A-4
	11	-	9 July	Practice bombing	Westover	A-4
	15	-	14 July	Bomb Rota	Westover	A-4
	20	2	20 July	Pumpkin bomb	Bock	C-13
	22	-	22 July	Practice bombing	Eatherly	C-11
	24	6	24 July	Pumpkin bomb	Westover	A-4
	33	-	2 August	Bomb Guguan	Westover	A-4
	38	14	8 August	Pumpkin bomb	Westover	A-4
	44	17	14 August	Pumpkin bomb	Westover	A-4
	46	-	18 August	Training	Westover	A-4
44-27301	*Straight Flush*		*Victor 85 (originally Victor 5)*			
	1	-	30 June	Calibration flight	Eatherly	C-11
	2	-	1 July	Bomb Rota	Eatherly	C-11
	3	-	2 July	Training	Eatherly	C-11
	4	-	2 July	Training – aborted	Eatherly	C-11
	5	-	3 July	Bomb Rota	Eatherly	C-11
	6	-	4 July	Bomb Rota	Eatherly	C-11
	8	-	6 July	Bomb Rota	Eatherly	C-11
	20	1	20 July	Pumpkin bomb	Eatherly	C-11
	24	7	24 July	Pumpkin bomb	Eatherly	C-11
	27	8	26 July	Pumpkin bomb	Eatherly	C-11
	30	12	29 July	Pumpkin bomb	Eatherly	C-11
	33	-	2 August	Bomb Guguan	Bock	C-13
	35	13	6 August	Weather/Hiroshima	Eatherly	C-11
	44	18	14 August	Pumpkin bomb	Albury	C-15
	46	-	18 August	Training	Eatherly	C-11
	47	-	20 August	Training	Eatherly	C-11
	48	-	22 August	Training	Zahn	C-12
44-27302	*Top Secret*		*Victor 72 (originally Victor 2)*			
	1	-	30 June	Calibration flight	McKnight	B-8
	2	-	1 July	Bomb Rota	McKnight	B-8
	4	-	2 July	Training	McKnight	B-8
	5	-	3 July	Bomb Rota	McKnight	B-8
	6	-	4 July	Bomb Rota	McKnight	B-8
	7	-	5 July	Bomb Truk	McKnight	B-8
	10	-	8 July	Practice bombing	McKnight	B-8
	11	-	9 July	Practice bombing	McKnight	B-8
	15	-	14 July	Bomb Rota	McKnight	B-8
	20	1	20 July	Pumpkin bomb	McKnight	B-8
	24	7	24 July	Pumpkin bomb	McKnight	B-8
	27	8	26 July	Pumpkin bomb	Westover	A-4
	30	10	29 July	Pumpkin bomb	McKnight	B-8
	33	-	2 August	Bomb Guguan	Hopkins	C-14
	38	15	8 August	Pumpkin bomb	Eatherly	C-11
	44	18	14 August	Pumpkin bomb	McKnight	B-8
	46	-	18 August	Training	McKnight	B-8
	47	-	20 August	Training	McKnight	B-8
	48	-	22 August	Training	McKnight	B-8

Appendix B

Serial Number	Opns Order	Combat Msn	1945 Date	Purpose of Mission	Airplane Commander	Crew
44-27303	*Jabit III*		*Victor 71 (originally Victor 1)*			
	1	-	30 June	Calibration flight	Wilson	B-6
	2	-	1 July	Bomb Rota	Wilson	B-6
	4	-	2 July	Training	Wilson	B-6
	5	-	3 July	Bomb Rota	Wilson	B-6
	6	-	4 July	Bomb Rota	Wilson	B-6
	7	-	5 July	Bomb Truk	Wilson	B-6
	9	-	7 July	Bomb Marcus	Wilson	B-6
	15	-	14 July	Bomb Rota	Wilson	B-6
	20	3	20 July	Pumpkin bomb	Wilson	B-6
	22	-	22 July	Practice bombing	Wilson	B-6
	25	-	24 July	Little Boy L2 test	Tibbets	A-5
	26	-	25 July	Little Boy L5 test	Tibbets	A-5
	27	9	26 July	Pumpkin bomb	Devore	A-3
	30	10	29 July	Pumpkin bomb	Wilson	B-6
	33	-	2 August	Bomb Guguan	Wilson	B-6
	35	13	6 August	Weather/Kokura	Wilson	B-6
	38	14	8 August	Pumpkin bomb	Wilson	B-6
	41	-	9 August	Return to U.S. for next Fat Man bomb	Wilson	B-6
44-27304	*Up An' Atom*		*Victor 88 (originally Victor 8)*			
	1	-	30 June	Calibration flight	Marquardt	B-10
	2	-	1 July	Bomb Rota	Marquardt	B-10
	4	-	2 July	Training	Marquardt	B-10
	5	-	3 July	Bomb Rota	Marquardt	B-10
	8	-	6 July	Bomb Rota	Marquardt	B-10
	10	-	8 July	Practice bombing	Marquardt	B10
	15	-	14 July	Bomb Rota	Marquardt	B-10
	20	1	20 July	Pumpkin bomb	Marquardt	B-10
	27	9	26 July	Pumpkin bomb	Marquardt	B-10
	30	12	29 July	Pumpkin bomb	Smith	A-5
	33	-	2 August	Bomb Guguan	Devore	A-3
	38	14	8 August	Pumpkin bomb	Lewis	B-9
	44	17	14 August	Pumpkin bomb	Hopkins	C-14
	48	-	22 August	Training	Marquardt	B-10
44-27353	*The Great Artiste*		*Victor 89 (originally Victor 9)*			
	6	-	4 July	Bomb Rota	Marquardt	B-10
	7	-	5 July	Bomb Truk	Bock	C-13
	9	-	7 July	Bomb Marcus	Bock	C-13
	12	-	9 July	Training	Albury	C-15
	13	-	11 July	Training	Sweeney	C-15
	14	-	12 July	Bomb Rota	Albury	C-15
	15	-	14 July	Bomb Rota	Albury	C-15
	18	-	18 July	Bomb Guguan	Albury	C-15
	19	-	19 July	Bomb Guguan	Eatherly	C-11
	20	2	20 July	Pumpkin bomb – aborted	Albury	C-15
	24	6	24 July	Pumpkin bomb	Albury	C-15
	30	11	29 July	Pumpkin bomb	Lewis	B-9
	35	13	6 August	Hiroshima/Instruments	Sweeney	C-15
	39	16	9 August	Nagasaki/Instruments	Bock	C-13

Silverplate B-29 Mission List (Tinian, 1945)

Serial Number	Opns Order	Combat Msn	1945 Date	Purpose of Mission	Airplane Commander	Crew
	46	-	18 August	Training	Albury	C-15
	47	-	20 August	Training	Albury	C-15
	48	-	22 August	Training	Westover	A-4
44-27354	**Big Stink**	*Victor 90 (originally Victor 10)*				
	6	-	4 July	Bomb Rota	Bock	C-13
	7	-	5 July	Bomb Truk	Bock	C-13
	9	-	7 July	Bomb Marcus	Bock	C-13
	12	-	9 July	Training	Classen	A-5
	13	-	11 July	Training	Classen	A-5
	14	-	12 July	Bomb Rota	Classen	A-5
	15	-	14 July	Bomb Rota	Classen	A-5
	18	-	18 July	Bomb Guguan	McKnight	B-8
	19	-	19 July	Bomb Guguan	Price	B-7
	20	3	20 July	Pumpkin bomb	Classen	A-4
	23	-	23 July	Little Boy L1 test	Tibbets	A-5
	27	8	26 July	Pumpkin bomb	Classen	A-5
	35	13	6 August	Iwo Jima backup	McKnight	B-8
	39	16	9 August	Nagasaki/photo	Hopkins	C-14
	45	-	15 August	Unknown	Eatherly	C-11
	46	-	18 August	Training	Zahn	C-12
	47	-	20 August	Training	Marquardt	B-10
44-86291	**Necessary Evil**	*Victor 91 (originally Victor 11)*				
	10	-	8 July	Bomb Marcus	Eatherly	C-11
	11	-	9 July	Practice bombing	Wilson	B-6
	16	-	17 July	Training	Ray	C-14
	17	-	18 July	Training	Ray	C-14
	18	-	18 July	Training	Ray	C-14
	19	-	19 July	Bomb Guguan	Devore	A-3
	21	-	21 July	Bomb Marcus	Ray	C-14
	22	-	22 July	Practice bombing	Marquardt	B-10
	24	6	24 July	Pumpkin bomb	Ray	C-14
	27	8	26 July	Pumpkin bomb	Ray	C-14
	30	11	29 July	Pumpkin bomb	Ray	C-14
	35	13	6 August	Hiroshima/photo	Marquardt	B-10
	46	-	18 August	Training	Ray	C-14
	48	-	22 August	Training	Ray	C-14
44-86292	**Enola Gay**	*Victor 82 (originally Victor 12)*				
	9	-	7 July	Bomb Marcus	Devore	A-3
	14	-	12 July	Bomb Rota	Price	B-7
	16	-	17 July	Training	Lewis	B-9
	17	-	18 July	Training	Lewis	B-9
	18	-	18 July	Bomb Guguan	Lewis	B-9
	19	-	19 July	Bomb Guguan	Wilson	B-6
	21	-	21 July	Bomb Marcus	Lewis	B-9
	22	-	22 July	Practice bombing	McKnight	B-8
	24	6	24 July	Pumpkin bomb	Lewis	B-8
	27	9	26 July	Pumpkin bomb	Lewis	B-8
	31	-	31 July	Little Boy L6 test	Tibbets	B-9
	35	13	6 August	Hiroshima/Little Boy L11	Tibbets	B-9
	39	16	9 August	Weather/Kokura	Marquardt	B-10

Appendix B

Serial Number	Opns Order	Combat Msn	1945 Date	Purpose of Mission	Airplane Commander	Crew
	47	-	20 August	Training	Lewis	B-9
	48	-	22 August	Training	Lewis	B-9
44-86346	*Not named on Tinian*		*Victor 94*			
	41	-	9 August	Return to U.S. for next Fat Man bomb	Classen	A-5
44-86347	*Laggin' Dragon*		*Victor 95*			
	35	16	6 August	Weather/Nagasaki	McKnight	B-8
	46	-	18 August	Training	Costello	A-2
	48	-	22 August	Training	Costello	A-2

APPENDIX C: CREW INFORMATION

Crew Summary

Crew	Normal Airplane Commander	Normally Assigned Airplane Name	Number	Missions (see footnote) Tng	PB	Pmk	Atom	Test	Total
A-1	Taylor	*Full House*	44-27298	4	8	5	2	0	19
A-2	Costello	*Laggin' Dragon*	44-86347	2	0	0	0	0	2
A-3	Devore	*Next Objective*	44-27299	4	9	4	0	0	17
A-4	Westover	*Strange Cargo*	44-27300	4	8	4	0	0	16
A-5	Classen	*Big Stink*	44-27354	2	2	3	0	3	10
B-6	Wilson	*Jabit III*	44-27303	2	9	3	1	0	15
B-7	Price	*Some Punkins*	44-27296	5	8	5	0	0	18
B-8	McKnight	*Top Secret*	44-27302	5	9	4	2	0	20
B-9	Lewis	*Enola Gay*	44-86292	4	2	4	1	1	12
B-10	Marquardt	*Up an' Atom*	44-27304	5	6	2	2	0	15
C-11	Eatherly	*Straight Flush*	44-27301	4	8	5	1	0	18
C-12	Zahn	*Luke the Spook*	44-86346	2	0	0	0	0	2
C-13	Bock	*Bockscar*	44-27297	4	11	4	1	0	20
C-14	Ray	*Necessary Evil*	44-86291	5	2	4	1	0	12
C-15	Albury	*The Great Artiste*	44-27353	4	3	3	2	5	17

Crew A-1

Flight Crew

Airplane Commander	Ralph R. Taylor, Jr.
Pilot	Raymond P. Biel
Navigator	Fred A. Hoey
Bombardier	Michael Angelich
Flight Engineer	Frank M. Briese
Radio Operator	Theodore M. Slife
Radar Operator	Nathaniel T. Burgwyn
Tail Gunner	Robert J. Valley
Ass't Eng/Scanner	Richard B. Anselme

Ground Crew

Glen Mahugh
Chester A. Hammond
Steve J. Kinosh, Jr.
William B. Reedy
Donald D. Fockler
Mario A. Litterio

"Tng" is training and orientation, "PB" is practice bombing, "Pmk" is pumpkin, "Atom" is atomic missions, "Test" is test drops of Little Boy or Fat Man units.

The Silverplate B-29 assigned to Crew A-1 was 44-27298 (*Full House*), Victor No. 83. After arriving on Tinian on about 16 June 1945, Crew A-1 flew 5 calibration and training missions and 7 practice bombing missions. This crew was credited with six combat missions, as shown below. 44-27298 was used on each mission. Ralph Taylor was the Aircraft Commander on each mission.

20 Jul 45 Per Operations Order 20, dropped a pumpkin bomb on the assigned primary target (an aluminum plant in the Toyama area), using visual bombing. The results were recorded as "poor."

24 Jul 45 Per Operations Order 24, dropped a pumpkin bomb on the assigned primary target (the Sumitomo Copper Refining plant in the Niihama area), using visual bombing. The results were recorded as "excellent."

26 Jul 45 Per Operations Order 27, dropped a pumpkin bomb on a target of oppor-

42. Crew A-1 on Tinian. *Top row (left to right):* 2nd Lt. Raymond P. Biel, Major Ralph R. Taylor, 1st Lt. Michael Angelich, 1st Lt. Fred A. Hoey. *Middle row (left to right):* S/Sgt. Theodore M. Slife, Cpl. Richard B. Anselme, T/Sgt. Robert J. Valley, M/Sgt. Frank M. Briese, Cpl. Nathaniel T. R. Burgwyn. *Bottom row (left to right):* Pfc. Donald D. Fockler, Cpl. William B. Reedy, Pfc. Mario A. Litterio, S/Sgt. Glen Mahugh, Jr., Sgt. Chester A. Hammond, Sgt. Steve J. Kinosh, Jr. (Air Force Museum)

tunity (railroad yards in the Yaizu area), using radar. The results were recorded as "poor."

29 Jul 45 Per Operations Order 30, dropped a pumpkin bomb on the assigned primary target (a nitrogen fertilizer plant in Ube area), using visual bombing. The results were recorded as "poor."

6 Aug 45 Per Operations Order 35, served as the advance weather reconnaissance over Nagasaki on the Hiroshima atomic bombing mission.

9 Aug 45 Per Operations Order 39, served as the backup aircraft at Iwo Jima on the Nagasaki atomic bombing mission.

43. Ralph R. Taylor, Airplane Commander of Crew A-1. (Leon D. Smith)

Crew A-2

Flight Crew
Airplane Commander   Edward M. Costello
Pilot   Harry B. Davis

Ground Crew
John C. Hansen
Robert J. Dowling

44. Crew A-2 on Tinian. *Top row (left to right):* Captain Edward M. Costello, 2nd Lt. Harry B. Davis, 2nd Lt. Robert J. Petrolli, 2nd Lt. Thomas H. Brumagin, 2nd Lt. John L. Downey. *Middle row (left to right):* Cpl. James R. Bryant, M/Sgt. Carleton A. McEachern, Sgt. Maurice J. Clark, Sgt. David Purdon. *Bottom row (left to right):* Pfc. James W. McGlennon, Sgt. Robert E. Holse, S/Sgt. Robert J. Dowling, Pfc. Fred D. Butler, Cpl. Robert R. Garn, Pfc. Charles W. Rich, M/Sgt. John C. Hansen. (Air Force Museum)

 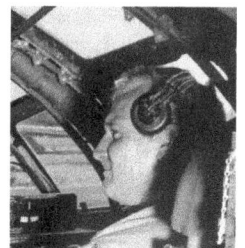 

45. *Left:* Edward M. Costello, Airplane Commander of Crew A-2. 46. *Middle:* Harry B. Davis, Pilot of Crew A-2. 47. *Right:* John L. Downey, Bombardier of Crew A-2. (Leon D. Smith)

Flight Crew		*Ground Crew*
Navigator	Robert J. Petrolli	Robert E. Holse
Bombardier	John L. Downey	Robert R. Garn
Flight Engineer	Thomas H. Brumagin	Fred D. Butler
Radio Operator	David Purdon	James W. McGlennon
Radar Operator	James R. Bryant	Charles W. Rich
Tail Gunner	Carleton C. McEachern	
Ass't Eng/Scanner	Maurice J. Clark	

The Silverplate B-29 assigned to Crew A-2 was 44-86347 (*Laggin' Dragon*), Victor No. 95. After arriving on Tinian on 2 August 1945, Crew A-2 flew 2 training missions, but did not fly any combat missions due to its late arrival on Tinian. 44-86347 was used on both missions. Edward Costello was the Aircraft Commander on each training mission.

Crew A-3

Flight Crew		*Ground Crew*
Airplane Commander	Ralph N. Devore	Forrest C. Anderson
Pilot	William J. Easton	Marion C. Fowler
Navigator	Franklin B. Wimer	Mack Newsom
Bombardier	Leon Cooper	James R. Womack
Flight Engineer	William T. Hulse	Jerry Grubaugh, Jr.
Radio Operator	Lee E. Palmert	Charles E. Schwab
Radar Operator	Michael B. Bohon	
Tail Gunner	Glenn S. Allison	
Ass't Eng/Scanner	Clarence E. Britt	

The Silverplate B-29 assigned to Crew A-3 was 44-27299 (*Next Objective*), Victor No. 86. After arriving on Tinian on about 16 June 1945, Crew A-3 flew 5 calibration and training missions and 9 practice bombing missions. This crew was credited with four combat missions, as shown below. One additional pumpkin mission was flown (on 8 August 1945) but it was aborted and combat credit was not given. 44-27299 was used on all missions except 26 July 1945 when 44-27303 was used. Ralph Devore was the Aircraft Commander on each mission.

20 Jul 45 Per Operations Order 20, dropped a pumpkin bomb on the assigned primary target (the Nippon Soda plant in the Toyama area), using visual bombing. The results were recorded as "very poor."

48. Crew A-3 on Tinian. *Top row (left to right):* 2nd Lt. Leon Cooper, 2nd Lt. William J. Easton, Capt. Ralph N. Devore, 2nd Lt. Franklin B. Wimer, 2nd Lt. William T. Hulse. *Middle row (left to right):* Cpl. Glenn S. Allison, Sgt. Michael G. Bohon, Sgt. Lee E. Palmert, Cpl. Clarence E. Britt, Cpl. George F. Robinson. *Bottom row (left to right):* Cpl. James R. Womack, Pfc. Charles E. Schwab, Sgt. Marion C. Fowler, T/Sgt. Forrest C. Anderson, Pfc. Jerry Grubaugh, Jr., Sgt. Mack Newsom. (Air Force Museum)

24 Jul 45   Per Operations Order 24, dropped a pumpkin bomb on a secondary target (the Sumitomo Rayon plant in the Niihama area), using visual bombing. The results were recorded as "excellent."

26 Jul 45   Per Operations Order 27, dropped a pumpkin bomb on a secondary target (urban area in the Osaka area), using visual bombing. The results were recorded as "Good."

14 Aug 45   Per Operations Order 44, dropped a pumpkin bomb on the assigned primary target (an arsenal factory in the Nagoya area), using visual bombing. The results were recorded as "poor."

Crew A-4

Flight Crew
Airplane Commander   Joseph E. Westover
Pilot   William J. Desmond

Ground Crew
Robert E. Smithson
Clyde R. Beecher

Appendix C

Flight Crew		*Ground Crew*
Navigator	John W. Dulin	Cleo E. Harter
Bombardier	Louis B. Allen	Filbert Reynolds
Flight Engineer	Robert M. Donnell	Derward A. Stevens
Radio Operator	James H. Doiron	John H. Hubeny, Jr.
Radar Operator	William J. Cotter	Francis J. Merry
Tail Gunner	Walter A. Spradlin	
Ass't Eng/Scanner	Samuel R. Wheeler	

The Silverplate B-29 assigned to Crew A-4 was 44-27300 (*Strange Cargo*), Victor No. 73. After arriving on Tinian on about 10 June 1945, Crew A-4 flew 4 calibration and training missions and 8 practice bombing missions. This crew was credited with four combat missions, as shown below. 44-27300 was used on all com-

49. Crew A-4 on Tinian. *Top row (left to right):* 2nd Lt. John W. Dulin, 2nd Lt. Louis B. Allen, Capt. Joseph E. Westover, 2nd Lt. William J. Desmond, 1st Lt. Robert M. Donnell. *Middle row (left to right):* Sgt. Samuel R. Wheeler, S/Sgt. William J. Spradlin, S/Sgt. James H. Doiron, S/Sgt. William J. Cotter. *Bottom row (left to right):* Cpl. Derward A. Stevens, Sgt. Cleo E. Harter, Pfc. Francis J. Merry, Pfc. John H. Hubeny, Jr., Sgt. Clyde R. Beecher, Cpl. Filbert Reynolds, M/Sgt. Robert E. Smithson. (Air Force Museum)

   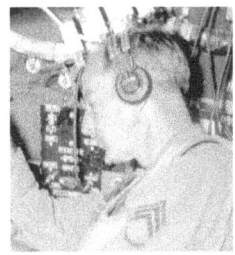

(Left to Right) 50. Joseph E. Westover, Airplane Commander of Crew A-4. 51. William J. Desmond, Pilot of Crew A-4. 53. Louis B. Allen, Bombardier of Crew A-4. 54. James H. Doiron, Radar Operator of Crew A-4. (Leon D. Smith)

52. Operations Officer Hopkins with Crew A-4. *Standing (left to right):* 2nd Lt. Louis B. Allen, 2nd Lt. John W. Dulin, Major James I. Hopkins, Jr., 2nd Lt. William J. Desmond, 1st Lt. Robert M. Donnell. *Kneeling (left to right):* S/Sgt. James H. Doiron, S/Sgt. William J. Cotter, Sgt. Samuel R. Wheeler, S/Sgt. William J. Spradlin. (Leon D. Smith)

bat missions except the one on 26 July 1945 when 44-27302 was used. Joseph Westover was the Aircraft Commander on each mission.

24 Jul 45 Per Operations Order 24, dropped a pumpkin bomb on the assigned primary target (Mitsubishi Heavy Industries plant), using visual bombing. The results were recorded as "excellent."

26 Jul 45 Per Operations Order 27, dropped a pumpkin bomb on a target of opportunity (Taira industrial area), using visual bombing. The results were recorded as "poor."

8 Aug 45   Per Operations Order 38, dropped a pumpkin bomb on a secondary target (Tsuruga chemical plant), using visual bombing. The results were recorded as "excellent."

14 Aug 45   Per Operations Order 44, dropped a pumpkin bomb on a target of opportunity (an arsenal factory in the Nagoya area), using visual bombing. The results were recorded as "excellent."

Crew A-5

Flight Crew		*Ground Crew*
Airplane Commander	Thomas J. Classen	Claude E. McLenon
Pilot	William M. Rowe	Roy K. Balliet
Navigator	William E. Wright	Donald E. Piehl
Bombardier	Bobby J. Chapman	Calvin B. Popwell
Flight Engineer	Floyd W. Kemner	Hinginio A. Baca
Radio Operator	Omar G. Strickland	
Radar Operator	George A. Weller	
Tail Gunner	Alfred A. Lewandowski	
Ass't Eng/Scanner	Lee E. Caylor	

55. Crew A-5 at Wendover. *Top row (left to right):* Cpl. George A. Weller, Cpl. Lee E. Caylor, S/Sgt. Alfred A. Lewandowski, 2nd Lt. William M. Rowe, Jr., T/Sgt. Omar G. Strickland. *Kneeling (left to right):* Lt. Col. Thomas J. Classen, Capt. William E. Wright, 1st Lt. Floyd W. Kemner, Capt. Bobby J. Chapman. (509th Pictorial Album)

The Silverplate B-29 assigned to Crew A-5 was 44-27354 (*Big Stink*), Victor No. 90. After arriving on Tinian on about 24 June 1945, Crew A-5 flew 2 training missions and 2 practice bombing missions with Classen as the Airplane Commander. This crew was also used in 3 Little Boy test missions in July with Tibbets as the Airplane Commander (one mission used 44-27354 and two missions were flown with 44-27303. Crew A-5 was credited with three combat missions, as shown below. 44-27354 was used on each mission except where noted. Classen was the Aircraft Commander on the first two missions; Elbert E. Smith was the Airplane Commander on the third mission.

20 Jul 45   Per Operations Order 20, dropped a pumpkin bomb on the assigned primary target (the Tsugami-Atagi Manufacturing Company in the Nagaoka area), using radar bombing. The results were recorded as "unobserved."

26 Jul 45   Per Operations Order 27, dropped a pumpkin bomb on a target of opportunity (a copper refinery in the Hitachi area), using visual bombing. The results were recorded as "good."

29 Jul 45   Per Operations Order 30, dropped a pumpkin bomb on a secondary target (an oil refinery in the Wakayama area), using visual bombing. The results were recorded as "unobserved." Aircraft 44-27304 was used on this mission.

Note: Per Operations Order 41, Crew A-5 and its associated ground crew departed Tinian for Wendover on 9 August 1945. Classen was the Airplane Commander and aircraft 44-86346 was used. The purpose of the mission was to be positioned at Wendover if the need arose to transport another Fat Man unit to Tinian.

Crew B-6

Flight Crew		*Ground Crew*
Airplane Commander	John A. Wilson	Charles J. Baker
Pilot	Ellsworth T. Carrington	Kenneth L. Baxter
Navigator	James S. Duva	Pasquale Lazzarino
Bombardier	Paul W. Gruning	William F. Jellick
Flight Engineer	James W. Davis	George I. Schreffer
Radio Operator	Glen H. Floweree	
Radar Operator	Vernon J. Rowley	
Tail Gunner	Chester A. Rogalski	
Ass't Eng/Scanner	Donald L. Rowe	

The Silverplate B-29 assigned to Crew B-6 was 44-27303 (*Jabit III*), Victor No. 71. After arriving on Tinian on about 10 June 1945, Crew B-6 flew 2 calibration and training missions and 10 practice bombing missions. This crew was credited with four combat missions, as shown below. 44-27303 was used on each combat mission. Wilson was the Aircraft Commander on each mission.

20 Jul 45   Per Operations Order 20, dropped a pumpkin bomb on a secondary tar-

56. Crew B-6 in Debriefing. *(Left to right):* Unidentified debriefing officer, Sgt. Vernon J. Rowley (hidden behind debriefing officer), Cpl. Donald L. Rowe, S/Sgt. Glen H. Floweree, M/Sgt. James W. Davis, 2nd Lt. Paul W. Gruning, 2nd Lt. Ellsworth T. Carrington, Major John A. Wilson, 2nd Lt. James S. Duva, Cpl. Chester A. Rogalski. (Robert W. Krauss)

get (the Taira urban area), using radar bombing. The results were recorded as "unobserved."

29 Jul 45 Per Operations Order 30, dropped a pumpkin bomb on the assigned primary target (the Nippon Oil Company plant in the Ube area), using visual bombing. The results were recorded as "poor."

6 Aug 45 Per Operations Order 35, served as the advance weather reconnaissance over Kokura on the Hiroshima atomic bombing mission.

8 Aug 45 Per Operations Order 38, dropped a pumpkin bomb on a secondary target (an assembly plant in the Uwajima area), using visual bombing. The results were recorded as "good."

Note: Per Operations Order 41, Crew B-6 and its associated ground crew departed Tinian for Wendover on 9 August 1945. Wilson was the Airplane Commander and aircraft 44-27303 was used. The purpose of the mission was to be positioned at Wendover if the need arose to transport another Fat Man unit to Tinian.

57. Crew B-7 on Tinian. *Top row (left to right):* 1st Lt. William Collinson, Capt. James N. Price, Jr., 2nd Lt. Thomas F. Costa, 2nd Lt. Everist I. Bednorz. *Middle row (left to right):* Cpl. Clyde L. Bysom, S/Sgt. Robert H. Byrd, Sgt. Fred E. Brown, M/Sgt. James A. Adkins, Cpl. Joe R. Brown. *Bottom row (left to right):* Cpl. Joe M. Madrid, Pfc. Edward M. Josefiak, Cpl. William R. Crotty, S/Sgt. Raymond G. St. Myers, Pfc. Donald E. Miller, S/Sgt. Russell D. Carrigan. Cpl. William R. Compronio of the ground crew is not in the photograph. (Air Force Museum)

Crew B-7

Flight Crew		*Ground Crew*
Airplane Commander	James N. Price, Jr.	Russell D. Carrigan
Pilot	Everist L. Bednorz	Raymond G. St. Myers
Navigator	William J. Collinson	William R. Compronio
Bombardier	Thomas F. Costa	William R. Crotty
Flight Engineer	James A. Adkins	Joe M. Madrid
Radio Operator	Robert H. Byrd	Edward M. Josefiak
Radar Operator	Joe R. Brown	Donald E. Miller
Tail Gunner	Clyde L. Bysom	
Ass't Eng/Scanner	Frederick E. Brown	

The Silverplate B-29 assigned to Crew B-7 was 44-27296 (*Some Punkins*), Victor No. 84. After arriving on Tinian on about 13 June 1945, Crew B-7 flew 5 calibration and training missions and 7 practice bombing missions. This crew was credited with five combat missions, as shown below. 44-27296 was used on each mission. Price was the Aircraft Commander on each mission.

 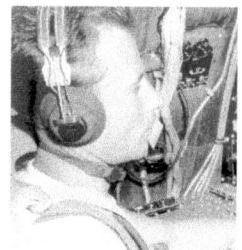

58. *Left:* Thomas F. Costa, Bombardier on Crew B-7. 59. *Right:* James A. Adkins, Flight Engineer on Crew B-7. (Leon D. Smith)

20 Jul 45 Per Operations Order 20, dropped a pumpkin bomb on the assigned primary target (the Fujikoshi Steel Products plant in the Yoyama area), using radar bombing. The results were recorded as "unobserved."

24 Jul 45 Per Operations Order 24, dropped a pumpkin bomb on the assigned primary target (the Ogaki urban area), using radar bombing. The results were recorded as "unobserved."

26 Jul 45 Per Operations Order 27, dropped a pumpkin bomb on a secondary target (the Shimoda urban area), using visual bombing. The results were recorded as "very poor."

8 Aug 45 Per Operations Order 38, dropped a pumpkin bomb on the assigned primary target (a converted textile mill in the Yokkaichi area), using visual bombing. The results were recorded as "poor."

14 Aug 45 Per Operations Order 44, dropped a pumpkin bomb on the assigned primary target (an arsenal factory in the Nagoya area), using visual bombing. The results were recorded as "poor."

Crew B-8

Flight Crew

Airplane Commander	Charles F. McKnight	
Pilot	Jacob Y. Bontekoe	
Navigator	Jack Widowsky	
Bombardier	Franklin H. MacGregor	
Flight Engineer	George H. Cohen	
Radio Operator	Lloyd J. Reeder	
Radar Operator	William F. Orren	
Tail Gunner	Roderick E. Legg	
Ass't Eng/Scanner	Donald O. Cole	

Ground Crew

Arnold E. Sleipnes
Carmine A. Genova
Chester J. Krajewski
Oscar J. Thigpen
Francis J. Schramke
Frank E. Sutton

The Silverplate B-29 assigned to Crew B-8 was 44-27302 (*Top Secret*), Victor No. 72. After arriving on Tinian on about 10 June 1945, Crew B-8 flew 5 calibration and training missions and 8 practice bombing missions. This crew was credited with six combat missions, as shown below. 44-27302 was used on all combat missions

60. Crew B-8 on Tinian. *Top row (left to right):* 2nd Lt. Franklin H. MacGregor, 2nd Lt. Jacob Y. Bontekoe, Capt. Charles F. McKnight, 2nd Lt. Jack Widowsky, 1st Lt. George H. Cohen. *Middle row (left to right):* Sgt. Roderick E. Legg, Sgt. Lloyd J. Reeder, T/Sgt. William F. Orren, Jr., Cpl. Donald O. Cole. *Bottom row (left to right):* Cpl. Oscar J. Thigpen, Pfc. Frank E. Sutton, Sgt. Carmine A. Genova, Cpl. Chester J. Krajewski, Pfc. Francis J. Schramke, T/Sgt. Arnold E. Sleipnes. (Air Force Museum)

except the one on 6 August 1945 when 44-86347 was used and the one on 9 August 1945 when 44-27354 was used. McKnight was the Aircraft Commander on all missions.

20 Jul 45   Per Operations Order 20, dropped a pumpkin bomb on a secondary target (the Otsu urban area), using radar bombing. The results were recorded as "unobserved."

24 Jul 45   Per Operations Order 24, dropped a pumpkin bomb on a secondary target (a heavy industry in the harbor of Yokkaichi), using visual bombing. The results were recorded as "excellent."

29 Jul 45   Per Operations Order 30, dropped a pumpkin bomb on the assigned primary target (Industrial Soda Company plant in the Ube area), using visual bombing. The results were recorded as "excellent."

6 Aug 45   Per Operations Order 35, served as the backup aircraft at Iwo Jima on the Hiroshima atomic bombing mission.

61. *Left:* George H. Cohen, Flight Engineer on Crew B-8. 62. *Right:* Jack Widowsky, Navigator on Crew B-8. (Leon D. Smith)

9 Aug 45 Per Operations Order 39, served as the advance weather reconnaissance over Nagasaki on the Nagasaki atomic bombing mission.

14 Aug 45 Per Operations Order 44, dropped a pumpkin bomb on the assigned primary target (the Toyoda Auto Works in the Koromo area), using visual bombing. The results were recorded as "poor."

Crew B-9

Flight Crew		*Ground Crew*
Airplane Commander	Robert A. Lewis	Steve C. Lizak
Pilot	Richard McNamara	Leonard W. Markley
Navigator	Harold J. Rider	Jean S. Cooper
Bombardier	Stewart W. Williams	Winfield C. Kinkade
Flight Engineer	Wyatt E. Duzenbury	John E. Jackson
Radio Operator	Richard H. Nelson	John J. Lesniewski
Radar Operator	Joseph S. Stiborik	Harold R. Olson
Tail Gunner	George R. Caron	
Ass't Eng/Scanner	Robert H. Shumard	

The Silverplate B-29 assigned to Crew B-9 was 44-86292 (*Enola Gay*), Victor No. 82. After arriving on Tinian on 6 July 1945, Crew B-9 flew 4 calibration and training missions and 2 practice bombing missions. This crew also flew one Little Boy drop test mission with Paul Tibbets as the Airplane Commander. Crew B-9 was credited with five combat missions, as shown below. The aircraft used on each mission was as noted. Lewis was the Airplane Commander on all combat missions except the Hiroshima atomic bombing mission on 6 August 1945. The crew changes for this mission are noted below.

24 Jul 45 Per Operations Order 24, dropped a pumpkin bomb on the assigned primary target (a steel works in the Kobe area), using visual bombing. The results were recorded as "unobserved." Aircraft 44-86292 was used on this mission.

26 Jul 45 Per Operations Order 27, dropped a pumpkin bomb on a secondary target (the Nagoya urban area), using radar bombing. The results were recorded as "unobserved." Aircraft 44-86292 was used on this mission.

63. Crew B-9 on Tinian. *Top row (left to right):* 2nd Lt. Richard McNamara, Capt. Robert A. Lewis, 1st Lt. Stewart W. Williams, 2nd Lt. Harold J. Rider. *Middle row (left to right):* S/Sgt. Joe S. Stiborik, T/Sgt. George R. Caron, Cpl. Richard M. Nelson, Sgt. Robert H. Shumard, T/Sgt. Wyatt E. Duzenbury, S/Sgt. Walter F. McCaleb. *Bottom row (left to right):* Pfc. Harold R. Olson, Sgt. Leonard W. Markley, Pfc. John E. Jackson, Pfc. John J. Lesniewski, Sgt. Steve C. Lizak, Cpl. Jean S. Cooper, Cpl. Winfield C. Kinkade. (Air Force Museum)

29 Jul 45   Per Operations Order 30, dropped a pumpkin bomb on the assigned primary target (Koriyama marshalling yards), using visual bombing. The results recorded as "excellent." Aircraft 44-27353 was used on this mission.

6 Aug 45   Per Operations Order 35, a modified crew B-9 flew 44-86292 to drop the Little Boy atomic bomb on Hiroshima. Paul Tibbets was the Airplane Commander, Lewis was the Pilot, Theodore Van Kirk was the Navigator, and Thomas Ferebee was the Bombardier. Additional details on the mission can be found in chapter 3.

8 Aug 45   Per Operations Order 38, dropped a pumpkin bomb on a target of opportunity (a light industry in the Tokushima area), using visual bombing. The results were recorded as "poor." Aircraft 44-27304 was used on this mission.

Crew B-10

Flight Crew

Airplane Commander	George W. Marquardt
Pilot	James M. Andeson
Navigator	Russell E. Gackenbach
Bombardier	James W. Strudwick
Flight Engineer	James R. Corliss
Radio Operator	Warren L. Coble
Radar Operator	Joseph M. DiJulio
Tail Gunner	Melvin H. Bierman
Ass't Eng/Scanner	Anthony D. Capua

Ground Crew

Joseph I. Gulick
George J. Brown
Matthew W. Huddleston
George P. Hammons
Frank W. Berzinis
Aram E. Bezdegian
Carl C. Mason

The Silverplate B-29 assigned to Crew B-10 was 44-27304 (*Up An' Atom*), Victor No. 88. After arriving on Tinian on about 16 June 1945, Crew B-10 flew 5 calibration and training missions and 7 practice bombing missions. This crew was credited with four combat missions, as shown below. 44-27304 was used on the two pumpkin missions. The aircraft used on the two atomic bombing missions were as shown. Marquardt was the Aircraft Commander on all missions.

64. Crew B-10 on Tinian. *Top row (left to right):* Capt. George W. Marquardt, 2nd Lt. James M. Anderson, 2nd Lt. Russell Gackenbach, Capt. James W. Strudwick. *Middle row (left to right):* T/Sgt. James R. Corliss, Sgt. Warren L. Coble. *Bottom row (left to right):* Cpl. George P. Hammons, Pfc. Carl C. Mason, Pfc. Aram E. Bezdegian, Pfc. Grank W. Berzinis, Sgt. Matthew W. Huddleston, T/Sgt. Joseph L. Gulick, Sgt. George J. Brown. (Air Force Museum)

20 Jul 45   Per Operations Order 20, dropped a pumpkin bomb on a secondary target (the Taira urban area), using radar bombing. The results were recorded as "unobserved."

26 Jul 45   Per Operations Order 27, dropped a pumpkin bomb on a secondary target (the Hamamatsu urban area), using radar bombing. The results were recorded as "unobserved."

6 Aug 45   Per Operations Order 35, flew aircraft 44-86291 as the photo airplane on the Hiroshima atomic bombing mission.

9 Aug 45   Per Operations Order 39, flew aircraft 44-86292 as the advance weather reconnaissance over Kokura on the Nagasaki atomic bombing mission.

Crew C-11

Flight Crew

Airplane Commander	Claude R. Eatherly
Pilot	Ira C. Weatherly
Navigator	Francis D. Thornhill
Bombardier	Frank K. Wey
Flight Engineer	Eugene S. Grennan
Radio Operator	Pasquale Baldasaro
Radar Operator	Albert G. Barsumian
Tail Gunner	Gillen T. Niceley
Ass't Eng/Scanner	Jack Bivans

Ground Crew

Donald D. Beaudette
Howard A. Thompson
Yive J. H. Ping
William E. Smith
Chester s. Chudy
Harold E. Knisley
William J. Jacks

The Silverplate B-29 assigned to Crew C-11 was 44-27301 (*Straight Flush*), Victor No. 85. After arriving on Tinian on about 13 June 1945, Crew C-11 flew 6 calibration and training missions and 6 practice bombing missions. This crew was credited with six combat missions, as shown below. 44-27300 was used on all combat missions except the one on 8 August 1945 when 44-27302 was used. Eatherly was the Aircraft Commander on all missions.

20 Jul 45   Per Operations Order 20, dropped a pumpkin on a target of opportunity (a railroad station in Tokyo), using radar bombing. The results were recorded as "unobserved."

24 Jul 45   Per Operations Order 24, dropped a pumpkin bomb on a secondary target (the Toyo Rayon Factory in the Otsu area), using visual bombing. The results were recorded as "excellent."

26 Jul 45   Per Operations Order 27, dropped a pumpkin bomb on a target of opportunity (an identified target in the Tsugawa area), using visual bombing. The results were recorded as "poor."

29 Jul 45   Per Operations Order 30, dropped a pumpkin bomb on a secondary target (the naval base at Maizuru), using visual bombing. The results were recorded as "excellent."

65. Crew C-11 on Tinian. *Top row (left to right):* 2nd Lt. Ira J. Weatherly, 2nd Lt. Franklin Wey, Major Claude R. Eatherly, Captain Francis D. Thornhill, 2nd Lt. Thomas Grennan. *Middle row (left to right):* Sgt. Jack Bivans, Sgt. Gillon T. Niceley, S/Sgt. Pasquale Baldasaro, Sgt. Albert Barsumian. *Bottom row (left to right):* Cpl. Yive J.H. Ping, Pfc. Harold E. Knisley, Pfc. Chester S. Chudy, Sgt. Howard A. Thompson, T/Sgt. Donald D. Beaudette, Cpl. William E. Smith. (Air Force Museum)

6 Aug 45 Per Operations Order 35, served as the advance weather reconnaissance over Hiroshima on the Hiroshima atomic bombing mission.

8 Aug 45 Per Operations Order 38, dropped a pumpkin bomb on the assigned primary target (a heavy industry plant in the Yokkaichi harbor area), using visual bombing. The results were recorded as "poor."

Crew C-12

Flight Crew		*Ground Crew*
Airplane Commander	Herman S. Zahn	Elbert E. Owens
Pilot	Gilbert B. Dickman	Carl W. Rein
Navigator	Henry Deutsch	Gerald J. Corcoran
Bombardier	Francis R. Ormond	Francis A. Pellegrino
Flight Engineer	James K. Elder	Lavern L. Holmes
Radio Operator	Leander J. Baur	

66. Crew C-12 on Tinian. *Top row (left to right):* F/O Francis R. Ormond, 1st Lt. Henry Deutsch, Capt. Herman S. Zahn, 2nd Lt. Gilbert B. Dickman. *Middle row (left to right):* S/Sgt. Leander J. Baur, T/Sgt. James K. Elder, Jr., Sgt. Neil R. Corey, Sgt. Gerald F. Clapso, Sgt. Raymond E. Allen. *Bottom row (left to right):* Sgt. Francis A. Pellegrino, Sgt. Gerald J. Corcoran, M/Sgt. Elbert E. Owens, S/Sgt. Carl W. Rein, Cpl. Lavern L. Holmes. (509th Pictorial Album)

Crew C-12

Flight Crew

Radar Operator	Gerald F. Clapso
Tail Gunner	Raymond E. Allen
Ass't Eng/Scanner	Neil R. Corey

The Silverplate B-29 assigned to Crew C-12 was 44-86346 (not given a name on Tinian, but named *Luke the Spook* later at Roswell), Victor No. 94. After arriving on Tinian on 2 August 1945, Crew C-12 only flew 2 training missions, using 44-27301 and 44-27354. It did not fly any practice bombing missions or combat missions. When Classen and crew A-5 flew 44-86346 back to Tinian on 9 August 1945, Zahn and crew C-12 were assigned aircraft 44-27354 (the aircraft previously assigned to crew A-5).

Crew C-13

Flight Crew

Airplane Commander	Frederick C. Bock
Pilot	Hugh C. Ferguson
Navigator	Leonard A. Godfrey
Bombardier	Charles Levy
Flight Engineer	Roderick F. Arnold
Radio Operator	Ralph D. Curry
Radar Operator	William C. Barney
Tail Gunner	Robert J. Stock
Ass't Eng/Scanner	Ralph D. Belanger

Ground Crew

Frederick D. Clayton
Robert L. McNamee
John L. Willoughby
Robert M. Haider
Rudolph H. Gerken

The Silverplate B-29 assigned to Crew C-13 was 44-27297 (*Bockscar*), Victor No. 77. After arriving on Tinian on about 16 June 1945, Crew C-13 flew 5 calibration and training missions and 11 practice bombing missions. This crew was cred-

67. Crew C-13 on Tinian. *Top row (left to right):* 2nd Lt. Hugh C. Ferguson, 2nd Lt. Leonard A. Godfrey, Capt. Frederick C. Bock, 1st Lt. Charles Levy. *Middle row (left to right):* Sgt. Ralph D. Curry, Sgt. William C. Barney, Sgt. Ralph D. Belanger, M/Sgt. Roderick F. Arnold, Sgt. Robert J. Stock. *Bottom row (left to right):* Sgt. Robert L. McNamee, Sgt. John L. Willoughby, S/Sgt. Frederick D. Clayton, Pfc. Rudolph H. Gerken, Cpl. Robert M. Haider. (Air Force Museum)

ited with five combat missions, as shown below. The aircraft used on the combat missions are as noted. Bock was the Aircraft Commander on all missions.

20 Jul 45 Per Operations Order 20, dropped a pumpkin bomb on the assigned primary target (a light industry plant in the Fukushima area), using radar bombing. The results were recorded as "unobserved." Aircraft 44-27300 was used on this mission.

24 Jul 45 Per Operations Order 24, dropped a pumpkin bomb on the assigned primary target (Sumitomo aluminum plant in the Niihama area), using visual bombing. The results were recorded as "excellent." Aircraft 44-27297 was used on this mission.

29 Jul 45 Per Operations Order 30, dropped a pumpkin bomb on a secondary target (Nakajima aircraft engine factory in the Tokyo-Musashino area), using visual bombing. The results were recorded as "poor." Aircraft 44-27297 was used on this mission.

9 Aug 45 Per Operations Order 39, flew 44-27353 as the instrument aircraft on the Nagasaki atomic bombing mission.

14 Aug 45 Per Operations Order 44, dropped a pumpkin bomb on the assigned primary target (the Toyoda Auto Works in the Koromo area), using visual bombing. The results were recorded as "good." Aircraft 44-27298 was used on this mission.

Crew C-14

Flight Crew		*Ground Crew*
Airplane Commander	Norman W. Ray	William E. Egger
Pilot	John E. Cantlon	Richard E. Blouse
Navigator	Stanley G. Steinke	Woitto T. Laine
Bombardier	Myron Faryna	Paul C. Schafhauser
Flight Engineer	George L. Brabenec	Barton B. Crespin
Radio Operator	Francis X. Dolan	Edgar A. Poe
Radar Operator	Richard F. Cannon	Troy B. Scott
Tail Gunner	Martin G. Murray	
Ass't Eng/Scanner	Thomas A. Bunting	

69. *Left:* Norman W. Ray, Airplane Commander of Crew C-14. 70. *Right:* John E. Cantlon, Pilot of Crew C-14. (Leon D. Smith)

68. Crew C-14 on Tinian. *Top row (left to right):* 2nd Lt. Myron Faryna, 2nd Lt. Stanley G. Steinke, Capt. Norman W. Ray, 2nd Lt. John E. Cantlon. *Middle row (left to right):* Sgt. Martin G. Murray, Sgt. Thomas A. Bunting, M/Sgt. George L. Brabanec, Cpl. Richard F. Cannon, Sgt. Francis X. Dolan. *Bottom row (left to right):* Pfc. Edgar A. Poe, Jr., Pfc. Troy B. Scott, Cpl. Woitto T. Laine, Pfc. Barton B. Crespin, Cpl. Richard E. Blouse, S/Sgt. William E. Egger, Cpl. Paul C. Schafhauser. (Air Force Museum)

The Silverplate B-29 assigned to Crew C-14 was 44-86291 (*Necessary Evil*), Victor No. 91. After arriving on Tinian on about 2 July 1945, Crew C-14 flew 5 calibration and training missions and 2 practice bombing missions. This crew was credited with five combat missions, as shown below. 44-86291 was used on all combat missions except where noted. Ray was the Airplane Commander except for the missions on 9 and 14 August. He was ill during this period of time. James I. Hopkins, Jr., the 509th Operations Officer, acted as Airplane Commander on these two missions.

24 Jul 45 Per Operations Order 24, dropped a pumpkin bomb on the assigned primary target (Kawasaki Locomotive and Car Company in the Kobe area), using visual bombing. The results were recorded as "excellent."

26 Jul 45 Per Operations Order 27, dropped a pumpkin bomb on a secondary target (the Kashiwazaki urban area), using radar bombing. The results were recorded as "unobserved."

29 Jul 45 Per Operations Order 30, dropped a pumpkin bomb on the assigned pri-

mary target (a light industry in the Koriyama area), using visual bombing. The results were recorded as "poor."

9 Aug 45 Per Operations Order 39, Hopkins and crew C-14 flew 44-27304 as the photo airplane on the Nagasaki atomic bombing mission.

14 Aug 45 Per Operations Order 44, Hopkins and crew C-14 flew 44-27304 to drop a pumpkin bomb on the assigned primary target (an arsenal factory in the Nagoya area), using visual bombing. The results were recorded as "poor."

Crew C-15

Flight Crew		*Ground Crew*
Airplane Commander	Charles D. Albury	Chester V. Pawiak
Pilot	Fred J. Olivi	Charles B. Rinard

71. Crew C-15 on Tinian. *Top row (left to right):* Capt. Charles D. Albury, Capt. Kermit K. Beahan, Major Charles W. Sweeney, Capt. James F. Van Pelt, Jr., 2nd Lt. Fred J. Olivi. *Middle row (left to right):* Sgt. Abe M. Spitzer, S/Sgt. Edward K. Buckley, M/Sgt. John D. Kuharek, S/Sgt. Albert T. Dehart, Sgt. Raymond G. Gallagher. *Bottom row (left to right):* Cpl. Claude C. Gilliam, Pfc. Robert E. Davenport, Cpl. Allan L. Moore, S/Sgt. Chester V. Pawiak, Pfc. Theron L. Blaisdell, Cpl. James J. Reilly, S/Sgt. Charles B. Rinard. (Air Force Museum)

   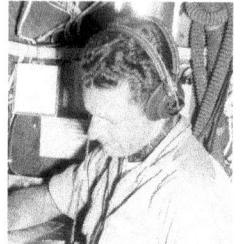

Left to right: 72. Charles D. Albury, Airplane Commander of Crew C-15. 73. Charles W. Sweeney, Airplane Commander of Crew C-15 for Nagasaki Mission. 74. Fred J. Olivi, Pilot of Crew C-15. 75. Abe M. Spitzer, Radio Operator of Crew C-15. (Leon D. Smith)

Flight Crew		*Ground Crew*
Navigator	James F. Van Pelt	Claude C. Gilliam
Bombardier	Kermit K. Beahan	Allan L. Moore
Flight Engineer	John D. Kuharek	James J. Reilly
Radio Operator	Abe M. Spitzer	Theron L. Blaisdell
Radar Operator	Edward K. Buckley	Robert E. Davenport
Tail Gunner	Albert T. Dehart	
Ass't Eng/Scanner	Raymond G. Gallagher	

The Silverplate B-29 assigned to Crew C-15 was 44-27353 (*The Great Artiste*), Victor No. 89. After arriving on Tinian on about 27 June 1945, Crew C-15 flew 4 calibration and training missions and 3 practice bombing missions. The crew also flew 2 Little Boy drop test missions in 44-27299 and 3 Fat Man drop test missions in 44-27297. Charles W. Sweeney was the Airplane Commander on all of the test missions. This crew was credited with five combat missions, as shown below. One additional pumpkin mission was flown (on 20 July 1945) but it was aborted and combat credit was not given. 44-27353 was used on all missions except where noted. Albury was the Aircraft Commander on each mission except where noted.

24 Jul 45 Per Operations Order 24, dropped a pumpkin bomb on the assigned primary target (railroad yards in the Kobe area), using visual bombing. The results were recorded as "excellent."

26 Jul 45 Per Operations Order 27, dropped a pumpkin bomb on a secondary target (urban area in the Toyama area), using radar bombing. The results were recorded as "unobserved." Aircraft 44-27297 was used on this mission.

6 Aug 45 Per Operations Order 35, Sweeney and crew C-15 used 44-27353 as the instrument aircraft on the Hiroshima atomic bombing mission.

9 Aug 45 Per Operations Order 39, Sweeney and crew C-15 used 44-27297 to drop the Fat Man atomic bomb on Nagasaki.

14 Aug 45 Per Operations Order 44, dropped a pumpkin bomb on the assigned primary target (the Toyoda Auto Works in the Koromo area), using visual bombing. The results were recorded as "poor." Aircraft 44-27301 was used on this mission.

APPENDIX D:
509TH COMPOSITE GROUP AND PROJECT ALBERTA ROSTER (TINIAN, 1945)

This roster of the men of the 509th Composite Group and Project Alberta who were based on Tinian in July–August 1945 was prepared by compiling a list of names from the unit photographs and accompanying captions included in the *509th Pictorial Album*. The names of the men who came to Tinian from the Los Alamos Laboratory of the Manhattan Project were taken from Harlow Russ's *Project Alberta: The Preparation of Atomic Bombs for Use in World War II*. Additional information on Project Alberta can be found in Appendix E.

The unit abbreviations, full names, number of men assigned, and the unit Commanding Officers are as follows:

	Unit	*Size*	*Commanding Officer*
509HQ	Headquarters, 509th Composite Group	98	Col. Paul W. Tibbets, Jr.
393rd	393rd Bombardment Squadron (VH)	535	Major Charles W. Sweeney
1st	1st Ordnance Squadron, Special Aviation	296	Major Charles F.H. Begg
320th	320th Troop Carrier Squadron	149	Capt. John J. Casey, Jr.
390th	390th Air Service Group	189	Lt. Col. John W. Porter
603rd	603rd Air Engineering Squadron	227	Capt. Earl O. Casey
1027th	1027th Air Materiel Squadron	141	Major Guy Geller
1395th	1395th Military Police Company (Aviation)	133	Capt. Louis Schaffer
Proj A	Project Alberta	51	Capt. William S. Parsons (U.S. Navy)
HQ	Washington Representatives	2	
		Total 1,821	

The number of men in each unit of the 509th Composite Group and in the Project Alberta contingent is given in the "Size" column above. The Washington Representatives were Brigadier General Thomas F. Farrell (deputy to General Groves) and Rear Admiral William R. Purnell (Navy member of the Military Policy Committee). Other than the above listing of the Commanding Officers of the nine units, no attempt was made to include rank, duty, or other information in this roster. Ranks were not given in many of the unit photographs in the source material and promotions did occur while the 509th was on Tinian.

509th Composite Group and Project Alberta Roster
Tinian, 1945

Name	Unit	Name	Unit	Name	Unit
Abraham, Sheffe	1st	Asseff, R. T.	390th	Beecher, Clyde R.	393rd
Acker, John G.	320th	Astarita, Thomas	1st	Beeler, Kenneth E.	1st
Adams, Bob	1395th	Atkielski, Joseph R.	393rd	Bega, Joe	1027th
Adams, L. J., Jr.	390th	Aungst, Sharon	1st	Begg, Charles F. H.	1st
Adams, Ronald K.	320th	Ayers, Robert L.	393rd	Begnoche, Raymond	1st
Adams, Scott C.	390th	Babock, James W., Jr.	320th	Behr, R. B.	509HQ
Adams, Vernon	1395th	Baca, Hinginio A.	393rd	Belanger, Ralph D.	393rd
Adkins, James A.	393rd	Back, Lawrence L.	393rd	Belasco, Daniel M.	1st
Agnew, Harold	Proj A	Bacon, Charles E.	1st	Belcher, Ray	1395th
Albright, Lee S.	1027th	Bagley, Winton	1395th	Bell, Edwin M.	393rd
Albury, Charles D.	393rd	Baiago, Joseph	1027th	Bell, Francis III	509HQ
Alexander, Adair M.	603rd	Bailey, Kenneth E.	393rd	Bell, W., Jr.	390th
Alexander, Albert D.	1st	Baker, Charles J.	393rd	Bellamy, Sidney J.	393rd
Alexander, John	1st	Baker, Charles P.	Proj A	Benbrook, Robert E.	393rd
Alger, Frank A.	509HQ	Baker, Delbert R.	320th	Benenati, Frank J.	393rd
Aljian, Edward	390th	Baker, George S.	393rd	Benjamin, Farron P.	1027th
Allen, Louis B.	393rd	Baldasaro, Pasquale	393rd	Bennett, Cecil	390th
Allen, Raymond E.	393rd	Baldwin, Robert F., Jr.	1027th	Bennett, Ralph M.	393rd
Allen, Sam, Jr.	320th	Ball, Walter A.	1027th	Benson, Bernard F.	320th
Allison, Glenn S.	393rd	Balliet, Roy K.	393rd	Benson, Robert A.	603rd
Allison, Noah C.	1027th	Bandick, R. N.	390th	Berardo, D. J.	509HQ
Allshouse, Dorsey	1st	Bandy, Ray C.	509HQ	Berg, E. C.	390th
Almon, Jabez W.	320th	Bankoski, Edward	603rd	Bergamo, Frank	1395th
Alvarez, Luis	Proj A	Barbera, James J.	320th	Berger, Ralph C.	603rd
Amentt, Michael J.	603rd	Bardecker, Irving E.	393rd	Berkanholtz, I.	390th
Ames, Robert N.	320th	Barker, Curtis T.	1st	Berkeley, Theodore	1395th
Anderson, David	Proj A	Barker, John O.	320th	Berkoff, Louis	603rd
Anderson, Edsel	1395th	Barnard, Harry N.	320th	Bernath, Glen A.	393rd
Anderson, Forest C.	393rd	Barnes, Philip M.	1st	Berry, Kenneth E.	1st
Anderson, Howard J.	390th	Barney, Arthur G.	393rd	Berzinis, Frank W.	393rd
Anderson, James F.	393rd	Barney, William C.	393rd	Beser, Jacob	393rd
Anderson, James J.	393rd	Barrett, Orin R.	393rd	Best, Warren	393rd
Anderson, James M.	393rd	Barsumian, Albert	393rd	Betes, Manual	393rd
Anderson, Jonie	603rd	Barthelomew, Stanley M.	603rd	Betts, Loyal E.	1st
Andrews, Lester W.	1395th	Bartholomew, W. E.	390th	Bever, Theodore G.	603rd
Andrews, Sam G.	509HQ	Bartlett, Albert L.	393rd	Bezdegian, Aram E.	393rd
Andritsis, Harry D.	393rd	Bateman, Rao H.	603rd	Biel, Raymond P.	393rd
Angeli, Russell F.	320th	Batt, Kenneth L.	320th	Bierman, Melvin H.	393rd
Angelich, Michael	393rd	Baugh, Aaron C.	393rd	Biggio, William D.	393rd
Anselme, Richard B.	393rd	Baur, Leander J.	393rd	Bingman, Sandy M.	603rd
Anstine, Calvin C.	393rd	Baxter, Kenneth L.	393rd	Birch, Francis A.	Proj A
Anthony, Michael A.	1027th	Baxter, Marcus W.	393rd	Birkenkamp, Allen A.	1st
Apgar, Stanley C.	393rd	Bayrik, Mark L., Jr.	320th	Bishop, Gilbert W.	393rd
Arena, John L.	393rd	Beahan, Kermit K.	393rd	Bishop, William E.	393rd
Armijo, Cicilio	603rd	Bean, Bernard H.	1027th	Bissonnette, George	390th
Armstrong, James S.	1027th	Bean, Gerald E.	509HQ	Bivans, Jack	393rd
Arnold, Alvin R.	1027th	Beatson, James A.	1st	Black, Norman	393rd
Arnold, George L.	393rd	Beatty, James A.	320th	Black, Richard	1395th
Arnold, Marvin H., Jr.	320th	Beaty, Marvin O.	393rd	Blaisdell, Theron L.	393rd
Arnold, Roderick F.	393rd	Beaudette, Donald D.	393rd	Blakely, Earl	1st
Arnson, Robert J.	1st	Bederson, Benjamin B.	Proj A	Blakney, Earl J.	603rd
Artripe, Asper A.	603rd	Bednorz, Everist L.	393rd	Blandine, Alfred H.	393rd
Ashworth, Frederick L.	Proj A	Beebe, Vernon C.	393rd	Blankenship, Vester	1395th

509th Composite Group and Project Alberta Roster (Tinian, 1945)

Blasingame, Thomas E.	1027th	Brown, Frank S.	1st	Carmichael, D. D.	390th
Bloam, James C.	1st	Brown, Fred E.	393rd	Carol, Andrew	393rd
Block, George	1st	Brown, George J.	393rd	Caron, George R.	393rd
Block, Otto C., Jr.	393rd	Brown, Joe R.	393rd	Carpenter, Charles E.	320th
Bloomfield, Ralph	603rd	Brown, Leland A.	320th	Carr, Charley C.	393rd
Blouse, Richard E.	393rd	Brown, Richard	1st	Carrasco, T.	390th
Blower, Joseph, Jr.	393rd	Brown, Venard	1027th	Carrigan, Russell D.	393rd
Blum, J. E.	509HQ	Brown, William E.	393rd	Carrington, Ellsworth T.	393rd
Blumenfeld, Leonard M.	393rd	Bruenger, Fred E.	320th	Carroll, William E.	390th
Blyler, Ernest J.	509HQ	Brumagin, Thomas H.	393rd	Carter, Malla	1395th
Bobinson, J. R.	509HQ	Brumfield, Abram A.	1027th	Carwile, William M.	1027th
Bock, Frederick C.	393rd	Bruno, N. F.	509HQ	Cary, Delbert P.	1st
Boehm, W. A., Jr.	390th	Bryan, John C.	1st	Casci, Peter	1st
Bohine, S. H.	509HQ	Bryant, Claude E.	393rd	Casey, Donald M.	603rd
Bohon, Michael G.	393rd	Bryant, James R.	393rd	Casey, Earl O.	603rd
Bolles, William H.	320th	Buchner, Charles	1st	Casey, John J., Jr.	320th
Bolstad, Milo	Proj A	Buckley, Edward K.	393rd	Cash, Bertram S.	393rd
Bonadies, Anthony	393rd	Budai, Stephen	1st	Castater, John W.	320th
Bonczek, Walter J.	393rd	Budmen, Bernard H.	1st	Castellitto, Adam J.	393rd
Bonds, John E.	390th	Bunting, Thomas A.	393rd	Catt, Grover H.	393rd
Bonjour, Glenn	1st	Burford, Kermit	1st	Caylor, Lee E.	393rd
Bontekoe, Jacob Y.	393rd	Burgener, Fred E.	320th	Cetti, Bob	1395th
Borger, Joseph B.	603rd	Burgess, E. A.	390th	Chadwick, B.	509HQ
Borgerson, William H.	393rd	Burgmeir, William D.	1st	Chambers, C. F.	390th
Borgstadt, William C.	393rd	Burgwyn, Nathaniel T. R.	393rd	Chaney, Edgar	393rd
Born, W. R.	509HQ	Burns, Billy B.	509HQ	Chapman, Bobby J.	393rd
Bossert, Frederick	1st	Burns, Ernest C.	393rd	Chapman, Elzie	1395th
Bost, Avery C.	320th	Burns, James A.	393rd	Chase, Ralph E.	320th
Boucher, Charles E., Jr.	393rd	Burris, Donald E.	1st	Chatt, John O.	509HQ
Bourre, John P.	393rd	Busang, Joseph S.	320th	Chaussy, Pern J.	1st
Bowen, H. D.	390th	Buscher, Joseph D.	509HQ	Chavez, Alfredo	1395th
Bowen, Harry	393rd	Bush, Neal W.	1395th	Chavez, Henry G.	320th
Bower, Robert	603rd	Bushee, Joseph C.	1027th	Cheek, Ples M.	1st
Bowman, Lester E.	393rd	Butensky, S. J.	390th	Cheeseman, John L.	1027th
Boyle, Ray N., Jr.	393rd	Butler, Fred D.	393rd	Chelnik, D.	390th
Brabenec, George L.	393rd	Butterfield, Harold	1st	Childs, Raymond	1395th
Bradley, Guy C.	603rd	Buxton, Carl E.	1st	Chisom, R. C.	509HQ
Bradley, James H.	1st	Byczynski, Edmund S.	393rd	Chiuchiolo, Michael	320th
Bradley, Max W.	320th	Byler, George G., Jr.	1st	Christensen, John E.	1027th
Brady, Frank J.	320th	Byrd, Robert H.	393rd	Christie, D. T.	509HQ
Bramer, Bill	1395th	Byrnes, William	1st	Chudy, Chester S.	393rd
Branfeld, J. G.	390th	Bysom, Clyde L.	393rd	Churchill, Deane G.	320th
Breeding, William	1st	Caddell, Curtis W.	1st	Ciaccio, B. P.	509HQ
Brending, Edward	1395th	Cagle, Howard L.	1395th	Cirami, Salvatore P.	1027th
Brevelle, Curtley, J. B.	1027th	Cain, William R.	320th	Clancy, Joseph L.	393rd
Brewster, Leon J.	1027th	Caleca, Vincent	Proj A	Clapso, Gerard F.	393rd
Brice, George F.	393rd	Callahan, Cordell W.	1st	Clark, C. C.	390th
Bridges, James H.	393rd	Camac, Morton	Proj A	Clark, Ernest K.	1st
Briese, Frank M.	393rd	Camden, Paul M.	1027th	Clark, Joe L.	1st
Briggs, Stephen W., Jr.	320th	Campbell, John M.	393rd	Clark, Maurice J.	393rd
Bright, J. L.	509HQ	Campeau, Edward J.	603rd	Classen, Thomas J.	509HQ
Brightman, Stanton H.	1395th	Canby, Joel S.	509HQ	Clay, R. L.	393rd
Brin, Raymond	Proj A	Cangilla, Maurice C.	1st	Clayton, Frederick D.	393rd
Brininger, Ralph A.	1st	Canjar, Mathew H.	320th	Cleary, John P.	1027th
Brinkley, Raymond	1st	Cannon, Richard F.	393rd	Clemens, J. C. W.	390th
Britt, Clarence E.	393rd	Cantlon, John E.	393rd	Clement, Jackson M.	393rd
Brooks, Charles W.	603rd	Capua, Anthony D., Jr.	393rd	Clements, William M.	393rd
Broussard, V.	509HQ	Carling, Francis A.	320th	Clifton, Robert L.	1st
Brower, V.	509HQ	Carlo, Frank C.	320th	Clifton, Robert R.	603rd
Brown, Andrew A.	393rd	Carlon, Earl L.	603rd	Cloepfil, John K.	320th
Brown, Asa H.	1st	Carlson, Edward G.	Proj A	Coble, Warren L.	393rd
Brown, Dale M.	320th	Carlson, Per E.	603rd	Codatta, Antonio, Jr.	393rd
Brown, David S.	1st	Carlson, Russell R.	1027th	Coffman, Lynn P.	1st

Name	Unit	Name	Unit	Name	Unit
Cohen, George H.	393rd	Czaja, Leo J.	603rd	Dodge, William W.	1027th
Cole, Donald O.	393rd	D'Alessio, L. M.	390th	Dodgen, Roy E.	393rd
Cole, Gerald F.	1st	Dacorte, Antone M.	1st	Doine, Harold G.	603rd
Cole, Leon	393rd	Daggett, Ralph	603rd	Doiron, James H.	393rd
Colella, Joseph, Jr.	1st	Dahl, Newell E.	603rd	Dolan, Francis X.	393rd
Collins, Arthur W.	Proj A	Daloisio, Albert R.	603rd	Dolan, John J.	393rd
Collins, John E.	393rd	Daly, James R.	1395th	Doll, Edward B.	Proj A
Collins, Kenneth	603rd	Damask, Arthur C.	603rd	Donnell, Robert M.	393rd
Collins, William Q.	509HQ	Damron, Chester	603rd	Dorsch, Allen R.	1027th
Collinson, William	393rd	Danahy, James C.	603rd	Dorsey, Alan G.	320th
Collinsworth, James	603rd	Danby, Jack I. H.	509HQ	Doss, Maxie H.	393rd
Combs, Archie G., Jr.	1st	Daniel, James	390th	Doss, Victor H.	393rd
Compronio, William R.	393rd	Darby, G. C., Jr.	509HQ	Doty, Wayne	1st
Conkle, Arthur R.	393rd	Darre, Eugene W.	603rd	Doubek, Van, Jr.	320th
Conley, Robert C.	393rd	Davenport, Robert E.	393rd	Dowling, Robert J.	393rd
Connaughton, Joseph L.	393rd	Davidson, James E.	1027th	Downey, John L.	393rd
Conner, Lloyd G.	393rd	Davis, Albert	1st	Downey, William B.	390th
Cooke, R. K.	390th	Davis, Grover	1st	Downs, T.	390th
Cooper, George	1395th	Davis, Harold	1st	Drag, John W.	1st
Cooper, Grover G., Jr.	393rd	Davis, Harry B.	393rd	Drainer, William C.	393rd
Cooper, Hubert L., Jr.	1395th	Davis, James W.	393rd	Dramby, Arthur E.	393rd
Cooper, Jean S.	393rd	Davis, Robert K.	320th	Dreckshage, Charles	603rd
Cooper, Kenneth J.	1st	Davis, Wiley H.	1st	Driesel, Joel	1st
Cooper, Leon	393rd	Davis, William J.	1027th	Dube, H. W.	390th
Cooper, W. J.	509HQ	Davison, Benjamin D.	393rd	Duffy, Frank K.	393rd
Cope, Curtis	1395th	Dawson, Robert W.	Proj A	Duga, Paul	1st
Coppola, Jack J.	393rd	Day, Joe B.	509HQ	Dugger, James	1st
Corcoran, Gerald J.	393rd	Deacon, Richard S.	1st	Dulin, John W.	393rd
Corey, Neil R.	393rd	Deal, S. J.	390th	Dunlap, Harold T.	603rd
Corliss, James R.	393rd	DeFuir, Laurence E.	1st	Dunnagan, William	603rd
Cornett, Pearl	320th	Dehart, Albert T.	393rd	Dunsing, Leonard W.	393rd
Corrigan, Bruce G.	1st	Deis, Bert	1st	Duquette, Ovila J.	320th
Corson, Norman O.	393rd	DeLaney, J. Slade	320th	Duran, Jewel	1395th
Cortez, Leonides C.	1027th	Delehanty, James F.	1395th	Durey, Dale H.	603rd
Cortez, Louis Y.	1st	Delmar, John C., Jr.	603rd	Durham, Francis	1st
Cosimano, Anthony	393rd	DeLong, E. E.	509HQ	Durrum, Robert C.	1st
Costa, Thomas F.	393rd	Deming, R. O., III	509HQ	Duva, James S.	393rd
Costello, Edward M.	393rd	Demo, Andrew G.	393rd	Duzenbury, Wyatt E.	393rd
Cothran, J. G.	390th	Denham, Joel S., Jr.	393rd	Dyer, Arthur F.	393rd
Cotter, William J.	393rd	Denman, Howard B.	393rd	Easterly, Elliott	1st
Cotton, Ira J.	393rd	Denton, Freddie	1st	Easton, William J.	393rd
Cottrill, Harold W.	1027th	Depner, Michael	393rd	Eatherly, Claude R.	393rd
Coury, Harry J.	603rd	Deprang, Raleigh K.	393rd	Eberle, R. G.	390th
Covatto, Armand C.	603rd	Desmond, William J.	393rd	Echert, John P.	393rd
Covington, Guy	1st	Deutsch, Henry	393rd	Eckley, James N.	1st
Coy, Seth	320th	DeVito, J.	390th	Edgecomb, Jesse	1395th
Cozad, Ellis E.	1st	Devore, Ralph N.	393rd	Edwards, James	1395th
Craft, Cecil W.	1st	DeWoody, Bill J.	603rd	Edwards, Roy R., Jr.	393rd
Crawford, William D.	1027th	Dhonau, John E.	393rd	Edwards, William, Jr.	320th
Creed, J. D.	320th	Dial, Walter E.	1st	Egger, William E.	393rd
Crespin, Barton B.	393rd	Dickman, Gilbert B.	393rd	Eidnes, Kenneth L.	393rd
Crisp, George W.	393rd	DiJulio, Joseph M.	393rd	Eilers, Herbert	1395th
Crotty, William R.	393rd	Dike, Sheldon	Proj A	Elam, Robert	393rd
Crouse, Stanley, Jr.	509HQ	DiLeonardo, J. J.	390th	Elder, James K., Jr.	393rd
Crow, Harvey J.	603rd	Dillinger, Dwight	1st	Elder, Stanley P., Jr.	393rd
Crusenberry, L.	390th	Dillman, Richard J.	393rd	Eley, John F.	1st
Csome, Andrew, Jr.	1027th	Dimoush, Melvin E.	1395th	Ellerman, Leslie A.	603rd
Cullom, Homer L.	603rd	DiPalantino, Dominic J.	603rd	Elliott, Merle E.	393rd
Cummins, Joseph H.	320th	DiRienzo, Vito	1st	Ellis, George W.	1st
Cunningham, Loren L.	393rd	Disparti, Joseph C.	1st	Ellis, Lloyd F.	393rd
Curry, Ralph D.	393rd	Dispensa, Joseph S.	393rd	Ellis, Roger J.	603rd
Custer, Glen L.	603rd	DiTullio, Arthur J.	1027th	Ellison, Jackson V.	1027th
Cybert, E., Jr.	390th	Doane, Philip E.	1st	Ellison, O. J.	390th

509th Composite Group and Project Alberta Roster (Tinian, 1945)

Ellison, Tom G.	1st	Fox, Miles V.	1st	Gleason, George D.	393rd
Elvidge, Russell P.	320th	Francis, R. E.	390th	Gleneski, John	320th
Emerson, Clarence G.	320th	Franckowiak, Aloysious L.	603rd	Glick, Harold B.	603rd
Ender, Kenneth A.	1027th	Frank, Joseph J.	603rd	Glore, Charles E.	1395th
Engle, John P.	1st	Frank, Meyer	1st	Glore, Ralph A.	1027th
Ensle, Cecil H.	603rd	Franz, Paul J.	1st	Glosser, Saul H.	393rd
Epperson, Silas M.	1395th	Fredlund, Ronald D.	390th	Gmach, Edward J.	1st
Erickson, Carl R.	320th	Freet, Robert	1395th	Godfrey, Leonard A., Jr.	393rd
Esposito, Ignatius J.	393rd	French. L. C.	390th	Godfrey, Paul E.	1st
Esten, Edward T.	1st	Frese, Gilbert S.	320th	Goff, Stanley P., Jr.	393rd
Evans, William P.	1st	Frey, Ernest W.	393rd	Gold, Oliver W.	320th
Ewell, Leighton B.	393rd	Fricker, Glen E.	320th	Goodman, Walter	Proj-A
Fabinack, Charles C.	603rd	Friedman, Robert A.	603rd	Goodwin, Alvin P.	1st
Faidley, Clarence A.	1st	Frisbie, George	603rd	Gorecki, Walter M.	390th
Faist, Leonard W.	1st	Frohn, Charles E.	1027th	Gosnell, Samuel, Jr.	603rd
Faith, Randal L.	603rd	Fry, Ralph D.	603rd	Gostovich, Mike	1st
Falks, Albert L.	1st	Frye, Thomas	1395th	Gottwig, T. P.	390th
Farmway, Edgar F., Jr.	1027th	Fuller, Willis E.	320th	Gowans, Daniel M.	1st
Farrell, Thomas F.	HQ	Funwela, Pasquale E.	393rd	Grady, James E.	1st
Faryna, Myron	393rd	Furman, Ralph A.	603rd	Green, Clifford O.	1st
Faucitano, J. N.	390th	Futschik, August F.	393rd	Green, Fred	1st
Fawcett, Jay W.	1395th	Gabor, John	1395th	Green, George W.	1395th
Feally, Frank J.	1st	Gackenbach, Russell	393rd	Grennan, Thomas	393rd
Feiler, Edgar	603rd	Gagnon, Joseph A. R.	320th	Griebe, Norman	1395th
Felblinger, Robert J.	320th	Galati, V. G.	390th	Griep, Hugo	1395th
Felchlia, Albert O.	320th	Galbreath, James E.	390th	Griffin, Francis E.	320th
Fellwock, Robert A.	1027th	Galdarisi, Joseph, Jr.	1st	Griffin, Michael F.	1027th
Femmel, A. H.	390th	Gallagher, Raymond G.	393rd	Griffin, Thomas R., Jr.	393rd
Ferebee, Thomas W.	509HQ	Galusha, Howard J.	393rd	Grill, I. P.	390th
Ferguson, Hugh C.	393rd	Gamelier, Michael J.	603rd	Grimes, James B., Jr.	1027th
Ferguson, William N.	393rd	Ganley, John H.	603rd	Grimm, Harley L.	320th
Ferre, Keith W.	603rd	Garinger, P. L., Jr.	390th	Grossman, Elmer G.	1027th
Ferst, Kenneth C.	603rd	Garman, Kenneth J.	1st	Grosso, Josepf P.	393rd
Fetterman, R. A.	509HQ	Garn, Robert R.	393rd	Groves, Elery M.	1027th
Field, J.	390th	Garner, Carl M.	393rd	Groves, Paul P.	393rd
Filichia, Joe L.	603rd	Garner, R. E.	390th	Grubaugh, Jerry, Jr.	393rd
Firneno, Michael J.	1st	Garrett, John E.	1027th	Gruning, Paul W.	393rd
Fischer, Karl R.	393rd	Gaskins, W. E.	390th	Grzywinski, Edward	1395th
Fish, Anthony J.	390th	Gaskins, Willard E.	509HQ	Gulick, Joseph I.	393rd
Fisher, Earl W.	603rd	Gasser, Adolph	390th	Gunderson, Rex E.	603rd
Fisher, John E.	320th	Gaughey, Glenn	1395th	Gurly, James R.	393rd
Fisher, William T.	603rd	Gayeski, J. S.	390th	Guszak, Matthew A.	1395th
Fithian, Thomas H.	320th	Gehrke, V. P.	509HQ	Hagan, Ralph V.	1st
Flanagin, Rollin L.	1st	Gehrken, J. S.	390th	Hagar, Nelson F.	393rd
Fleischman, Howard A.	390th	Geller, Guy	1027th	Haider, Robert M.	393rd
Fletcher, J., Jr.	390th	Genova, Carmine A.	393rd	Halbur, Edwin	1395th
Florer, Darrell W.	1st	Geren, Theodore R.	603rd	Halden, Kermit W.	603rd
Flournoy, Cecil B.	603rd	Gerken, Rudolph H.	393rd	Hale, Samuel E.	393rd
Floweree, Glen H.	393rd	Gerster, Clarence W.	320th	Halein, Floyd	393rd
Flowers, C. L.	390th	Gibavitch, Albert J.	1st	Hall, Norman	1395th
Fockler, Donald D.	393rd	Gibbs, Charlie L.	1027th	Haluska, Michael J.	1027th
Fogarty, George R.	393rd	Gibson, Adam L.	393rd	Hamilton, LeRoy	1395th
Forman, Glenn	1027th	Giguere, William C.	603rd	Hammond, Chester A.	393rd
Fortine, Frank J.	Proj A	Gilbert, Charles M.	390th	Hammons, George P.	393rd
Foss, Richard H.	1st	Gililland, Cecil C.	1st	Hancock, Lonnie B.	393rd
Foster, Clifford E.	603rd	Gilliam, Claude C.	393rd	Hannah, Robert D.	320th
Foster, Wallace A.	320th	Gilliam, Claude W.	393rd	Hannert, William J.	393rd
Fowler, Calvin B.	1st	Gills, Rodney L.	393rd	Hanse, Eugene L.	1st
Fowler, Curtis P.	1027th	Gilmet, James H.	393rd	Hansen, James T.	393rd
Fowler, Marion C., Jr.	393rd	Giroux Joseph W.	1st	Hansen, John C.	393rd
Fowler, Percy	1395th	Gitnick, Edwin I.	320th	Hansen, N. B.	390th
Fox, James L., Jr.	320th	Glanz, Arthur	1395th	Hanson, Arthur R.	320th
Fox, Lawrence	1395th	Glazer, Sam	1027th	Hanson, James H.	603rd

Name	Unit	Name	Unit	Name	Unit
Harbuck, Atward J.	1027th	Holse, Robert E.	393rd	Johnson, James J.	603rd
Hardin, Glen G.	1395th	Holub, E. J.	509HQ	Johnson, M.	390th
Harding, Lonnie T.	1027th	Homa, Elroy C.	393rd	Johnson, Willard	1395th
Hardy, Leonard	603rd	Homer, Michael	390th	Johnston, Lawrence H.	Proj A
Harman, Billy J.	603rd	Hooker, James A.	393rd	Johnston, William J.	1027th
Harms, Donald C.	Proj A	Hopkins, James I., Jr.	509HQ	Jolly, James W.	393rd
Harrigan, Cornelius	603rd	Hopkins, Melvin G.	1st	Jones, Charles C.	393rd
Harrington, John H., Jr.	393rd	Hopkins, Vincent P.	603rd	Jones, Dale W.	603rd
Harris, Brooks H.	603rd	Hopper, John D.	Proj A	Jones, Glenn E.	1027th
Harris, Jack E.	393rd	Horn, Bobby E.	1st	Jones, Henry I.	393rd
Harris, James M.	320th	Hornicak, Joseph A.	1st	Jones, Melvin A.	320th
Harris, Peter T.	393rd	Horton, Leon	393rd	Jones, Paul W.	1st
Harter, Cleo E.	393rd	Hoss, H. L.	509HQ	Jones, Weston W.	320th
Hartley, Granville K.	1027th	Houser, Loy F.	393rd	Jones, William A.	1st
Hartman, Clarence W.	393rd	Hovsepian, David P.	1027th	Josefiak, Edward M.	393rd
Hartnick, Milton	603rd	Howard, Jim D.	393rd	Josephson, Arthur E.	390th
Hartpence, Jack	1395th	Howle, B. A.	509HQ	Joyce, Patrick J.	393rd
Harty, Frank R.	393rd	Howley, Daniel J.	1st	Juchno, Joseph	1395th
Harvey, Leonard	1027th	Hubbs, J. H.	390th	Judkins, Gordon D.	393rd
Harwell, Leon	1395th	Hubeny, John H., Jr.	393rd	Juntti, Melvin W.	603rd
Hassel, Robert T.	1st	Hubly, James W.	509HQ	Kaddatz, Carl	1st
Hatch, Floyd L.	1027th	Huddleston, Matthew W.	393rd	Kade, Bertram J.	393rd
Havekotte, Curt J.	1st	Hudgens, Edwin C.	1st	Kainz, Frank C.	603rd
Hayes, Robert R.	320th	Hudson, Ernie	1395th	Kamla, John L.	320th
Headrick, A. L.	390th	Hudson, Jack	1st	Kammerer, Philip E.	1st
Heath, Robert F.	393rd	Huey, Lankford	603rd	Kanapaux, Eugene F.	393rd
Heathcote, Kenneth S.	393rd	Hull, Claud E.	320th	Kandel, Edwin	393rd
Heddy, Thomas L.	320th	Hulse, William T.	393rd	Kansella, Howard R.	1st
Hefferman, Louis J.	1395th	Hunt, Robert L.	603rd	Kapitz, Richard J.	1st
Heideman, Melville	1st	Hurst, Farr L.	603rd	Kaplan, S.	390th
Heimer, R. K.	390th	Hutnick, Paul G.	603rd	Kapral, Andrew	603rd
Hemmel, C. H., Jr.	390th	Hylton, William H.	1st	Kapusta, M.	390th
Henderson, Arthur D.	320th	Inaprucker, Raymond	1395th	Karl, Allan L.	393rd
Hendren, Charles H.	603rd	Inzer, Luke	1395th	Karnes, Thomas L.	509HQ
Hengen, James F.	1395th	Iorio, Joseph	1st	Kasalek, Carl	1st
Hennes, Robert J.	509HQ	Iosco, D.	390th	Kasik, Joe	1395th
Henze, Wilbur S.	393rd	Irick, Edward B.	320th	Katlarz, Bruno A.	393rd
Herbert, Maurice D.	1395th	Irwin, Ted C.	393rd	Katz, Seymour S.	603rd
Herman, Harry	1395th	Jacks, Robert B.	320th	Kauffman, John R.	509HQ
Hess, C. W.	509HQ	Jacks, William J.	393rd	Keene, Francis W.	603rd
Hess, D. A.	509HQ	Jackson, A. D.	390th	Keister, Robert E.	393rd
Hesse, Richard M.	393rd	Jackson, D. M.	390th	Kelleher, John R.	1st
Higgins, Thomas L.	320th	Jackson, Goble	603rd	Keller, John E.	603rd
Hill, C. F.	509 HQ	Jackson, John E.	393rd	Kelly, Daniel J.	1027th
Hill, James	1st	Jackson, Severn A.	1st	Kemner, Floyd W.	393rd
Hill, Thomas P., III	393rd	Jacobson, I. H.	390th	Kennedy, John B.	393rd
Hill, Thomas	1st	Jacobson, Q. L.	390th	Kern, F.	390th
Hillhouse, Murray M.	1027th	James, David B., Jr.	1st	Keyser, John H.	393rd
Hills, Clayton	1st	Jameson, D. L.	390th	Kiedrowski, Stanley A.	393rd
Hinchey, James J.	393rd	Jay, Edward	1395th	Kieltyka, Stanley L.	393rd
Hintz, Norman S.	603rd	Jellick, William F.	393rd	Kimber, Charles E.	390th
Hochlerner, Arnold H.	1027th	Jenceleski, William J.	603rd	Kimme, Harold E.	393rd
Hodson, Carl	603rd	Jenkins, William, Jr.	603rd	King, Cecil N.	393rd
Hoey, Fred A.	393rd	Jensen, Maurice	1st	King, Herbert L.	1st
Hofstede, John C.	393rd	Jensen, Ray	1395th	King, Horace	1395th
Hogan, Patrick J.	603rd	Jensen, W. F.	390th	King, J. T.	509HQ
Hogg, Rudolph W.	1st	Jeppson, Morris R.	1st	King, J. W.	509HQ
Hogue, Melvin L.	1st	Jernigan, Norris N.	393rd	King, John A.	393rd
Hollinger, Frank	1395th	Johanson, Ross H.	603rd	King, Joseph R.	603rd
Hollis, Fontaine O.	603rd	Johnson, A. J.	390th	Kingston, Earl, Jr.	603rd
Holmes, James F.	390th	Johnson, Arthur J.	390th	Kinkade, Winfield C.	393rd
Holmes, John G., Jr.	1st	Johnson, Frankie R.	393rd	Kinnaman, John	1395th
Holmes, Lavern L.	393rd	Johnson, Howard V.	1st	Kinosh, Steve J., Jr.	393rd

509th Composite Group and Project Alberta Roster (Tinian, 1945)

Kirby, Harold W.	1st	Lauer, Ronald C.	603rd	Lyon, Wilbur H.	320th
Kirby, Wesley	1st	Laurino, J.	390th	Maas, Robert H.	603rd
Kirk, Dixon P.	1st	Lawler, James A., Jr.	603rd	MacGregor, Franklin	393rd
Klement, Edmund M.	393rd	Lawrence, Albert B.	1st	Machen, Arthur B.	Proj A
Kling, Werner	1395th	Lawrence, Kenneth	1395th	Madden, Joseph H.	603rd
Kloss, Emil	1027th	Lawrence, Virginia	390th	Maddux, Emos E.	1st
Knapp, Raymond G.	1st	Lazzarino, Pasquale	393rd	Madrid, Joe M.	393rd
Knaub, Baird D.	603rd	Leach, Paul E.	393rd	Magby, Charles H.	393rd
Knauth, Edgar	393rd	Leazer, Chloe S., Jr.	393rd	Mahon, Newton R. E.	320th
Knisley, Harold E.	393rd	Lee, Jimmie F.	393rd	Mahugh, Glen, Jr.	393rd
Knowles, Rellie R.	1st	Lee, Louis M.	390th	Malcolm, L. R.	390th
Knox, Edward S.	320th	Leffler, Raymond W.	1395th	Maling, A. S.	509HQ
Knox, Willard G.	603rd	Legg, Roderick E.	393rd	Mallory, K. L.	509HQ
Koester, George A.	1st	Lemley, Floyd A.	603rd	Malnek, Edward	1395th
Kogler, L. F.	390th	Lentz, Paul	390th	Maloney, Anthony J., Jr.	509HQ
Kohn, Armine E.	320th	Leon, Diego	393rd	Manganielo, R. R.	509HQ
Kolasinski, Peter P., Jr.	1395th	Lesniewski, John J.	393rd	Mann, Virgil I.	320th
Kolesky, Leonard	390th	Levy, Charles	393rd	Manning, Glenn B.	1027th
Konkle, Edwin W.	320th	Lewandowski, Alfred A.	393rd	Manuel, Howard G.	1027th
Koons, William W.	603rd	Lewandowski, S. R.	390th	Marcello, Paul L.	320th
Kopka, Frederick D.	1027th	Lewinson, R. J.	509HQ	Marchese, James R.	603rd
Koplets, Theodore F.	1st	Lewis, Darwin C.	509HQ	Marchlewski, Raymond A.	1st
Korthals, Ernest W.	1027th	Lewis, Henry E.	1027th	Markley, Leonard W.	393rd
Kosh, Stephen	603rd	Lewis, Joseph R.	603rd	Marks, Marvin	603rd
Kotoff, Nick G.	390th	Lewis, Robert A.	393rd	Marmolejo, R.	390th
Kotzian, Francis S.	1st	Lincoln, Drexel	1st	Marquardt, George W.	393rd
Kowalski, Frank V.	1027th	Lindau, Harold F.	393rd	Marshall, Stanley J.	1st
Kozlowski, Charles	393rd	Lindemann, Herbert E.	509HQ	Marstellar, John	603rd
Krajczynski, Chester S.	603rd	Lindsay, Harold J.	393rd	Martin, Herbert L.	1st
Krajewski, Chester J.	393rd	Lindsey, Charles, Jr.	603rd	Martin, John B.	1st
Krause, Eugene H.	320th	Lindsey, Jack D.	320th	Martinez, Juan	1027th
Krauss, Roy H.	390th	Linschitz, Henry	Proj A	Mason, Carl C.	393rd
Kregar, Edward E.	1st	Linton, John T.	1395th	Masoner, Lee R.	603rd
Kroes, John J.	1st	Lipschitz, Max	393rd	Massengill, Joe M.	603rd
Kruba, J.	390th	Liptak, August S.	1027th	Mastick, Donald	Proj A
Krug, Frederick C.	393rd	Litowitz, M. M.	390th	Matheny, C. S.	509HQ
Krug, Robert E., Jr.	393rd	Litterio, Mario A.	393rd	Mathews, Robert P.	Proj A
Kuck, Leslie C.	603rd	Littlejohn, William	603rd	Mathison, Clarke C.	320th
Kugler, Richard D.	393rd	Liukkonen, William	603rd	Matranga, Phil	1395th
Kuharek, John D.	393rd	Lizak, Steve C.	393rd	Matson, Lee W.	1st
Kuhlman, M.	390th	Locke, Buford L.	1st	Matson, Thomas C.	393rd
Kuhn, Howard L.	1395th	Loden, Charles A.	603rd	Matthews, Malcom E.	1027th
Kuhner, Roy D.	1st	Loder, Burnell M.	1027th	Mauldion, Don A.	393rd
Kupferberg, Jesse	Proj A	Long, William G., Jr.	1st	Maynard, Thomas C.	393rd
Kurowski, Adam	1st	Longwell, B. R.	390th	Mazuco, N. E.	509HQ
Kushner, Theodore	393rd	Lonnquist, Vincent	1st	McBride, Chester G.	393rd
Kvam, Dale D.	1st	Lonsinger, G. W.	390th	McCabe, Edward	603rd
Kwiatkowski, John	603rd	Loomis, John F.	603rd	McCain, Clarence D.	1027th
Kwiatokowski, B. F.	390th	Lovstad, Stanley	1395th	McCaleb, Walter F.	393rd
LaCombe, Henry R.	1st	Lowder, James L.	603rd	McCall, Ivan J.	390th
LaCroix, Russell J.	393rd	Loyacono, Patsy	1395th	McClary, Robert C.	393rd
Laine, Woitto T.	393rd	Luccionihony, Anthony	393rd	McClung, Samuel A.	1st
Laitala, Harold M.	393rd	Lucero, Mauricio G.	1027th	McComas, Wayne L.	1st
Lambert, Rufus J.	1027th	Lucke, E. G.	509HQ	McCoy, Earl W.	1st
Lane, John H. A.	393rd	Luckert, Alton L.	1027th	McCoy, Ralph R.	393rd
Lang, Chester	1395th	Ludwig, Melvin R.	1st	McCright, H. S.	390th
Lang, William O., Jr.	1st	Luguet, G. A.	509HQ	McCullough, J. B.	509HQ
Lange, Victor W.	320th	Lundgren, John L.	393rd	McCurley, Robert E.	320th
Langer, Lawrence	Proj A	Lunn, Ralph W.	603rd	McCutcheon, Clifford C.	1st
Lanuti, Carl A.	393rd	Lyberger, George N.	1st	McDivitt, John V.	390th
Largur, Joseph	603rd	Lydon, John C., Jr.	603rd	McDuffie, Lewis W.	603rd
Larkin, William J.	Proj A	Lynch, James R.	393rd	McEachern, Carleton A.	393rd
Lathrop, Wendell B.	393rd	Lynch, Laverne L.	1st	McFall, J.	390th

McFarland, Clyde R.	1st	Mockler, Bernard W.	1027th	Nyhan, Dennis J.	1st
McGlennon, James W.	393rd	Moe, Robert	603rd	O'Callaghan, Homer M.	1st
McGurrin, Francis J.	393rd	Mohr, Royal H.	393rd	O'Hara, Clement J.	1027th
McIntosh, F. D.	509HQ	Moore, Allan L.	393rd	O'Hara, Franklin B.	1st
McIntosh, Norman B.	393rd	Moore, Billy	1395th	O'Keefe, B. J.	Proj A
McKee, Dean W.	1st	Moore, Everett L.	1st	O'Neal, Gail	1395th
McKenny, Charles A.	393rd	Moore, Jesse	1395th	Oakley, Eldridge W.	603rd
McKey, Irvine	603rd	Moorehead, Harold	603rd	Oakley, Terry D.	1027th
McKinney, Edgar P., Jr.	320th	Moorehead, Ralph	603rd	Olin, H. F.	390th
McKnight, Charles F.	393rd	Moose, Dewey H.	603rd	Olivi, Fred J.	393rd
McKnight, Walter A.	1027th	Morawa, Leo P.	393rd	Olmstead, Thomas H.	Proj A
McLachlan, G. E.	390th	Moreau, William A.	603rd	Olson, Harold R.	393rd
McLaughlin, Frank	1st	Morrison, Lennie	1395th	Olsson, Frank A.	603rd
McLaury, William J.	1st	Morrison, Philip	Proj A	Opsahl, Arthur S.	603rd
McLenon, Claude E.	393rd	Morton, Hector	1st	Ormond, Francis R.	393rd
McMahan, Allen P.	320th	Moseley, Clarence T.	320th	Orr, Leonard	1395th
McManus, John J.	603rd	Motichko, Leonard	Proj A	Orr, Wilford A.	320th
McMillan, F. E.	509HQ	Mullany, Gerald	603rd	Orren, William F.	393rd
McNamara, Richard	393rd	Mulligan, J. J.	390th	Ortega, Leo A., Jr.	393rd
McNamee, Robert L.	393rd	Mullins, Bob B.	603rd	Ortiz, Frank E.	603rd
McNary, Spencer G.	1027th	Mullins, Clyde	393rd	Osborne, James	1395th
McNaught, Joseph	603rd	Mullins, D. J.	390th	Ossip, Jerome J.	509HQ
McNeely, Richard	1395th	Mulvey, R. E.	390th	Overman, Robert	603rd
McNeiece, Robert L.	320th	Munivez, S.	509HQ	Ovesey, Lionel	390th
McNitt, David B.	1027th	Muretic, Matthew S.	320th	Owen, H.	390th
McOmber, John P.	320th	Murphy, James H.	1395th	Owens, Elbert E.	393rd
McQueen, D. L.	390th	Murphy, William L.	Proj A	Owens, Owen	1027th
McVay, Burdette R.	320th	Murray, Herman C.	603rd	Oxley, Charles R.	1027th
McWherter, Ned	1st	Murray, Joseph, Jr.	1027th	Page, Joseph G.	1027th
Meeson, Phip	1395th	Murray, Martin G.	393rd	Painter, Earl	320th
Melton, Linton W.	320th	Muscolo, Annibale	1st	Pair, Aubrey	393rd
Mendl, John J.	1st	Nabors, Robert C.	393rd	Pake, Tom T.	603rd
Merkle, William R.	603rd	Nagy, John P.	1st	Palmer, Donald W.	320th
Merry, Francis J.	393rd	Napier, Omar E.	1st	Palmert, Lee E.	393rd
Mersky Jacob	603rd	Napoli, Louis J.	1027th	Parker, Edison, Jr.	603rd
Metcalf, Bob	1395th	Nardi, Flavio H.	1027th	Parr, Howard T.	603rd
Metro, Paul	393rd	Nash, William L.	603rd	Parson, Q.	390th
Meyer, Dale R.	603rd	Naughton, R. R.	509HQ	Parsons, Earnest C.	603rd
Meyer, Morris	603rd	Neas, Harry C.	1027th	Parsons, William S.	Proj A
Meyers, Gene H.	393rd	Nelson, Emmert L.	603rd	Paschall, R. L.	509HQ
Meyers, Jack	1027th	Nelson, Frederick H.	1st	Patrick, James	1st
Michaels, Fred H.	393rd	Nelson, Lloyd H.	320th	Patten, Davis I.	1st
Mickelson, Mont J.	603rd	Nelson, Richard M.	393rd	Patten, George A.	320th
Migneco, Victor	1st	Nesseth, Arvid T.	1027th	Patterson, Archie	1395th
Mikulenka, J. E.	390th	Newman, Jack E.	603rd	Patterson, J. P.	390th
Miller, A.	509HQ	Newsom, Mack	393rd	Patusch, Eric P.	320th
Miller, Arthur, Jr.	603rd	Nicely, Gillon T.	393rd	Paulauskas, John	1395th
Miller, Donald E.	393rd	Nichols, Cecil C., Jr.	393rd	Paulikonis, Peter P.	320th
Miller, Lawrence J.	393rd	Nicholson, Oscar C.	1st	Pavone, Theodore C.	320th
Miller, Leon R.	1027th	Nicklaus, Roy C.	1st	Pawiak, Chester V.	393rd
Miller, Parke N.	320th	Nicola, Frank E.	603rd	Payne, James H.	1st
Miller, R. P.	509HQ	Nieme, Eugene E.	320th	Payne, Kenneth	603rd
Miller, Raymond L.	390th	Noble, Frank N., Jr.	1st	Payton, Lawrence S.	320th
Miller, Robert C.	1st	Nolan, James F.	Proj A	Pearson, Morris J.	1st
Miller, Victor A.	Proj A	Nolte, Harry W.	603rd	Pegram, James I.	393rd
Miller, William L., Jr.	320th	Nooker, Eugene L.	Proj A	Pellegrino, Francis A.	393rd
Milligan, Harvey R.	1st	Norder, Herbert	393rd	Pellow, W. J.	390th
Mills, Gordon W.	1st	Norman, Hyatt D., Jr.	393rd	Pembroke, Milo E.	603rd
Mills, Loren W.	320th	Norman, Thomas W.	390th	Penney, W. G.	Proj A
Mingin, Lester W.	1st	Norris, Francis W.	320th	Penninger, Harry	393rd
Mitchell, Robert W.	393rd	Nottingham, Lee F.	393rd	Pepe, Henry J.	1st
Mize, Charles E.	603rd	Nowels, A. Wilson, Jr.	390th	Perez, J. M.	390th
Mize, Earney	1395th	Nunnemaker, Earl R.	393rd	Perez, Jacob	1395th

509th Composite Group and Project Alberta Roster (Tinian, 1945)

Name	Unit	Name	Unit	Name	Unit
Perlman, Theodore	Proj-A	Quigley, Wilbur W.	393rd	Rosenberger, Earl E.	603rd
Perry, Charles A.	393rd	Raffel, LeRoy R.	603rd	Rosenthal, Howard	1st
Pescho, M.	390th	Rainey, Milton F.	1027th	Rosenthal, Hudson D.	1st
Peters, John G.	393rd	Ramsey, Norman F.	Proj A	Ross, Floyd E.	390th
Peters, O. H.	390th	Rara, Edward J.	320th	Ross, Frederick	1395th
Peterson, Clarence	603rd	Raub, Leo G., Jr.	1st	Ross, Joseph L.	393rd
Peterson, Kenneth C.	390th	Ray, Norman W.	393rd	Ross, Kirby	393rd
Peterson, Wesley P.	390th	Rayome, Clayton J.	320th	Rothenberg, Meyer	603rd
Petrolli, Robert J.	393rd	Reale, Natalie	1395th	Rothschild, John A.	393rd
Petroski, John H.	603rd	Reames, D. G.	390th	Rotunno, C.	390th
Pettengill, Leland F.	393rd	Rebol, R. R.	509HQ	Rouse, Berndon N.	390th
Pettigrew, Elliott, Jr.	603rd	Reed, Vestle O.	393rd	Rovello, A. J.	390th
Pettit, Paul R.	390th	Reeder, Lloyd J.	393rd	Rowe, Donald L.	393rd
Pfaff, Thomas J.	1395th	Reedy, William B.	393rd	Rowe, Glenn O.	1st
Pfeiffer, John C., Jr.	393rd	Reese, Thaddeous L.	320th	Rowe, William M., Jr.	393rd
Pfister, Kurt	1395th	Reidelbach, Stanley F.	1395th	Rowley, Vernon J.	393rd
Pharr, Gordon C.	1st	Reilly, James J.	393rd	Roy, Carl R.	393rd
Phillips, William S.	320th	Reimers, W. H., Jr.	390th	Rubis, Andrew	1st
Phipps, John E.	393rd	Rein, Carl W.	393rd	Rudgers, M. T.	509HQ
Piehl, Donald D.	393rd	Renfro, Floyd K.	1st	Ruscio, John L.	320th
Piepho, Harvey L.	1st	Rentschler, Stanley	1395th	Rush, R. B.	390th
Pierce, K. L.	390th	Repko, Mike	1395th	Russ, Harlow W.	Proj A
Pilgrim, Audave C.	603rd	Reynolds, Clarence	1027th	Russell, John	1st
Pinchot, Albert	1st	Reynolds, Filbert	393rd	Russell, Paul V.	1027th
Ping, Yive J. H.	393rd	Reynolds, George T.	Proj A	Russell, Vernon	1st
Pirkle, Chester G.	1027th	Reynolds, Grover	1st	Russo, John A.	1st
Plato, Peter P.	393rd	Rice, William H.	1st	Ruzzo, Pasquale C.	393rd
Podolsky, Richard J.	1st	Rich, C. D.	390th	Ryan, Edward A., Jr.	1st
Poe, Edgar A., Jr.	393rd	Rich, Charles W.	393rd	Ryder, Roland E.	603rd
Poehls, I. H.	390th	Richard, G. W., Jr.	509HQ	Rzepinski, Marshall	1st`
Poehls, Irvin F.	390th	Richards, Lyndon	1st	Sabatura, Harry	1395th
Pogue, Charles E.	1st	Richardson, Harold H.	1027th	Salyer, Everett L.	320th
Polakowski, Joseph	603rd	Richardson, Porter A.	393rd	Sanborn, P., Jr.	390th
Poli, A. J.	509HQ	Richardson, Willard H.	1st	Sanders, David M.	603rd
Politi, Carmine V.	393rd	Richardson, William H.	320th	Sanders, Jason E.	603rd
Polito, John	1st	Richotte, Donald C.	320th	Sanders, M. A.	390th
Poole, Quinton	1027th	Rider, Harold J.	393rd	Sanders, Ray	1st
Popp, George F.	603rd	Rigby, Henry	1395th	Sanders, Rex	1395th
Popwell, Calvin B.	393rd	Rigler, Robert B.	1st	Sands, Earl E.	1027th
Porter, George A.	1st	Rinard, Charles B.	393rd	Sanfratello, Salvatore S.	1027th
Porter, John W.	390th	Rissbacher, Frank	1027th	Sapunka, Joseph S.	393rd
Poslof, Anton	1027th	Ritchie, Floyd J.	1027th	Sarni, Tony	393rd
Pratt, Robert H., Jr.	393rd	Ritchie, M. E.	390th	Saunders, Charles O	509HQ
Prebel, Edward	393rd	Rivera, Trinidad	1395th	Saunders, Harold N.	1st
Presser, E. J.	390th	Roark, F.	390th	Savage, Evell G.	603rd
Price, Edward A.	603rd	Robbins, Patrick J.	393rd	Savage, Frank L.	1027th
Price, James B., Jr.	320th	Robertson, R. F.	390th	Schaffer, Louis	1395th
Price, James N., Jr.	393rd	Robertson, Robert D.	1st	Schafhauser, Paul C.	393rd
Prince, R. I.	390th	Robey, John D.	393rd	Schaller, J. G.	390th
Pringle, John C.	603rd	Robinson, Aubrey C.	1st	Scharf, S. W.	390th
Prohs, W. R.	Proj A	Robinson, George F.	393rd	Schauer, L. M. E.	390th
Prout, Charles H.	603rd	Robinson, Rowland E.	320th	Scheer, George F.	320th
Puckett, D. W.	509HQ	Rodolico, Thomas A.	393rd	Scheuern, John A.	1st
Puckett, James A.	393rd	Rodriguez, B. R.	390th	Schiavone, Alexander G.	390th
Pugh, Charles J.	320th	Roebuck, Kenneth O.	1st	Schick, John A.	320th
Pugh, Lyle E.	390th	Rogalski, Chester A.	393rd	Schiller, William	1st
Pulfer, Carl A.	603rd	Rogers, Clarence E.	1st	Schlesinger, Edward P.	393rd
Purdon, David	393rd	Rogers, Joel B.	1st	Schlessel, Walter	320th
Purdum, John M	603rd	Rogers, Rudolph E.	1st	Schmidtke, Paul C.	393rd
Purnell, W. R.	HQ	Roland, Whitney G.	603rd	Schneider, Sidney S.	1027th
Putsch, Charles P.	1027th	Romine, Kermit H.	1027th	Schramke, Francis J.	393rd
Quartana, Oakley P.	1st	Ronfeld, B. H.	509HQ	Schreffer, George I.	393rd
Quiggin, Edward R.	1027th	Ronk, Edwin A.	1st	Schreiber, Raemer E.	Proj A

Appendix D

Schrodt, Sterling F.	603rd	Smith, Albert E.	509HQ	Strandholm, H. S.	390th
Schultz, William T.	1st	Smith, Charles W.	393rd	Strasburg, Lawrence F.	393rd
Schwab, Charles E.	393rd	Smith, Earnest P.	1027th	Strayer, C.	390th
Schwab, Charles W.	393rd	Smith, Elbert B.	393rd	Streaker, Frederick H.	1st
Scoggin, Maurice L.	390th	Smith, Harry D.	393rd	Strickland, Omar G.	393rd
Scott, John B.	603rd	Smith, Henry L.	393rd	Stringfellow, William	1st
Scott, Troy B.	393rd	Smith, J. I.	390th	Strudwick, James W.	393rd
Scott, W. T.	390th	Smith, Jesse F.	393rd	Stuewe, William C.	393rd
Scott, Wilbur G.	603rd	Smith, John	1395th	Sullivan, Charles	1st
Scully, Charles H.	1027th	Smith, Leon D.	1st	Sullivan, James B.	393rd
Scully, J. B.	390th	Smith, Newton R., Jr.	320th	Sullivan, Joseph G.	320th
Seaman, Harold F.	603rd	Smith, Paul C.	1st	Sullivan, Joseph M.	1st
Seay, M. L.	393rd	Smith, Robert C.	393rd	Sullivan, Maurice	1395th
Sedor, Joseph	390th	Smith, Roger M.	1st	Supienko, Joe	1027th
Seely, R. L.	509HQ	Smith, Sawdon S.	603rd	Sutton, Frank E.	393rd
Sekeres, E. J.	509HQ	Smith, Seth I.	1st	Swafford, H.	390th
Sekeres, Elmer C.	393rd	Smith, William E.	393rd	Swasey, Herbert D.	603rd
Selander, Walter	1395th	Smith, William, Jr.	393rd	Swatha, E. J.	390th
Sells, Robert M.	1027th	Smithson, Robert E.	393rd	Sweeney, Charles W.	393rd
Sensibaugh, William P.	1027th	Snider, Glasgow	1st	Sweitzer, Lawrence J.	1027th
Serber, Robert`	Proj A	Snyder, Frank E.	393rd	Switalski, Leonard	1st
Serrietella, Rocco F.	393rd	Snyder, Murray	1027th	Switzer, Carl	1st
Severinsen, Leslie A.	1395th	Snyder, W. W., Jr.	509HQ	Sylvia, Michael H.	393rd
Seweryniak, Thaddeus J.	1st	Sorci, Anthony J.	320th	Szczepanik, Eugene F.	1027th
Shackelton, LeRoy	1st	Sosna, A. B.	390th	Szczuka, Mitchell S.	393rd
Shade, Robert L.	1st	Sowers, Wilson C.	393rd	Taeger, Glenn M.`	1027th
Shakespeare, Howard V.	1027th	Sparrow, Jimmie	390th	Tagliabue, Richard F.	320th
Shaller, Joseph G.	393rd	Spiker, Chlorus M.	603rd	Tardiff, B. A.	390th
Shamlian, Armen	390th	Spitzer, Abe M.	393rd	Taylor, George E.	1027th
Shaw, Earl	1395th	Spradlin, William J.	393rd	Taylor, Jack	1395th
Sheehan, William P.	509HQ	Sprague, Willis N., Jr.	390th	Taylor, James R., Jr.	393rd
Sheets, Donald L.	603rd	Sprouse, Milton C.	393rd	Taylor, John B.	509HQ
Shepherd, Harry G.	1027th	Spurling, Harold M.	320th	Taylor, Ralph R., Jr.	393rd
Shepler, Clarence M.	393rd	St. Myers, Raymond G.	393rd	Teckentien, W. R.	390th
Sherwood, John J.	603rd	Stafford, James, Jr.	603rd	Teel, James E.	1st
Shields, Wilson D.	320th	Staley, Clifford L.	1027th	Tenzer, Harold N.	603rd
Shmiske, Paul C.	603rd	Stanek, Frank	1st	Teuton, Edwin	1395th
Shofield, Edgar F.	393rd	Stankevitch, Robert	1st	Theno, J. B.	390th
Showalter, Frederic	1st	Stasiak, Lawrence J.	509HQ	Thetford, Oscar L.	1027th
Shropshire, William O.	1st	Stasink, Thomas J.	390th	Thigpen, Oscar J.	393rd
Shryer, William G.	1027th	Staton, Raymond	1395th	Thomas, Leslie	1395th
Shuhmaker, I.	390th	Stein, Arthur C.	320th`	Thompson, Howard A.	393rd
Shults, John H.	1027th	Steinke, Stanley G.	393rd	Thompson, Howard B.	393rd
Shumard, Robert H.	393rd	Stephenson, Edward	Proj A	Thompson, John M.	1395th
Shvegel, Edward P.	603rd	Steur, Paul W.	393rd	Thompson, Virgil	1395th
Sibulski, George P.	603rd	Stevans, Howard H.	390th	Thornhill, Francis D.	393rd
Sidebottom, Mobly A.	1027th	Stevens, Derward A.	393rd	Thornton, Gunnar	Proj A
Siegle, Calvin G.	1027th	Stevens, George E.	1st	Thornton, Robert E.	1027th
Simanovich, Nicholas	393rd	Stevenson, Robert L.	1027th	Thorstrom, Earl	1395th
Simon, Stanley	1st	Stewart, F. H.	509HQ	Tibbets, Paul W., Jr.	509HQ
Simpson, Leonard	1395th	Stewart, Ivan H.	393rd	Tigner, Richard O.	393rd
Skaggs, Glen F.	393rd	Stiber, Andrew J.	1027th	Tijerina, Thomas T.	393rd
Skidmore, George A	1st	Stiborik, Joe S.	393rd	Tilley, James P.	393rd
Skora, Walter, J.	393rd	Stiegman, John L.	1st	Tillman, Paul L.	393rd
Skrupsky, Metro	509HQ	Stillwell, B.	390th	Timberly, Harold E.	603rd
Skull, William G.	1027th	Stinnette, William S.	1st	Tippett, Clarence E.	1395th
Slaby, Joseph	320th	Stock, Robert J.	393rd	Tirabassi, Louis	1395th
Sleipnes, Arnold E.	393rd	Stockwell, Vaughn	603rd	Tison, Ralph R.	393rd
Slife, Theodore M.	393rd	Stolsonburg, William G.	393rd	Tobias, Joe P.	1395th
Slusky, Joseph	509HQ	Stone, Charley L.	603rd	Toldness, Robert H.	320th
Slussar, Walter J.	1st	Storey, James M.	393rd	Tortosa, Aubrey	393rd
Smallwood, E. R.	509HQ	Stough, Harold L.	390th	Trainer, Jesse W.	1027th
Smiley, Doyle. C.	1st	Stradford, Leroy	1st	Travis, Frank H., Jr.	1st

509th Composite Group and Project Alberta Roster (Tinian, 1945)

Travis, William	1st	Weaver, Alvin O.	393rd	Williams, Stewart W.	393rd
Troutner, Leon C.	603rd	Webb, E. W.	390th	Willis, John W.	1st
Truhlar, Lewis	393rd	Webb, William F.	320th	Willis, Robert D.	603rd
Tucker, John L.	Proj A	Weeks, Alfred R.	1st	Willison, Clifford E.	1027th
Tuggle, Thomas E.	1027th	Weichel, Edgar	603rd	Willoughby, John L.	393rd
Turner, Claude A.	603rd	Weigandt, George J.	393rd	Wilson, John A.	393rd
Turner, John M.	320th	Weimer, Thomas J.	393rd	Wilson, Robert	393rd
Turner, Merle C.	320th	Weiner, M. B.	390th	Wimer, Franklin B.	393rd
Tuttle, Donald D.	393rd	Weiss, Harold L.	509HQ	Winslow, Warren W.	1027th
Twork, Chester	393rd	Welle, Raymond	1395th	Wisnewski, Joseph A.	1st
Twyford, William	603rd	Weller, George A.	393rd	Witherell, John H.	320th
Ursch, John	1395th	Wellman, Merl L.	1027th	Wlodarski, John	603rd
Utley, Arthur M., Jr.	1st	Wells, James L.	1027th	Wolf, Donald L.	603rd
Valazquez, Edward G.	1027th	Wells, Robert L.	393rd	Wolfe, Charles R.	603rd
Valley, Robert J.	393rd	Wendlandt, L. W.	390th	Wolfe, Theodore E.	393rd
Van Pelt, James F.	393rd	Werney, Morris	1027th	Wolff, Russell R.	390th
Vanderhoof, Ronal	1st	Wertz, Keith	603rd	Womack, James R.	393rd
VanDerHorn, H.	390th	Wertz, Kenneth	390th	Wong, Patrick P.	393rd
Vandermale, Carl A.	1st	Wescott, George W.	509HQ	Woodard, Carlie, Jr.	603rd
VandeVoort, John H.	390th	West, Billy A.	1st	Woodbury, J. K.	390th
VanKirk, Theodore J.	509HQ	Westcott, Kermit F.	509HQ	Worley, Howard C.	603rd
VanMeter, Glen	1395th	Westmark, Robert J.	1st	Worthington, Clark	320th
Varga, Charles A.	603rd	Westover, Joseph E.	393rd	Wrede, William L.	1st
Vavro, J. A.	509HQ	Wey, Franklin K.	393rd	Wren, William H.	603rd
Vedder, Spencer	393rd	Whan, Orval	603rd	Wright, Alex V., Jr.	393rd
Vella, James	603rd	Wheeler, Samuel R.	393rd	Wright, David B.	603rd
Vernon, Chester	1st	Wheelock, Phillip T.	1st	Wright, John W.	393rd
Vertz, Richard W.	1st	Wherland, E. J.	390th	Wright, Philip L.	393rd
Vester, Donald W.	1st	Whitaker, Baxter L.	393rd	Wright, R. M.	390th
Villarreal, Marion M.	603rd	Whitaker, Loy G., Jr.	393rd	Wright, William E.	393rd
Vitale, L. W.	390th	Whitaker, W. M.	390th	Wrzesienski, Alfred	1st
Vrana, Leon J.	320th	White, Charles	603rd	Wysocki, Thaddeus	603rd
Wacowski, Charley	1395th	White, Clifford C.	393rd	Yeager, Homer L.	1027th
Waggoner, Wilber L.	320th	White, Everett E.	603rd	Yeagley, Clyde	1395th
Wagner, Edgar G.	393rd	White, James H.	1395th	Young, A. F.	509HQ
Wainscott, James J.	393rd	White, William J.	393rd	Young, Donald A.	393rd`
Waldman, Bernard	Proj A	Whitehead, R. H.	509HQ	Young, William E.	393rd`
Walgamotte, N. L.	390th	Widowsky, Jack	393rd	Zachary, James	1395th
Walk, Paul W.	393rd	Wierenga, Russell G.	1395th	Zafonte, A.	390th
Walters, Aaron	1395th	Wierman, F. C.	509HQ	Zahn, Herman S., Jr.	393rd
Walz, Jack	1st	Wilbur, John A.	1st	Zammarrelli, N. J.	390th
Ward, Elvern	1395th	Wilkerson, Fred	1395th	Zangre, Joseph A.	390th
Ward, George T.	1st	Williams, Albert J.	320th	Zauratsky, Joseph F.	1st
Warga, Edward	1st	Williams, Andrew	603rd	Zechman, George	1395th
Warner, Roger S.	Proj A	Williams, J. C.	390th	Zeinfeld, V. W.	509HQ
Warner, Stanley	1027th	Williams, John O.	603rd	Ziegler, Arthur B.	1395th
Wasz, Robert H.	320th	Williams, John V.	320th	Zimmerli, Frederick H.	Proj A
Wayland, Clarence R.	320th	Williams, Marion L.	603rd	Zimmerman, Harry	320th
Wayland, R. C.	390th	Williams, Perry O.	1st	Zozom, Frank, Jr.	1027th
Weatherly, Ira J.	393rd	Williams, Ray	1st	Zweber, Emmery H.	1395th

APPENDIX E:
PROJECT ALBERTA

The success of the Silverplate B-29 in carrying out the atomic bombing missions was due largely to the efforts of the Los Alamos personnel that made up the group called Project Alberta. Also known as Project A, the important role of this organization in the development and combat operations of the Silverplate B-29 has never been fully appreciated. The purpose of this appendix is to shed some light on this phase of the Manhattan Project.

A detailed account of the organization and activities of Project Alberta can be found in *Critical Assembly* by Hoddeson, Henriksen, Meade, and Westfall. Another excellent source of information regarding Project Alberta is *Project Y: The Los Alamos Story* by Hawkins, Truslow, and Smith.

Project Alberta was established in March 1945 as an independent element of the Manhattan Project at Los Alamos in order to provide an organizational mechanism for preparing and delivering a combat atomic bomb on an enemy target. The forerunner of Project Alberta was Group E-7 of the Ordnance Division at Los Alamos. Group E-7 was established in October 1943 under the direction of Norman F. Ramsey, Jr. to manage the integration of design and delivery of combat atomic bombs.

Project A was responsible for three primary tasks. The most immediate task in the beginning was to manage the completion of design, procurement, and preliminary assembly of bomb units that would be complete and ready for use with active materials. A parallel task was the continuation of the Wendover test program. Finally, Project Alberta was responsible for preparation for overseas operations and support to the 509th Composite Group on Tinian (known to the Los Alamos personnel as Destination) in the conduct of the combat missions.

Selection of Tinian as the base of operations in the Pacific for the 509th was a joint decision of U.S. Army Air Forces and Project Alberta personnel. Commander Frederick L. Ashworth visited Tinian in February 1945 and selected the locations for Project Alberta and 509th operations. Personnel assigned to Project Alberta began leaving Los Alamos for Tinian on 1 July 1945. Fifty-one Los Alamos scientists, engineers, technicians, and administrative officers were involved in Project A operations on Tinian.

Their primary job was to receive equipment, components, and parts from the

76. *Left:* Norman F. Ramsey (left) and Navy Captain William S. Parsons (right). 77. *Middle:* Navy Captain William S. Parsons, Officer-in-Charge of Project Alberta. 78. *Right:* Commander Frederick L. Ashworth, Operations Officer of Project Alberta. (Air Force Historical Research Agency)

United States and prepare bomb units for test drops and the strike missions to Hiroshima and Nagasaki.

In addition, Captain William S. Parsons served as the weapon officer on the Hiroshima mission and Commander Ashworth performed the same function on the Nagasaki mission.

Scientists from Project Alberta also flew on the instrument aircraft on both missions to operate monitoring equipment that received data from the diagnostic canisters dropped from the instrument aircraft. Project Alberta specialists were also assigned to fly on the photographic aircraft to operate cameras on both missions.

Because of the administrative complexities created by the presence of so many Manhattan Project personnel (many of them civilians) on Tinian, the War Department established the First Technical Service Detachment, to which Project Alberta personnel were assigned. Lt. Colonel Peer de Silva was named Commanding Officer of the Detachment.

Also present on Tinian during the July-August 1945 period, although not officially members of Project Alberta, were Brigadier General Thomas F. Farrell (deputy to and personal representative of General Groves), Rear Admiral William R. Purnell (Navy member of the Manhattan Project Military Policy Committee), and Colonel Elmer E. Kirkpatrick (alternate to General Farrell and the officer in charge of construction of Alberta and 509th facilities).

General Farrell and Admiral Purnell maintained liaison and communications with the Manhattan Project in Washington, primarily with General Groves, but also with his staff. For security reasons, communications between Project Alberta and Los Alamos were routed through the Manhattan Project offices in Washington.

The responsibilities of Project personnel were to provide and test certain bomb components, to assemble and test Little Boy and Fat Man units, to supervise and assist in the loading and testing of the bombs, and to provide advice and recommendations about the use of the weapons. As stated above, personnel of Project Alberta were also directly involved in the conduct of the atomic missions as crew members performing essential duties.

The organization of Project Alberta as it existed on Tinian is shown below. Ranks shown are those in effect at that time. AUS indicates U.S. Army, USN is U.S.

Navy, and USNR is U.S. Navy Reserve (on active duty). Where no rank is given, the individual was a civilian.

Project Alberta Organization

Officer-in-Charge	Captain William S. Parsons, USN
Operations Officer and Deputy To Officer-in-Charge	Commander Frederick L. Ashworth, USN
Scientific and Technical Deputy To Officer-in-Charge	Norman F. Ramsey
Fat Man Assembly Team	Roger S. Warner, Jr.
Little Boy Assembly Team	A. Francis Birch, USNR
Fusing Team	Edward B. Doll
Electrical Detonation Team	Commander Edward C. Stevenson, USNR
Pit Team	Philip Morrison & Charles P. Baker
Observation Team	Luis W. Alvarez & Bernard Waldman
Aircraft Ordnance Team	Sheldon H. Dike

Special consultants included on the Project Alberta team included Robert Serber, William G. Penney (representative of Great Britain), and Captain James F. Nolan of the U.S. Army (medical expert).

Other Project personnel included the following (T/5 is Army enlisted rank of Technician with a following class number; T/Sgt is Technical Sergeant):

Agnew, Harold	Linschitz, Henry
Anderson, David L., Ensign	Machen, Arthur B.
Bederson, Benjamin B. T/5	Mastick, Donald, Ensign
Bolstad, Milo M.	Matthews, Robert P., T/3
Brin, Raymond, T/Sgt	Miller, Victor A., Lieutenant
Caleca, Vincent, T/Sgt	Motichko, Leonard L., T/3
Camec, Morton, T/Sgt	Murphy, William L., T/Sgt
Carlson, Edward G., T/Sgt	Nooker, Eugene L., T/Sgt
Collins, Arthur, T/4	O'Keefe, Bernard J., Ensign
Dawson, Robert W., T/Sgt	Olmstead, Thomas H.
Fortine, Frank J., T/Sgt	Perlman, Theodore
Goodman, Walter, T/3	Prohs, Wesley R., Ensign
Harms, Donald C., T/3	Reynolds, George T., Ensign
Hopper, John D., Lieutenant	Russ, Harlow W.
Johnston, Lawrence H.	Schreiber, Raemer E.
Kupferberg, Jesse, T/Sgt	Thornton, Gunnar, T/Sgt
Langer, Lawrence	Tucker, John L., Ensign
Larkin, William J., T/Sgt	Zimmerli, Frederick H., T/4

Although not a member of the Project Alberta group, Corps of Engineers Colonel Elmer E. Kirkpatrick played a key role in preparations for Project and 509th operations on Tinian. Selected by General Groves to manage the acquisition and construction of facilities for both units, he was highly successful in providing the best accommodations possible under the circumstances.

Four members of Project Alberta flew on the Hiroshima mission. Bernard Waldman was on the photographic aircraft, *Necessary Evil*, to operate a special Los Alamos

79. Project Alberta Personnel and Instrumentation Canister. *Standing (left to right):* Harold Agnew, Luis W. Alvarez. *Kneeling (left to right):* Lawrence H. Johnston, Bernard Waldman. (Los Alamos National Laboratory)

camera (for some reason, the film from the Fastax camera did not produce any images). Luis Alvarez, Harold Agnew, and Lawrence Johnston were on the instrument aircraft, *The Great Artiste*, to operate equipment that received blast measurement data from diagnostic canisters dropped from the instrument aircraft at the same time as the Little Boy bomb was released.

Appendix F: Silverplate B-29 Summary

Summary Statistics

Number produced 65
Initial assignment to test program 14   Produced at Martin-Omaha 57
Initial assignment to 509th 51   Produced at Boeing-Wichita 8
Number still in existence in museums 2
Stored and scrapped 16
Stored then converted to trainer 1
Converted to other configurations 31
Lost in accidents 12
Miscellaneous dispositions 3

Serial Number	Delivered To USAAF	Silverplate Start	Silverplate End	Usage 509	Usage Test	Silverplate Disposition	Out of Inventory
42-6259	30 Nov 43	Feb 44	Jan 45		x	To storage/converted	May 48
42-65209	29 Aug 44	Nov 44	Feb 45	x		To storage/scrapped	Jan 52
42-65216	15 Sep 44	Oct 44	Apr 45	x		To storage/scrapped	Aug 50
42-65217	16 Sep 44	Oct 44	Mar 45	x		To storage/scrapped	May 47
42-65234	18 Oct 44	Nov 44	Apr 50		x	Converted to TB-29	Aug 60
42-65235	18 Oct 44	Nov 44	Jan 46		x	To storage/scrapped	May 54
42-65236	24 Oct 44	Nov 44	May 45	x	x	To storage/scrapped	May 52
42-65237	26 Oct 44	Nov 44	May 45	x		To storage/scrapped	Jun 52
42-65238	26 Oct 44	Nov 44	May 45	x		To storage/scrapped	Jun 52
42-65239	26 Oct 44	Nov 44	May 45	x		To storage/scrapped	May 54
42-65240	31 Oct 44	Nov 44	Mar 45	x		To storage/scrapped	May 52
42-65258	13 Nov 44	Dec 44	Apr 46		x	To storage/scrapped	Jul 53
42-65259	11 Nov 44	Dec 44	May 45	x	x	To storage/scrapped	Jul 54
42-65260	14 Nov 44	Dec 44	Jul 45	x	x	To storage/scrapped	May 54
42-65261	14 Nov 44	Dec 44	Mar 45	x		To storage/scrapped	Jul 54
42-65262	14 Nov 44	Dec 44	Apr 45	x	x	To storage/scrapped	Apr 53
42-65263	15 Nov 44	Dec 44	Feb 45	x		To storage/scrapped	Sep 50
42-65264	15 Nov 44	Dec 44	Feb 45	x		To storage/scrapped	Jun 52
42-65384	15 Feb 45	Apr 45	Apr 50		x	Converted to TB-29	Jul 54
42-65385	15 Feb 45	Apr 45	Jan 47		x	Lost in accident	Apr 47
42-65386	15 Feb 45	Apr 45	Mar 47		x	To Hanscom Field	Apr 56
42-65387	15 Feb 45	Apr 45	Mar 46		x	Lost in accident	Mar 46
44-27295	19 Mar 45	Apr 45	Mar 49		x	Converted to TB-29	Jun 59

Serial Number	Delivered To USAAF	Silverplate Start	Silverplate End	Usage 509	Test	Silverplate Disposition	Out of Inventory
44-27296	19 Mar 45	Apr 45	Mar 46	x		Lost in accident	Aug 46
44-27297	19 Mar 45	Apr 45	Sep 46	x		To museum	Sep 46
44-27298	20 Mar 45	Apr 45	Apr 50	x		Converted to TB-29	Nov 56
44-27299	20 Mar 45	Apr 45	May 49	x		Lost in accident	Jul 49
44-27300	2 Apr 45	Apr 45	Aug 49	x		Converted to WB-29	Aug 57
44-27301	2 Apr 45	Apr 45	Apr 50	x		Converted to TB-29	Jul 54
44-27302	2 Apr 45	Apr 45	Apr 50	x		Converted to TB-29	Jul 54
44-27303	3 Apr 45	Apr 45	Sep 45	x		Lost in accident	Apr 46
44-27304	3 Apr 45	Apr 45	Apr 50	x		Converted to TB-29	Nov 56
44-27353	20 Apr 45	May 45	Sep 48	x		Lost in accident	Sep 49
44-27354	20 Apr 45	May 45	Apr 50	x		Converted to TB-29	Feb 60
44-86263	17 May 45	Nov 47	Apr 50	x		Converted to TB-29	Mar 60
44-86291	18 May 45	Jun 45	Apr 50	x		Converted to TB-29	Nov 56
44-86292	18 May 45	Jun 45	Aug 46	x		To museum	Aug 46
44-86346	15 June 45	Jul 45	Apr 50	x		Converted to TB-29	Jul 60
44-86347	15 June 45	Jul 45	Apr 50	x		Converted to TB-29	Jul 60
44-86382	26 July 45	Aug 45	Apr 50	x		Converted to TB-29	Dec 53
44-86383	30 July 45	Aug 45	Aug 48	x		Lost in accident	Aug 48
44-86384	27 July 45	Aug 45	Apr 50	x		Converted to TB-29	Jul 57
44-65394	24 July 45	Dec 47	Apr 50	x		Converted to TB-29	Jul 56
44-86401	30 July 45	Mar 47	Apr 50	x		Converted to TB-29	Sep 56
44-86430	27 Aug 45	Oct 45	Apr 50	x	x	Converted to TB-29	Oct 58
44-86431	28 Aug 45	Aug 45	Aug 47	x		Lost in accident	Aug 47
44-86432	30 Aug 45	Oct 45	Apr 50	x	x	Converted to TB-29	Oct 55
44-86437	24 Aug 45	May 47	May 50	x		Converted to TB-29	Jun 57
44-86439	24 Aug 45	Jan 47	Apr 50	x		Converted to TB-29	May 54
44-86440	28 Aug 45	Jan 47	Apr 50	x		Converted to TB-29	Oct 56
44-86443	30 Aug 45	Dec 47	Apr 50	x		Converted to TB-29	Sep 58
44-86444	29 Aug 45	Jun 47	Apr 50		x	Converted to TB-29	Jul 56
44-86445	29 Aug 45	Jul 47	May 50	x		Converted to TB-29	Oct 56
44-86447	10 Sep 45	Jun 47	Apr 50		x	Converted to TB-29	Nov 55
44-86448	31 Aug 45	Jan 47	Apr 50	x		Converted to TB-29	Jul 54
44-86451	31 Aug 45	Aug 47	Apr 50	x		To 8th Air Force	May 54
44-86472	2 Oct 45	Oct 45	Jun 47	x		Lost in accident	Jun 47
44-86473	2 Oct 45	Oct 45	Apr 46	x		Lost in accident	Apr 46
44-87752	10 Jul 45	Sep 47	Apr 50	x		Converted to TB-29	Sep 54
44-87771	17 Jul 45	Aug 47	Nov 51	x		To 9th Bomb Wing	Jul 56
44-87774	18 Jul 45	Mar 47	Apr 50	x		Converted to TB-29	Mar 52
45-21707	26 Jul 45	Mar 47	Apr 50	x		Lost in accident	Aug 49
45-21736	1 Aug 45	May 47	Aug 50	x		Lost in accident	Aug 50
45-21739	3 Aug 45	Sep 47	May 50	x		Converted to TB-29	Oct 56
45-21818	28 Aug 45	Jul 47	Mar 49		x	Converted to TB-29	Sep 55

APPENDIX G:
INDIVIDUAL SILVERPLATE
B-29 HISTORIES

The delivery, assignment, and disposition information included in the Silverplate B-29 histories provided in this appendix is based on data extracted from aircraft record cards by Archie DiFante of the Air Force Historical Research Agency at Maxwell Air Force Base in Montgomery, Alabama.[1] Additional information from numerous other sources was used to make each airplane's history as complete as possible. The histories are presented in serial number sequence. The notation "Phase" in the header for each history refers to the phases used in chapter 2.

B-29-1-BW-42-6259   Delivered to USAAF: 30 Nov 43[2]   Phase 1

42-6259 was the prototype Silverplate B-29. Manufactured at the Boeing Wichita plant, it was first assigned to the 468th Bombardment Group at Smoky Hill Army Air Field (KS) in December 1943. Almost immediately after arriving at Smoky Hill, it was reassigned to Wright Army Air Field (OH) for modification to the initial Silverplate configuration. See chapter 2 for details on the prototype modifications.

With the changes completed in February 1944, it was flown to Muroc Army Air Base (CA), later Edwards Air Force Base, for use in drop tests of atomic bomb development models at Muroc. During a mission on 16 March 1944, a Thin Man test bomb released prematurely and the bomb bay doors were damaged.[3] After repairs at Wright Field, it was used in a second series of tests at Muroc in June 1944.

The Los Alamos drop test program shifted to Wendover Army Air Field (UT) and the Salton Sea (CA) bombing range in the fall of 1944. After further modifications, 42-6259 was officially assigned to the 216th Base Unit at Wendover in October 1944. It was damaged in a landing accident in late 1944 and was not used again for bomb drop tests.[4]

It was assigned to the 4105th Base Unit at Davis-Monthan Army Air Field (AZ) in January 1945 for storage. In August 1946 it was removed from storage and reassigned to the 233rd Base Unit at Fort Worth Army Air Field (TX) in August 1946 as a TB-29 instructional aircraft. In December 1946, it was assigned to the 7th Bombardment Group at the same field for the same purpose.

Disposition: Salvaged at Carswell Air Force Base in May 1948.

80. Prototype Silverplate B-29 (42-6259). (Los Alamos National Laboratory)

B-29-5-MO-42-65209   Delivered to USAAF: 29 Aug 44   Phase 2

42-65209 was the first of the initial group of Silverplate B-29s assigned to Wendover Army Air Field (UT). Originally delivered to Oklahoma City Air Depot as a TB-29, it was assigned to Herrington Army Air Field (KS) in October 1944, and then almost immediately reassigned to the 393rd Bombardment Squadron at Wendover in November 1944. It was used by the 393rd for training purposes until February 1945, when it was assigned to the 4105th Base Unit at Davis-Monthan Army Air Field (AZ) for storage.

Disposition: Declared surplus and scrapped at Davis-Monthan in January 1952.

B-29-10-MO-42-65216   Delivered to USAAF: 15 Sep 44   Phase 2

42-65216 was the first of the initial group of Silverplate B-29s delivered direct from the Glenn L. Martin Aircraft Plant in Omaha (NE) to the 393rd at Wendover Army Air Field in Utah. Originally designated as a TB-29, it was assigned to the 393rd in October 1944 and was used for training purposes. When the 393rd began receiving improved Silverplate versions in the spring of 1945, it was reassigned to the 4136th Base Unit at Tinker Army Air Field (OK) in April 1945.

It was assigned to the 2532nd Base Unit at Randolph Army Air Field (TX) in August 1945, to the 236th Base Unit at Pyote Army Air Field (TX) in November 1945, and to the 4141st Base Unit at Pyote in March 1946 for storage.

Disposition: Declared surplus and scrapped at Pyote Air Force Base in August 1950.

B-29-10-MO-42-65217   Delivered to USAAF: 16 Sep 44   Phase 2

42-65217 was one of the initial group of Silverplate B-29s delivered to the 393rd at Wendover Army Air Field (UT). Originally designated as a TB-29, it was assigned to the 393rd in October 1944. When the 393rd began receiving improved Silverplate versions in the spring of 1945, it was reassigned to the 331st Bomb Group at McCook Army Air Field (NE) in March 1945. It was assigned to the 245th Base Unit at McCook in August 1945, the 4196th Base Unit at Victorville Army Air Field (CA) in November 1945, and the 4141st Base Unit at Pyote Army Air Field (TX) in May 1947 for storage.

Disposition: Declared surplus and scrapped at Pyote Air Force Base in August 1950.

B-29-15-MO-42-65234   Delivered to USAAF: 18 Oct 44   Phase 2

One of the initial group of Silverplate B-29s, 42-65234 was assigned to the 216th Base Unit at Wendover Army Air Field (UT) in November 1944 for use in the Los Alamos test program. It was used at Wendover for this purpose until February 1946, when it was reassigned to the 428th Base Unit at Kirtland Army Air Field (NM) for further bomb development testing. Photograph 81 shows 42-65234 next to a loading pit at Kirtland after the end of World War II.[5] A Fat Man test unit is resting in the loading pit ready to be hoisted into the bomb bay after the aircraft is rotated over the pit.

In March 1949, it was assigned to the 2758th Base Unit at Kirtland as an EB-29 and to the 3078th Base Unit at Kirtland in July 1949. In October 1949 it was assigned to the 97th Bomb Group at Biggs Air Force Base (TX) and in April 1950 to the Oklahoma City depot at Tinker Air Force Base (OK).

After conversion to a TB-29, it was assigned overseas duty to the 10th Radar Calibration Squadron at Yokota Air Base (Japan) in June 1952. Other assignments overseas included the 6023rd Radar Evaluation Flight at Yokota in March 1954, to Johnson Air Base (Okinawa) in July 1956, to Naha Air Base (Okinawa) in July 1958, and to the 6431st Air Base Group at Naha in December 1959.

Disposition: Declared surplus and scrapped at Naha Air Base in August 1960.

B-29-15-MO-42-65235   Delivered to USAAF: 18 Oct 44   Phase 2

One of the initial group of Silverplate B-29s, 42-65235 was assigned to the 216th Base Unit at Wendover Army Air Field (UT) in November 1944 for use in the Los Alamos bomb drop testing program. While on a mission on 21 February 1945, an engine fire made an emergency landing necessary and the crew evacuated the aircraft as soon as it came to a stop on the runway.[6]

The damage from the fire was considerable and 42-65235 was never used in the test program again. It was eventually repaired and reassigned to the 4105th Base Unit at Davis Monthan Army Air Field (AZ) in January 1946 for storage.

Disposition: Declared surplus and scrapped at Davis-Monthan in May 1954.

81. Silverplate B-29 42-65234 at Kirtland Army Air Field. (Los Alamos National Laboratory)

B-29-20-MO-42-65236   Delivered to USAAF: 24 Oct 44   Phase 2

42-65236 was one of the initial group of Silverplate B-29s assigned to the 393rd Bombardment Squadron at Wendover Army Air Field (UT). Originally designated as a TB-29, it was assigned to the 393rd in November 1944. In late February 1945, when the Los Alamos drop test program needed additional aircraft for its tests, 42-65236 was reassigned to the 216th Base Unit at Wendover.

When the 216th began receiving improved Silverplate versions in the spring of 1945, it was reassigned to the 2132nd Base Unit at Maxwell Army Air Field (AL) in May 1945. In November 1945 it was assigned to the 4141st Base Unit at Pyote Army Air Field (TX) for storage.

Disposition: Declared surplus and scrapped at Pyote in May 1952.

B-29-20-MO-42-65237   Delivered to USAAF: 26 Oct 44   Phase 2

One of the initial group of Silverplate B-29s delivered to Wendover Army Air Field (UT), 42-65237 was assigned to the 393rd in November 1944. When the 393rd began receiving improved Silverplate versions in the spring of 1945, it was reassigned to the 2510th Base Unit at Brooks Army Air Field (TX) in May 1945. It was assigned to the 2532nd Base Unit at Randolph Army Air Field (TX) as a TB-29 in July 1945, and then to the 4105th Base Unit at Davis-Monthan Army Air Field (AZ) in November 1945 for storage.

Disposition: Declared surplus and scrapped at Davis-Monthan in June 1952.

B-29-20-MO-42-65238   Delivered to USAAF: 26 Oct 44   Phase 2

One of the initial group of Silverplate B-29s delivered to Wendover Army Air Field (UT), 42-65238 was assigned to the 393rd in November 1944 and was one of the B-29s flown to Batista Field in Cuba in January 1945 by Airplane Commander Frederick C. Bock and crew C-13 for training. When the 393rd began receiving improved Silverplate versions in the spring of 1945, it was reassigned to the 2510th Base Unit at Brooks Army Air Field (TX) in May 1945. It was assigned to the 2532nd Base Unit at Randolph Army Air Field (TX) as a TB-29 in June 1945, and then to the 4105th Base Unit at Davis-Monthan Army Air Field (AZ) in November 1945 for storage.

Disposition: Declared surplus and scrapped at Davis-Monthan in June 1952.

B-29-20-MO-42-65239   Delivered to USAAF: 26 Oct 44   Phase 2

Assigned to Wendover Army Air Field (UT) in November 1944, 42-65239 was one of the initial group of Silverplate B-29s delivered to the 393rd Bombardment Squadron. As the 393rd began receiving improved Silverplate versions in the spring of 1945, it was reassigned to the 3502nd Base Unit at Chanute Army Air Field (IL) as a TB-29 in May 1945. It was assigned to the 4105th Base Unit at Davis-Monthan Army Air Field (AZ) for storage in December 1946.

Disposition: Declared surplus and scrapped at Davis-Monthan in May 1954.

B-29-20-MO-42-65240   Delivered to USAAF: 31 Oct 44   Phase 2

One of the initial group of Silverplate B-29s delivered to Wendover Army Air Field (UT), 42-65240 was assigned to the 393rd Bombardment Squadron in November 1944. As the 393rd began to receive improved Silverplate versions in the spring of 1945, it was reassigned to the 245th Base Unit at McCook Army Air Field (NE) in March 1945. It was then assigned to the 244th Base Unit at Harvard Army Air Field (NE) in May 1945 and the 2132nd Base Unit at Maxwell Army Air Field (AL) in June 1945. In November 1945, it was assigned to the 4141st Base Unit at Pyote Army Air Field (TX) for storage.

Disposition: Declared surplus and scrapped at Pyote in May 1952.

B-29-20-MO-42-65258   Delivered to USAAF: 13 Nov 44   Phase 2

One of the initial group of Silverplate B-29s, 42-65258 was assigned to Wendover Army Air Field (UT) in December 1944 for use in the Los Alamos bomb drop testing program. Assigned to the 216th Base Unit, it was used for this purpose at Wendover until October 1945, when it was reassigned to the 237th Base Unit at Kirtland Army Air Field (NM) for further bomb development testing.

It was assigned to the 428th Base Unit at Kirtland in February 1946. In April 1946, it was reassigned to the 444th Bomb Group at Castle Army Air Field (CA) and was deployed to Davis-Monthan Army Air Field (AZ) before being assigned to the 482nd Base Unit at Castle in June 1946. In November 1946, it was assigned to the 4141st Base Unit at Pyote Army Air Field (TX) for storage.

Disposition: Declared surplus and scrapped at Pyote in July 1953.

B-29-20-MO-42-65259   Delivered to USAAF: 11 Nov 44   Phase 2

One of the initial group of Silverplate B-29s delivered to Wendover Army Air Field (UT), 42-65259 was assigned to the 393rd Bombardment Group in December 1944. In late February 1945, when the Los Alamos drop test program needed additional aircraft for its tests, it was reassigned to the 216th Base Unit at Wendover.

When the 216th began receiving improved Silverplate versions in the spring of 1945, it was reassigned to Maxwell Army Air Field (AL) in May 1945 and then to the 4141st Base Unit at Pyote Army Air Field (TX) in November 1945 for storage.

Disposition: Declared surplus and scrapped at Pyote in July 1954.

B-29-20-MO-42-65260   Delivered to USAAF: 14 Nov 44   Phase 2

One of the initial group of Silverplate B-29s delivered to Wendover Army Air Field (UT), 42-65260 was assigned to the 393rd Bombardment Squadron in December 1944. In late February 1945, when the Los Alamos drop test program needed additional aircraft for its tests, it was reassigned to the 216th Base Unit at Wendover.

When the 216th began receiving improved Silverplate versions in the spring of 1945, it was no longer used in the Los Alamos test program. In July 1945 it was assigned to the 4105th Base Unit at Davis-Monthan Army Air Field (AZ) for storage.

Disposition: Declared surplus and scrapped at Davis-Monthan in May 1954.

B-29-20-MO-42-65261   Delivered to USAAF: 14 Nov 44   Phase 2

One of the initial group of Silverplate B-29s delivered to Wendover Army Air Field (UT), 42-65261 was assigned to the 393rd Bombardment Squadron in December 1944. As the 393rd began receiving improved Silverplate versions in the spring of 1945, it was reassigned to McCook Army Air Field (NE) in March 1945.

Further assignments included the 2132nd Base Unit at Maxwell Army Air Field (AL) in April 1945, the 4119th Base Unit at Brookley Army Air Field (AL) in May 1945, and the 245th Base Unit at McCook Army Air Field in July 1945. In November 1945 it was assigned to the 4141st Base Unit at Pyote Army Air Field (TX) for storage.

Disposition: Declared surplus and scrapped at Pyote in July 1954.

B-29-20-MO-42-65262   Delivered to USAAF: 14 Nov 44   Phase 2

One of the initial group of Silverplate B-29s delivered to Wendover Army Air Field (UT), 42-65262 was assigned to the 393rd Bombardment Squadron in December 1944. In late February 1945, when the Los Alamos drop test program needed additional aircraft for its tests, it was reassigned to the 216th Base Unit at Wendover. It was used in the test program until after the end of World War II. It was reassigned to the 4000th Base Unit at Wright Army Air Field (OH) in April 1945. It was then

assigned to the 4117th Base Unit at Robins Army Air Field (GA) in April 1946.
Disposition: Declared surplus and scrapped at Robins in April 1953.

B-29-20-MO-42-65263   Delivered to USAAF: 15 Nov 44   Phase 2

One of the last of the initial group of Silverplate B-29s delivered to Wendover Army Air Field (UT), 42-65263 was assigned to the 393rd Bombardment Squadron in December 1944. Even before the 393rd began receiving improved Silverplate versions in the spring of 1945, it was reassigned to Harvard Army Air Field (NE) in February 1945 and to Fairmont Army Air Field (NE) in March 1945.

Further assignments included the 271st Base Unit at Kearney Army Air Field (NE) in April 1945, the 4121st Base Unit at Kelly Army Air Field (TX) in May 1945, and the 2532nd Base Unit at Randolph Army Air Field (TX) in June 1945. It was assigned to the 4141st Base Unit at Pyote Army Air Field (TX) in November 1945 for storage.

Disposition: Declared surplus and scrapped at Pyote in September 1950.

B-29-25-MO-42-65264   Delivered to USAAF: 15 Nov 44   Phase 2

The last of the initial group of Silverplate B-29s delivered to Wendover Army Air Field (UT), 42-65264 was assigned to the 393rd Bombardment Squadron in December 1944. Even before the 393rd began receiving improved Silverplate versions in the spring of 1945, it was reassigned to the 242nd Base Unit at Grand Isle Army Air Field (NE) in February 1945. It was then assigned to 2532nd Base Unit at Randolph Army Air Field (TX) in August 1945 and to the 4105th Base Unit at Davis-Monthan Army Air Field (AZ) in November 1945 for storage.

Disposition: Declared surplus and scrapped at Davis-Monthan in June 1952.

B-29-36-MO-42-65384   Delivered to USAAF: 15 Feb 45   Phase 3

42-65384 was one of the first improved Silverplate versions delivered to Wendover Army Air Field (UT) in the spring of 1945. After delivery to the USAAF at the Omaha plant, it was immediately placed in the Omaha Modification Center and converted to the Silverplate configuration. After modification, its block number was changed from 30 to 36 to identify the special configuration. It was then delivered to Wendover in April 1945 and assigned to the 216th Base Unit for use in the Los Alamos bomb drop testing program. In February 1946 it was reassigned to the 428th Base Unit at Kirtland Army Air Field (NM) with deployments to Wright AAF (OH).

It was assigned to the 2758th Air Base Group at Kirtland in January 1949 and was redesignated as an EB-29 in March 1949. Additional assignments at Kirtland included the 3078th Air Base Group in July 1949 and the 4925th Special Weapons Group in December 1949. In April 1950 it was reassigned to the Oklahoma City depot at Tinker Air Force Base (OK) and redesignated as a TB-29. Further assignments included the 105th Radar Calibration Flight at Greenville Air Force Base (SC) in May 1952, US Air Forces in Europe at Laon Air Base (France) in July 1952, the 59th Air Depot Wing at RAF Burtonwood (UK) in August 1952, and the 105th Radar Calibration Flight at Nuebiburg Air Base (Germany) in October 1952.

In December, 42-65384 was assigned to Furstenfeldbruck Air Base (Germany), to Noussaur Air Base (Morocco) in January 1953, to Sidi Silimane Air Base (Morocco) in February 1953, and back to Furstenfeldbruck in April 1953. In August 1953 it was assigned to the 73rd Air Depot Wing at Chateauroux Air Base (France), and then to the 7373rd Air Base Group at the same base in January 1954. In February 1954, it was sent back to the United States to the 3040th Aircraft Storage Squadron at Davis-Monthan Air Force Base (AZ).

Disposition: Dropped from inventory as salvage at Davis-Monthan in July 1954.

B-29-36-MO-42-65385   Delivered to USAAF: 15 Feb 45   Phase 3

42-65385 was one of the first improved Silverplate versions delivered to Wendover Army Air Field (UT) in the spring of 1945. After delivery to the USAAF, it was placed in the Omaha Modification Center in February 1945 and converted to the Silverplate configuration. After modification, its block number was changed from 30 to 36 to identify the special configuration. It was then delivered to Wendover in April 1945 and assigned to the 216th Base Unit for use in the Los Alamos bomb drop testing program.

In October 1945 it was reassigned to the 237th Base Unit at Kirtland Army Air Field (NM). In February 1946 it was assigned to the 428th Base Unit at Kirtland and was used for Los Alamos bomb development testing. On 27 January 1947, 42-65385 crashed immediately after take-off from Kirtland on a routine maintenance test mission.[7] All twelve men on board were killed. See Chapter 5 for additional details of the accident.

Disposition: Recommended for salvage at Kirtland in January 1947 after the crash and dropped from inventory in April 1947 after reclamation was completed.

B-29-36-MO-42-65386   Delivered to USAAF: 15 Feb 45   Phase 3

42-65386 was one of the first improved Silverplate versions delivered to Wendover Army Air Field (UT) in the spring of 1945. After delivery to the USAAF, it was placed in the Omaha Modification Center in February 1945 and converted to the Silverplate configuration. After modification, its block number was changed from 30 to 36 to identify the special configuration. It was then delivered to Wendover in April 1945 and assigned to the 216th Base Unit for use in the Los Alamos bomb drop test program.

On 27 July 1945 three Silverplate B-29s were flown from Wendover to Kirtland Army Air Field (NM) for the start of a special mission. One of the aircraft was 42-65386 with William Hartshorn as the aircraft commander.[8] The other two were 44-86346 with Herman S. Zahn as the aircraft commander and 44-86347 with Edward M. Costello as the aircraft commander. The latter two B-29s were the last two aircraft of the 393rd Bombardment Squadron to be delivered from the Martin Omaha plant and be deployed to Tinian.

The reason for the B-29s stopping at Kirtland overnight was to load three Fat Man atomic bomb assemblies into their front bomb bays for transport to Tinian. None of the assemblies included the plutonium core. The three B-29s departed Kirtland on 28 July, and with several stops enroute arrived at Tinian on 2 August 1945 (Tinian date). One of the Fat Man units transported on this mission was the unit used in the Nagasaki mission. After the Fat Man units were off-loaded, Hartshorn and his crew flew 42-65386 back to Wendover.

In October 1945 it was assigned to the 237th Base Unit at Kirtland Army Air Field (NM), and then to the 428th Base Unit at Kirtland in March 1946. It was assigned to the Air Materiel Command in March 1947 with deployments to Wright Army Air Field (OH). Further assignments at Kirtland included the 2758th Air Base Group in February 1949 as an EB-29, to the 3078th Air Base Group in July 1949, the 4925th Special Weapons Group in December 1949, and the 4925th Test Group in July 1951.

In November 1952, it was redesignated as a B-29. It was assigned to the 6520th Test Wing at Hanscom Air Force Base (MA) in June 1953. In November 1955 it was redesignated as a TB-29.

Disposition: Dropped from inventory at Hanscom in April 1956 by transfer to the U.S. Army.

B-29-36-MO-42-65387   Delivered to USAAF: 15 Feb 45   Phase 3

42-65387 was one of the first improved Silverplate versions delivered to Wendover Army Air Field (UT) in the spring of 1945. After delivery to the USAAF, it was placed in the Omaha Modification Center in February 1945 and converted to the Silverplate configuration. After modification, its block number was changed from 30 to 36 to identify the special configuration. It was then delivered to Wendover in April 1945 and assigned to the 216th Base Unit for use in the Los Alamos bomb drop testing program. In January 1946 it was reassigned to the 237th Base Unit at Kirtland Army Air Field (NM), and then to the 428th Base Unit at Kirtland in February 1946.

On 7 March 1946, 42-65387 was used on a practice bombing mission from Kirtland to the Los Lunas bombing range southwest of Albuquerque, New Mexico. After dropping a 10,150 pound Pumpkin practice bomb, it disintegrated for reasons unknown and spun into the ground from about 32,000 feet.[9] All ten men on board died, including the bombardier, David Semple.

Semple was the bombardier on most of the drop test missions conducted from Wendover and Muroc in 1944 and 1945. The Silverplate B-29 (44-27354) that dropped the Fat Man atomic bomb in Test Able of Operation Crossroads in the Pacific on 1 July 1946 was given the name *Dave's Dream* in honor of him.

Disposition: Dropped from inventory as salvage at Kirtland in March 1946 following the crash.

B-29-36-MO-44-27295   Delivered to USAAF: 19 Mar 45   Phase 3

44-27295 was one of the first five improved Silverplate versions delivered to Wendover Army Air Field (UT) in the spring of 1945. It was one of ten B-29s built at the Martin Omaha plant with an original block number of 35, but which when modified to the Silverplate configuration was given block number 36.

While the Aircraft Record Card shows it being assigned to the 509th Composite Group in April 1945, it was actually assigned to the 216th Base Unit as were the other Silverplate B-29s used to support the Los Alamos test program. Sheldon Dike reported it as one of the B-29s used in the Los Alamos bomb drop testing program.

82. Silverplate B-29 44-27295 at Kirtland Army Air Field in 1946. (Los Alamos National Laboratory)

It was not deployed to Tinian as were the fifteen Silverplate B-29s delivered immediately following 44-27295.

In November 1945 it was reassigned to the 237th Base Unit at Kirtland Army Air Field (NM). It was assigned to the 4121st Base Unit at Kelly Army Air Field (TX) in January 1946, and then back to the 428th Base Unit at Kirtland in April 1946. In March 1949 it was assigned to the 2758th Air Base Group at Kirtland as an EB-29 and then transferred to the 3078th Air Base Group at Kirtland in July 1949.

In September 1949 it was redesignated as a B-29 and assigned to the 97th Bombardment Group at Biggs Air Force Base (TX). In April 1950 it was assigned to the Oklahoma City depot at Tinker Air Force Base (OK) and redesignated as a TB-29. It was then assigned to the 104th Radar Calibration Flight at Sewart Air Force Base (TN) in July 1952.

In October 1952 it was deployed overseas to Sidi Silimane Air Base (Morocco) and the 15th Radar Calibration Flight at Wiesbaden Air Base (Germany). It was also assigned to the 7366th Radar Evaluation Squadron at Furstenfeldbruck (Germany) in September 1956 before being transferred back to the U.S. in March 1957 to TEMCO at Majors Field (TX). Other assignments included the 4677th Radar Evaluation Flight at Hill Air Force Base (UT) in June 1957, the 4713th Radar Evaluation Flight at Griffiss Air Force Base (NY) in July 1958, and the 4713th Radar Evaluation Squadron at Griffiss in July 1958.

Disposition: Dropped from inventory at Griffiss in June 1959 by transfer to a school or museum, the identity of which is unknown.

B-29-36-MO-44-27296   Delivered to USAAF: 19 Mar 45   Phase 3

44-27296 was one of the fifteen Silverplate B-29s used by the 509th on Tinian. It was one of ten B-29s built at the Glenn L. Martin Aircraft Plant in Omaha (NE) plant as a block 35 B-29 but then given block number 36 to denote the special configuration. It was flown from Omaha to Wendover Army Air Field (UT) in April 1945 by one of the 393rd Bombardment Squadron crews, where it was assigned to airplane commander James N. Price, Jr. and crew B-7 of the 393rd. After being used in training and practice bombing missions at Wendover, it was flown from Wendover to Tinian by Price and crew B-7, departing Wendover on 8 June 1945.

On Tinian it was first assigned call sign Victor 4, and later Victor 84. It was given the nickname *Some Punkins* by crew B-7 and nose art was applied after the atomic bombing missions.[10] In June, July, and August 1945 it was used on Tinian on 13 training and practice bombing missions, and on five combat missions in which pumpkin bombs were dropped on Japanese targets. Listings showing the dates, crews, airplane commanders, and purposes of the missions in which 44-27296 was used on Tinian are included in chapter 3 and Appendix B.

83. Silverplate B-29 44-27296 (*Some Punkins*). (Leon D. Smith)

In November 1945, 44-27296 was flown back to the U.S. and assigned to the 509th Composite Group at Roswell Army Air Field (NM). In March 1946 it was assigned to Task Force 1.5 of Operation Crossroads, but it did not participate in the atomic bomb test in the Pacific due to an accident at Kirtland Army Air Field (NM) in which it was damaged.

Although there are references to Roswell as the site of the accident in some documents,[11] the circumstances of the incident and the assignment histories shown in both aircraft record cards for the aircraft involved lead to the conclusion that it happened at Kirtland.

On 1 March 1946, someone began to taxi another 509th B-29 (44-86473) on the Kirtland tarmac without properly energizing the hydraulic system for the landing gear brakes. Once in motion, 44-86473 could not be steered and could be stopped only by running into another object. That object happened to be the parked 44-27296. The accident resulted in considerable damage to both aircraft. After being reassigned to the 428th Base Unit at Kirtland in April 1946, it was burned in a firefighting demonstration at Kirtland in August of that year. See chapter 5 for more information on this accident.

Disposition: Dropped from inventory as surplus at Kirtland in August 1946 and used in a firefighting demonstration in which it was destroyed.

B-29-36-MO-44-27297   Delivered to USAAF: 19 Mar 45   Phase 3

44-27297 was one of the fifteen Silverplate B-29s used by the 509th on Tinian. It was one of ten B-29s built at the Glenn L. Martin Aircraft Plant in Omaha (NE) as a block 35 B-29 but then given block number 36 to denote the special configuration. It was flown from Omaha to Wendover Army Air Field (UT) in April 1945 by one of the 393rd Bombardment Squadron crews, where it was assigned to airplane commander Frederick C. Bock and crew C-13. After being used in training and practice bombing missions at Wendover, it was flown from Wendover to Tinian by Bock and crew C-13, departing Wendover on 11 June 1945.

On Tinian it was first assigned call sign Victor 7, and later Victor 77. It was named *Bockscar* and nose art was applied after the atomic bombing missions.[12] In June, July, and August 1945 it was used on Tinian on 13 training and practice bombing missions, three combat missions in which pumpkin bombs were dropped on Japanese targets, and three missions in which Fat Man test bombs were dropped. On 9 August 1945, it was used by Major Sweeney and crew C-15 to drop the Fat Man atomic bomb on Nagasaki. Listings showing the dates, crews, airplane commanders, and purposes of the missions in which 44-27297 was used on Tinian are included in chapter 3 and Appendix B.

In November 1945 it was flown back to the U.S. and assigned to the 509th Composite Group at Roswell Army Air Field (NM). In June 1946 it was assigned to Task Force 1.5 of Operation Crossroads, but there is no evidence that it participated in the atomic bomb test. In August 1946 it was reassigned to the 4105th Base Unit at Davis-Monthan Army Air Field (AZ) for storage. It was displayed at Davis-Monthan as the B-29 used to drop the Fat Man atomic bomb on Nagasaki, although it was given the identification markings of *The Great Artiste* (44-27353) with Victor number 89 on

84. Silverplate B-29 44-27297 (*Bockscar*). (Leon D. Smith)

the fuselage. The error in markings was the result of confusion on Tinian as to which B-29 actually carried and dropped the Fat Man bomb.[13]

Disposition: Dropped from inventory at Davis-Monthan in September 1946 by transfer of title to the Air Force Museum. It was flown to the museum on 26 September 1961 and is now on display with the correct markings.

B-29-36-MO-44-27298 Delivered to USAAF: 20 Mar 45 Phase 3

44-27298 was one of the fifteen Silverplate B-29s used by the 509th on Tinian. It was one of ten B-29s built at the Glenn L. Martin Aircraft Plant in Omaha (NE) as a block 35 B-29 but then given block number 36 to denote the special configuration. It was flown from Omaha to Wendover Army Air Field (UT) in April 1945 by one of the 393rd Bombardment Squadron crews, where it was assigned to airplane commander Ralph R. Taylor, Jr. and crew A-1.

Used in training and practice bombing missions at Wendover, it was flown from Wendover to Tinian by Taylor and crew A-1, departing Wendover on 11 June 1945. On Tinian it was first assigned call sign Victor 13, later changed to Victor 83. It was named *Full House* and nose art was applied after the atomic bombing missions. In June, July, and August 1945 it was used on 12 training and practice bombing mis-

85. Silverplate B-29 44-27298 (*Full House*). (Leon D. Smith)

sions, and on five combat missions in which pumpkin bombs were dropped on Japanese targets.

On 6 August 1945, it was used by Taylor and crew A-1 for weather reconnaissance over Nagasaki in conjunction with the Hiroshima bombing mission. On 9 August 1945, it was used by Taylor and crew A-1 as the standby aircraft on Iwo Jima in conjunction with the Nagasaki atomic bombing mission. Listings showing the dates, crews, airplane commanders, and purposes of the missions in which 44-27298 was used are included in chapter 3 and Appendix B.

In November 1945 it was flown back to the U.S. and assigned to the 509th Composite Group at Roswell Army Air Field (NM). In April 1946 it was assigned to Task Force 1.5 of Operation Crossroads with a deployment to Tinker Army Air Field (OK), but it did not participate in the atomic bomb test in the Pacific. In August 1946 it was reassigned to the 509th at Roswell with deployments to Rome Army Air Field (NY) and Mitchell Army Air Field (NY). In June 1949 it was assigned to the 97th Bombardment Group (later a Wing) at Biggs Air Force Base (TX).

In April 1950, 44-27298 was assigned to the Oklahoma City depot at Tinker Air Force Base (OK) via Kelly Air Force Base (TX) and redesignated as a TB-29. In August 1952 it was assigned to the 106th Radar Calibration Squadron at Sioux City Air Force Base (IA), and in September 1953 it was reassigned to the 7th Radar Calibration Squadron at the same base.

In December 1953, the 7th Radar Calibration Squadron moved to Hill Air Force

Base (UT). Additional assignments included the 4677th Radar Evaluation Flight at Hill in March 1954, the Mobile Air Materiel Area in Nashville (TN) in March 1955, the 17th Tow Target Squadron at Yuma County Airport (AZ) in June 1955, and the 4750th Air Defense Wing at the Yuma County Airport (later Vincent Air Force Base) in July 1955.

Disposition: Dropped from inventory by transfer to the U.S. Navy in November 1956 and flown to the Naval Ordnance Test Station at China Lake (CA) where it used as a target for Navy gunnery and bombing training.

B-29-36-MO-44-27299   Delivered to USAAF: 20 Mar 45   Phase 3

44-27299 was one of the fifteen Silverplate B-29s used by the 509th on Tinian. It was one of ten B-29s built at the Martin Omaha plant as a block 35 B-29 but then given block number 36 to denote the special configuration. It was flown from Omaha to Wendover Army Air Field (UT) in April 1945 by one of the 393rd Bombardment Squadron crews, where it was assigned to airplane commander Ralph N. Devore and crew A-3. Used in training and practice bombing missions at Wendover, it was flown from Wendover to Tinian by Devore and crew A-3, departing Wendover on 11 June 1945.

86. Silverplate B-29 44-272799 (*Next Objective*). (Leon D. Smith)

On Tinian it was first assigned call sign Victor 6, which was later changed to Victor 86. It was named *Next Objective* and nose art was painted on the nose after the atomic bombing missions. In June, July, and August it was used on 12 training and practice bombing missions, and on three combat missions in which pumpkin bombs were dropped on Japanese targets. One other pumpkin mission, on 8 August, was aborted and the bomb returned to Tinian. Listings showing the dates, crews, airplane commanders, and purposes of the missions in which 44-27299 was used on Tinian are included in chapter 3 and Appendix B.

In November 1945 it was flown back to the U.S. and assigned to the 509th Composite Group at Roswell Army Air Field (NM). It was deployed to Tinker Army Air Field (OK) for a short period of time and then assigned to Task Force 1.5 for use in Operation Crossroads. It is not known if 44-27299 actually deployed to the Pacific for the atomic bomb Test Able. In August 1946 it was reassigned to the 509th at Roswell with deployments to Rome Army Air Field (NY) and Mitchel Army Air Field (NY). In April 1949 it was assigned to the 97th Bombardment Group at Biggs Air Force Base (TX).

On 25 May 1949, 44-27299 was being used on a navigation and radar training mission out of Biggs. Shortly after takeoff and while climbing, a fire broke out in the right outboard engine. When the fire could not be extinguished, the crew bailed out. One crew member, the navigator, died when his parachute did not open (believed to be the result of the navigator striking his head on the nose-gear door operating assembly as he exited the aircraft). 44-27299 struck the ground 35 miles northeast of El Paso (TX) and exploded on impact. See chapter 5 for more information on this accident.[14]

Disposition: Dropped from inventory as salvage in July 1949.

B-29-36-MO-44-27300   Delivered to USAAF: 2 Apr 1945   Phase 3

44-27300 was one of the fifteen Silverplate B-29s used by the 509th on Tinian. It was one of ten B-29s built at the Glenn L. Martin Aircraft Plant in Omaha (NE) as a block 35 B-29 but then given block number 36 to denote the special configuration. It was flown from Omaha to Wendover Army Air Field (UT) in April 1945 by one of the 393rd Bombardment Squadron crews, where it was assigned to airplane commander Joseph E. Westover and crew A-4. Used in training and practice bombing missions at Wendover, it was flown from Wendover to Tinian by Westover and crew A-4, departing Wendover on 5 June 1945.

On Tinian it was first assigned call sign Victor 3, which was later changed to Victor 73. It was named *Strange Cargo* and nose art was painted on the nose after the atomic bombing missions. In June, July, and August it was used on 11 training and practice bombing missions, and on four combat missions in which pumpkin bombs were dropped on Japanese targets. It was not involved in either of the atomic bombing missions. Listings showing all of the dates, crews, airplane commanders, and purposes of the 44-27300 missions on Tinian are included in chapter 3 and Appendix B.

In November 1945 it was flown back to the U.S. and assigned to the 509th Composite Group at Roswell Army Air Field (NM). It was deployed to Tinker Army Air

87. Silverplate B-29 44-27300 (*Strange Cargo*). (Leon D. Smith)

Field (OK) for a short period of time and then assigned to Task Force 1.5 in April 1946 for use in Operation Crossroads. It is not known if 44-27300 actually deployed to the Pacific for the atomic bomb Test Able. It was assigned to the 509th at Roswell in August 1946 and was reassigned to the 97th Bombardment Group at Biggs Air Force Base (TX) in June 1949.

44-27300 was assigned to the Sacramento Air Materiel Area at McClellan Air Force Base (CA) in August 1949 where it was modified and redesignated as a WB-29. It was then assigned to the 513th Reconnaissance Squadron at Tinker Air Force Base (OK) in December 1950 and to the 374th Reconnaissance Squadron at McClellan in January 1951. In February 1951 it was assigned to the 57th Strategic Weather Squadron at Hickam Air Force Base (HI) and was used on deployments to Kwajalein Atoll in the Marshall Islands.

In May 1952 it was assigned to the Warner Robins Air Materiel Area at Robins Air Force Base (GA) for further modifications and was then assigned to the 58th Strategic Weather Squadron at Eielson Air Force Base (AK) in September 1952. In August 1954 it was reassigned to the Oklahoma City Air Materiel Area at Tinker and then to the Mobile Air Materiel Area at Nashville (TN) where it was modified and redesignated as a TB-29. In June 1955 it was flown to North Africa for assignment to the 5th Tow Target Squadron at Wheelus Air Base in Libya. Subsequent assignments included the 7280th Maintenance Group at Nouasseur Air Base in Morocco in October 1955, the 3150th Maintenance Group at Nouasseur in January 1956, and the 7235th Support Squadron at Wheelus in March 1956. In July 1957 it was assigned to the 3920th Air Base Group at RAF Brize Norton in the United Kingdom where it is believed to have been involved in an accident.

Disposition: Dropped from inventory as salvage in August 1957.

B-29-36-MO-44-27301   Delivered to USAAF: 2 Apr 1945   Phase 3

44-27301 was one of the fifteen Silverplate B-29s used by the 509th on Tinian. It was one of ten B-29s built at the Glenn L. Martin Aircraft Plant in Omaha (NE) as a block 35 B-29 but then given block number 36 to denote the special configuration. It was flown from Omaha to Wendover Army Air Field (UT) in April 1945 by one of the 393rd Bombardment Squadron crews, where it was assigned to airplane commander Claude R. Eatherly and crew C-11. Used in training and practice bombing missions at Wendover, it was flown from Wendover to Tinian by Eatherly and crew C-11, departing Wendover on 8 June 1945.

On Tinian it was first assigned call sign Victor 5, which was later changed to Victor 85. It was named *Straight Flush* and nose art was applied on the nose after the atomic bombing missions.[15] In June, July, and August it was used on 11 training and

88. Silverplate B-29 44-27301 (*Straight Flush*).

practice bombing missions, and on five combat missions in which pumpkin bombs were dropped on Japanese targets. On the Hiroshima atomic bombing mission on 6 August 1945, it was used by Eatherly and crew C-11 to scout the weather over Hiroshima about one hour before the actual strike. Listings showing the dates, crews, airplane commanders, and purposes of the missions in which 44-27301 was used on Tinian are included in chapter 3 and Appendix B.

In November 1945 it was flown back to the U.S. and assigned to the 509th Composite Group at Roswell Army Air Field (NM). It was deployed to Tinker Army Air Field (OK) for a short period of time and then assigned to Task Force 1.5 in April 1946 for use in Operation Crossroads. It is not known if 44-27301 actually deployed to the Pacific for the atomic bomb Test Able. In August 1946 it was reassigned to the 509th at Roswell with deployments to Rome Army Air Field (NY) and March Army Air Field (CA). In June 1949 it was assigned to the 97th Bombardment Group (later Wing) at Biggs Air Force Base (TX). 44-27301 was assigned to the Oklahoma City Air Materiel Area at Tinker Air Force Base (OK) in April 1950 where it was modified and redesignated as a TB-29.

In April 1953 it was assigned to the 2nd Radar Calibration Squadron at Elmendorf Air Force Base (AK), and then to the 5025th Maintenance Group at Elmendorf in August 1953. In December 1953 it was assigned to the 3040th Aircraft Storage Squadron at Davis-Monthan Air Force Base (AZ) for storage.

Disposition: Dropped from inventory as salvage at Davis-Monthan in July 1954.

89. Silverplate B-29 44-27302 (*Top Secret*). (Leon D. Smith)

B-29-36-MO-44-27302   Delivered to USAAF: 2 Apr 1945   Phase 3

44-27302 was one of the fifteen Silverplate B-29s used by the 509th on Tinian. It was one of ten B-29s built at the Glenn L. Martin Aircraft Plant in Omaha (NE) as a block 35 B-29 but then given block number 36 to denote the special configuration. It was flown from Omaha to Wendover Army Air Field (UT) in April 1945 by one of the 393rd Bombardment Squadron crews, where it was assigned to airplane commander Charles F. McKnight and crew B-8. Used in training and practice bombing missions at Wendover, it was flown from Wendover to Tinian by McKnight and crew B-8, departing Wendover on 5 June 1945.

On Tinian it was first assigned call sign Victor 2, which was later changed to Victor 72. It was named *Top Secret* and nose art was applied on the nose after the atomic bombing missions.[16] In June, July, and August it was used on 13 training and practice bombing missions, and on six combat missions in which pumpkin bombs were dropped on Japanese targets. Listings showing the dates, crews, airplane com-

90. *Top Secret* at Roswell Army Air Field. (Steve Pace)

manders, and purposes of the missions in which 44-27302 was used on Tinian are included in chapter 3 and Appendix B.

In November 1945 it was flown back to the U.S. and assigned to the 509th Composite Group at Roswell Army Air Field (NM). It was deployed to Tinker Army Air Field (OK) for a short period of time and then assigned to Task Force 1.5 in April 1946 for use in Operation Crossroads. It is not known if 44-27302 actually deployed to the Pacific for the atomic bomb Test Able. In August 1946 it was reassigned to the 509th at Roswell with deployments to Clovis Army Air Field (NM) and Rome Army Air Field (NY).

Photographs of 509th aircraft from this time period at Roswell, such as that shown in Photograph 90, indicate that the last four digits of the serial number were painted on the fuselage forward of the wing. It can also be seen in this photograph that nose art renditions were also retained.

In June 1949 it was assigned to the 97th Bombardment Group (later Wing) at Biggs Air Force Base (TX). 44-27302 was assigned to the Oklahoma City Air Materiel Area at Tinker Air Force Base (OK) in April 1950 where it was modified and redesignated as a TB-29.

In March 1953, 44-27302 was assigned to the 2nd Radar Calibration Squadron at Elmendorf Air Force Base (AK); then to the 5025th Maintenance Group at Elmendorf in August 1953. In September 1953 it was assigned to the 3040th Aircraft Storage Squadron at Davis-Monthan for storage.

Disposition: Dropped from inventory as salvage at Davis-Monthan in July 1954.

B-29-36-MO-44-27303   Delivered to USAAF: 3 Apr 1945   Phase 3

44-27303 was one of the fifteen Silverplate B-29s used by the 509th Composite Group on Tinian. It was one of ten B-29s built at the Glenn L. Martin Aircraft Plant in Omaha (NE) as a block 35 B-29 but then given block number 36 to denote the special configuration.

It was flown from Omaha to Wendover Army Air Field (UT) in April 1945 by one of the 393rd Bombardment Squadron crews, where it was assigned to airplane commander John A. Wilson and crew B-6. Used in training and practice bombing missions at Wendover, it was flown from Wendover to Tinian by Wilson and crew B-6, departing Wendover on 5 June 1945.

On Tinian it was first assigned call sign Victor 1, which was later changed to Victor 71. It was named *Jabit III* and nose art may have been applied on the nose sometime after it was flown back to the United States.[17] In June, July, and August it was used on 10 training and practice bombing missions, and on four combat missions in which pumpkin bombs were dropped on Japanese targets. In late–July it was used by Paul Tibbets and a special crew on two missions to drop test models of the Little Boy atomic bomb near Tinian. On the Hiroshima atomic bombing mission on 6 August 1945, it was used by Wilson and crew B-6 to scout the weather over Kokura, one of the alternate targets for that mission. Listings showing the dates, crews, airplane commanders, and purposes of the missions in which 44-27303 was used on Tinian are included in chapter 3 and Appendix B. More information on the Little Boy test drops is included in chapter 4.

91. Silverplate B-29 44-27303 (*Jabit III*) with unidentified crew members. (Air Force Museum)

On 9 August 1945, the same day as the Nagasaki mission, Wilson and crew B-6 departed Tinian in 44-27303, headed for Wendover on a special mission directed by 509th Operations Order number 41. Also flying this mission was 44-86346, manned by crew A-5 with Thomas J. Classen as the airplane commander. The ground crews for both airplanes accompanied the air crews on the mission to Wendover.

Arriving at Wendover on 11 August 1945, 44-27303 and 44-86346 were now positioned to fly to Kirtland Army Air Field on short notice and transport components of the third atomic bomb to Tinian if the need arose. The war with Japan ended shortly after their arrival at Wendover and they were never called upon to complete the transportation mission. Had an unforeseen event not happened, 44-27303 would have been flown to Roswell in November to rejoin the other aircraft of the 509th.

On 29 September 1945 while awaiting the return of the 509th from Tinian, Wilson and crew B-6 flew 44-27303 on a cross-country training mission. In landing at Chicago Municipal Airport (IL) that afternoon, it was involved in an accident that resulted in damage to the aircraft so severe that it was never repaired and flown again.[18]

In October 1945 it was assigned to the 4200th Base Unit at the airport while a disposition decision was being made. See Chapter 5 for more information on this accident.

Disposition: Dropped from inventory as salvage at the Chicago Municipal Airport in April 1946 as a result of the accident.

B-29-36-MO-44-27304   Delivered to USAAF: 3 Apr 1945   Phase 3

44-27304 was one of the fifteen Silverplate B-29s used by the 509th on Tinian. It was one of ten B-29s built at the Glenn L. Martin Aircraft Plant in Omaha (NE) as a block 35 B-29 but then given block number 36 to denote the special configuration. It was flown from Omaha to Wendover Army Air Field (UT) in April 1945 by one of the 393rd Bombardment Squadron crews, where it was assigned to airplane commander George W. Marquardt and crew B-10.

Used in training and practice bombing missions at Wendover, it was flown from Wendover to Tinian by Marquardt and crew B-10, departing Wendover on 11 June 1945. On Tinian it was first assigned call sign Victor 8, which was later changed to Victor 88. It was named *Up an' Atom* and nose art was applied on the nose after the atomic bombing missions.[19] In June, July, and August it was used on nine training and practice bombing missions, and on five combat missions in which pumpkin bombs were dropped on Japanese targets. Listings showing the dates, crews, airplane

92. Silverplate B-29 44-27304 (*Up an' Atom*). (Leon D. Smith)

commanders, and purposes of the missions in which 44-27304 was used on Tinian are shown in chapter 3 and Appendix B.

In November 1945 it was flown back to the U.S. and assigned to the 509th Composite Group at Roswell Army Air Field (NM). It was assigned to Task Force 1.5 in April 1946 for use in Operation Crossroads, and was deployed for short periods of time to Tinker Army Air Field (OK) and Topeka Army Air Field (KS). It is not known if 44-27304 was actually deployed to the Pacific for the atomic bomb Test Able on 1 July 1946. In August 1946 it was reassigned to the 509th at Roswell, with a deployment to Rome Army Air Field (NY).

In August 1949 it was assigned to the 97th Bombardment Group (later Wing) at Biggs Air Force Base (TX). It was assigned to the Oklahoma City Air Materiel Area at Tinker Air Force Base (OK) in April 1950 where it was modified and redesignated as a TB-29.

In October 1951 it was assigned to the 112th Radar Calibration Squadron at Hamilton Air Force Base (CA), and then to the 4th Radar Calibration Squadron at Hamilton in February 1953 and the 4754th Radar Evaluation Flight at Hamilton in March 1954. It was assigned to the Mobile Air Materiel Area facility at Nashville (TN) in March 1955 for modification, and then to the 17th Tow Target Squadron at Yuma County Airport, later Vincent Air Force Base (AZ) in May 1955.

Disposition: Dropped from inventory by transfer to the U.S. Navy in November 1956. 44-27304 was probably flown to the Naval Ordnance Test Station at China Lake (CA) and used as a target for Navy gunnery and bombing training.

B-29-40-MO-44-27353   Delivered to USAAF: 20 Apr 1945   Phase 3

44-27353 was one of the fifteen Silverplate B-29s used by the 509th on Tinian. Built at the Glenn L. Martin Aircraft Plant in Omaha (NE), it was flown from Omaha to Wendover Army Air Field (UT) in May 1945 by a crew from the 393rd Bombardment Squadron. It was assigned to airplane commander Charles D. Albury and crew C-15. Used in training and practice bombing missions at Wendover, it was flown from Wendover to Tinian by Albury and crew C-15, departing Wendover on 22 June 1945.

On Tinian it was first assigned call sign Victor 9, which was later changed to Victor 89. It was named *The Great Artiste* and nose art was applied on the nose after the atomic bombing missions.[20] In July and August 1945 it was used on 12 training and practice bombing missions, and on two combat missions in which pumpkin bombs were dropped on Japanese targets. One other pumpkin mission, on 20 July 1945, was aborted and the pumpkin bomb jettisoned near Iwo Jima. It was used on both atomic bombing missions as the aircraft carrying and dropping instrument packages. Charles W. Sweeney and crew C-15 used it for the Hiroshima mission and Frederick C. Bock and crew C-13 used it for the Nagasaki mission. Listings showing the dates, crews, airplane commanders, and purposes of the missions in which 44-27353 was used on Tinian are shown in chapter 3 and Appendix B.

In November 1945 it was flown back to the U.S. and assigned to the 509th Composite Group at Roswell Army Air Field (NM). It was assigned to Task Force 1.5 in April 1946 for use in Operation Crossroads, and was deployed for a short period of

93. Silverplate B-29 44-27353 (*The Great Artiste*). (Leon D. Smith)

time to Tinker Army Air Field (OK) for modifications. It is not known if 44-27353 was actually deployed to the Pacific for the atomic bomb Test Able on 1 July 1946. In August 1946 it was reassigned to the 509th at Roswell.

In September 1948 it was deployed with several other B-29s of the 509th to Goose Bay Air Base in Labrador for polar navigation training. During a routine navigation training flight on 3 September 1948, an engine problem resulted in the mission being aborted. The Airplane Commander, Artist H. Prichard, made a high approach downwind and touched down half way down the runway. The aircraft was unable to stop and left the runway onto an unfinished runway extension where it ground looped to avoid a tractor. Structural damage to the aircraft at the wing joint was so severe that it was never repaired and never flew again.[21] In September 1948 it was assigned to the 538th Air Base Group at Goose Bay, and in October 1948 was reassigned to the 1227th Air Base Group at Goose Bay. It is interesting to note that almost a year elapsed between the time of the accident and the action to drop the airplane from the inventory.

Disposition: Dropped from inventory at Goose Bay as salvage in September 1949 as a result of the accident.

B-29-40-MO-44-27354   Delivered to USAAF: 20 Apr 1945   Phase 3

44-27354 was one of the fifteen Silverplate B-29s used by the 509th on Tinian. Built at the Glenn L. Martin Aircraft Plant in Omaha (NE), it was flown from Omaha to Wendover Army Air Field (UT) in May 1945 by a crew from the 393rd Bombardment Squadron. It was assigned to airplane commander Thomas J. Classen and crew A-5. Used in training and practice bombing missions at Wendover, it was flown from Wendover to Tinian by Classen and crew A-5, departing Wendover on 19 June 1945.

On Tinian it was first assigned call sign Victor 10, which was later changed to Victor 90. It was named *Big Stink* and nose art was applied on the nose after the atomic bombing missions. In July and August 1945 it was used on 12 training and practice bombing missions, and on two combat missions in which pumpkin bombs were dropped on Japanese targets. On 23 July 1945 it was used in a mission in which a test model Little Boy atomic bomb was dropped near Tinian. Listings showing the dates, crews, airplane commanders, and purposes of the missions in which 44-27354 was used on Tinian are included in chapter 3 and Appendix B.

It was used as the back-up B-29 positioned at Iwo Jima for the Hiroshima atomic bombing mission on 6 August 1945, and was used as the photographic equipment

94. Silverplate B-29 44-27354 (*Big Stink*). (Leon D. Smith)

95. 44-27354 as *Dave's Dream*. *Back row (left to right):* Airplane Commander Major Woodrow Swancutt, Captain William Harrison, Major Harold H. Wood, Captain Paul Chenchar, Jr. *Front row (left to right):* Lt. Robert M. Glenn, Jack W. Cochran, Herbert Lyons, Roland Modlin. Not in the photograph is the electronics test officer flying with the crew, Leon D. Smith. (National Atomic Museum)

B-29 on the Nagasaki atomic bombing mission on 9 August 1945. When 44-86346 was assigned to Classen and crew A-5 for the mission on 9 August 1945 to return to Wendover to be ready to transport components of the third atomic bomb, 44-27354 was reassigned to Herman S. Zahn and crew C-12.

In November 1945 it was flown back to the U.S. and assigned to the 509th Composite Group at Roswell Army Air Field (NM). It was assigned to Task Force 1.5 in April 1946 for use in Operation Crossroads, and was deployed for a short period of time to Tinker Army Air Field (OK) for modifications. In March 1946, prior to its assignment to Task Force 1.5, an event occurred which had a direct effect on 44-27354.

On 7 March, a B-29 (42-65387) assigned to the 428th Base Unit at Kirtland AAF (NM) was being used on a practice bombing mission to the Los Lunas bombing range southwest of Albuquerque. After dropping a Fat Man practice bomb, it disintegrated for unknown reasons and spun into the ground from about 32,000 feet. All ten men on board died, including the bombardier, David Semple. Semple was

96. *Dave's Dream* in Operation Crossroads Markings. (Milford L. Foley)

the bombardier on most of the drop test missions conducted from Wendover and Muroc Army Air Field (CA) in 1944 and was scheduled to be the bombardier on one of the crews being considered for the honor of dropping the atomic bomb on Test Able of Operation Crossroads.

After being assigned to Task Force 1.5, the crew of 44-27354 renamed their airplane *Dave's Dream* in honor of David Semple. After a short deployment to Rome Army Air Field (NY), it deployed to the Pacific and was the B-29 that dropped the Fat Man unit in Test Able of Operation Crossroads on 1 July 1946. The nose art and crew of *Dave's Dream* are shown in Photograph 95. In July 1946, 44-27354 was flown back to Roswell to rejoin the 509th Composite Group.

In June 1949, 44-27354 was reassigned to the 97th Bombardment Group (later Wing) at Biggs Air Force Base (TX). It was assigned to the Oklahoma City Air Materiel Area at Tinker Air Force Base (OK) in April 1950 where it was modified and redesignated as a TB-29.

In October 1952 it was assigned to the 106th Radar Calibration Squadron at Sioux City Air Force Base (IA), and then to the 7th Radar Calibration Squadron at Sioux City in September 1953. It was reassigned to Hill Air Force Base (UT) in December 1953 and to the 4677th Radar Evaluation Flight at Hill in March 1954, with a deployment to Griffiss Air Force Base (NY). In June 1959 it was sent to Davis-Monthan Air Force Base (AZ) and assigned to the Arizona Aircraft Storage Branch for storage.

Disposition: Dropped from inventory at Davis-Monthan in February 1960 as salvage.

B-29-40-MO-44-86263   Delivered to USAAF: 17 May 1945   Phase 5

44-86263 was one of 19 B-29s produced in the regular B-29 configuration and later modified to the Silverplate version a year after the end of World War II when the U.S. atomic strike force was expanded. Produced at the Glenn L. Martin Aircraft Plant in Omaha (NE), it was flown to the Denver Modification Center (CO) in May 1945, and then to the San Antonio Air Depot (TX) in August 1945 and the Oklahoma City Air Depot at Tinker Army Air Field (OK) in October 1945. In November 1945 it was assigned to the 488th Base Unit at Chico Army Air Field (CA), and then in December 1945 to the 4196th Base Unit at Victorville Army Air Field (CA) for storage.

In April 1946 it was removed from storage and flown to McClellan Army Air Field (CA) and assigned to the 4127th Base Unit for modification to the Silverplate configuration in the Sacramento Air Depot facility. In November 1947 it was assigned to the 509th Bomb Group at Roswell (later Walker) Air Force Base (NM). While assigned to the 509th it was deployed to Biggs Air Force Base (TX), and in August 1949 it was assigned to the 97th Bomb Group at Biggs. It was assigned to the Oklahoma City Air Materiel Area at Tinker Air Force Base (OK) in April 1950 where it was modified and redesignated as a TB-29.

In July 1953 it was assigned to the 2nd Radar Calibration Squadron at Elmendorf Air Force Base (AK), and then to the 39th Air Base Wing at Elmendorf in September 1953. It was subsequently assigned to the 5015th Radar Evaluation Flight at Elmendorf and deployed to Yokota Air Base in Japan in October 1954. It was reassigned to the 5040th Consolidated Maintenance Group at Elmendorf in October 1957, and then to the 4713th Radar Evaluation Squadron at Griffiss Air Force Base (NY) in October 1958. In June 1959 it was assigned to the Arizona Aircraft Storage Branch at Davis-Monthan Air Force Base (AZ) for storage.

Disposition: Declared surplus and scrapped at Davis-Monthan in March 1960.

B-29-45-MO-44-86291   Delivered to USAAF: 18 May 1945   Phase 3

44-86291 was one of the fifteen Silverplate B-29s used by the 509th on Tinian. Built at the Glenn L. Martin Aircraft Plant in Omaha (NE), it was flown from Omaha to Wendover Army Air Field (UT) in June 1945 by one of the 393rd Bombardment Squadron crews where it was assigned to airplane commander Norman W. Ray and crew C-14. Used in training and practice bombing missions at Wendover, it was flown from Wendover to Tinian by Ray and crew C-14, departing Wendover on 27 June 1945.

On Tinian it was first assigned call sign Victor 11, which was later changed to Victor 91. It was named *Necessary Evil* and nose art was applied on the nose after the atomic bombing missions.[22] In July and August 1945 it was used on 10 training and practice bombing missions, and on three combat missions in which pumpkin bombs were dropped on Japanese targets. It was used on the Hiroshima atomic bombing mission on 6 August 1945 as the photographic equipment carrier with George W.

97. Silverplate B-29 44-86291 (*Necessary Evil*). (Leon D. Smith)

Marquardt as Airplane Commander with crew B-10. Listings showing the dates, crews, airplane commanders, and purposes of the missions in which 44-86291 was used on Tinian are included in chapter 3 and Appendix B.

In December 1945 it was flown back to the U.S. and assigned to the 509th Composite Group at Roswell Army Air Field (NM). It was assigned to Task Force 1.5 in April 1946 for use in Operation Crossroads, and was deployed for a short period of time to Tinker Army Air Field (OK) for modifications. It is not known if 44-86291 was actually deployed to the Pacific for the atomic bomb Test Able on 1 July 1946. In August 1946 it was reassigned to the 509th at Roswell, where it was used on deployments to Colorado Springs Army Air Field (CO) and Rome Army Air Field (NY). In June 1949 it was assigned to the 97th Bombardment Group (later Wing) at Biggs Air Force Base (TX).

44-86291 was assigned to the Oklahoma City Air Materiel Area at Tinker Air Force Base (OK) in April 1950 where it was modified and redesignated as a TB-29. In September 1952 it was assigned to the 1st Tow Target Squadron at Biggs, and then to the 1st Radar Calibration Squadron at Griffiss Air Force Base (NY) in March 1953. It was assigned to the 4713th Radar Evaluation Flight at Griffiss in March 1954 and then to the Mobile Air Materiel Area facility at Nashville (TN) in March 1955 for additional modifications. In June 1955 it was assigned to the 17th Tow Target

Squadron at the Yuma County Airport (AZ), and then to the 4750th Air Defense Wing at Yuma (later Vincent Air Force Base).

Disposition: Dropped from inventory by transfer to the U.S. Navy in November 1956. It is believed that 44-86291 was flown to the Naval Ordnance Test Station at China Lake (CA) and used as a target for Navy gunnery and bombing training.

B-29-45-MO-44-86292   Delivered to USAAF: 18 May 1945   Phase 3

44-86292 was one of the fifteen Silverplate B-29s used by the 509th on Tinian and is undoubtedly one of the most famous airplanes in aviation history because of its role in the atomic bombing of Hiroshima on 6 August 1945. Built at the Glenn L. Martin Aircraft Plant in Omaha (NE), it was personally selected on the assembly line by Colonel Paul W. Tibbets, the 509th Commanding Officer, on 9 May 1945 as the B-29 he would use when he flew missions.

On 14 June 1945 it was flown from Omaha to Wendover Army Air Field (UT) by airplane commander Robert A. Lewis and crew B-9, to whom it had been assigned. Used in training and practice bombing missions at Wendover, it was flown from Wendover to Tinian by Lewis and crew B-9, departing Wendover on 27 June 1945.

98. Silverplate B-29 44-86292 (*Enola Gay*). (Leon D. Smith)

After a layover on Guam for a bomb bay modification, it arrived on Tinian on 6 July 1945.

On Tinian it was first assigned call sign Victor 12, which was later changed to Victor 82. It was named *Enola Gay* by Colonel Tibbets (his mother's name). On the day before the Hiroshima mission, 5 August 1945, he had the name painted on the nose of the aircraft by Allan L. Karl, an enlisted man assigned to 509th operations.[23]

In July 1945 it was used on eight training and practice bombing missions, and on two combat missions in which pumpkin bombs were dropped on Japanese targets. On 31 July 1945 it was used by Tibbets and a special crew to drop a test model of the Little Boy atomic bomb near Tinian.

On 6 August 1945 it was flown by Tibbets and a special crew to drop the Little Boy atomic bomb on Hiroshima. Although it was generally believed that *Enola Gay* was not used on any combat missions after Hiroshima, the records show that it was used by George W. Marquardt and crew B-10 on the Nagasaki atomic bombing mission on 9 August 1945 to scout the weather over Kokura, the primary target for that mission. In August 1945 after the war had ended, it was used by Lewis and crew B-9 on two additional training missions. Listings showing the dates, crews, airplane commanders, and purposes of the missions in which 44-86292 was used on Tinian are included in chapter 3 and Appendix B.

99. Temporary *Enola Gay* Nose Art. (Robert W. Krauss)

Photograph 99 shows an inscription painted on the right side of the Enola Gay nose shortly after the Hiroshima mission. There are reports that Tibbets was very unhappy with the decoration and had it removed immediately.

On 6 November 1945, Lewis and crew B-9 departed Tinian in 44-86292 for the United States. They arrived at Roswell Army Air Field (NM) on 8 November to rejoin the other B-29s and crews of the 509th. In March 1946 it was assigned to Task Force 1.5 for use in Operation Crossroads and was flown to Kwajalein Island, departing Roswell on 29 April 1946 and arriving on Kwajalein on 1 May.

Tibbets and his crew were not selected to drop the Fat Man unit in Test Able of Operation Crossroads (see 44-27354), and immediately after the test on 1 July 1946 he and his crew departed Kwajalein in 44-86292 for the U.S, arriving at Fairfield-Suisun Army Air Field (CA) on 2 July 1945. 44-86292 was then assigned to the 4105th Base Unit at Davis-Monthan Army Air Field (AZ) on 24 July 1946 in preparation for storage. It was placed in storage at Davis-Monthan and dropped from the U.S. Army Air Forces inventory on 30 August 1946 by virtue of its title being transferred to the Smithsonian Institution.

On 3 July 1949 it was retrieved from storage and flown to Orchard Place Air Field in Park Ridge (IL) by Tibbets and a crew formed for this flight. On landing, it was accepted by the Smithsonian Institution for restoration and display. It was then stored at the field at Park Ridge, which later became the site of O'Hare International Airport. When the City of Chicago decided to build O'Hare airport, the Smithsonian was forced to find another location at which to store 44-86292. On 12 January 1952 it was flown from Park Ridge to Pyote Air Force Base (TX) for temporary storage.

Nearly a year later, on 2 December 1953, it was flown to Andrews Air Force Base (MD) outside Washington, DC, for what was called temporary storage. It remained uncovered and unattended in a remote part of the base for the next six and a half years. On 10 August 1960 Smithsonian personnel began the disassembly of the *Enola*

100. *Enola Gay* in Operation Crossroads Markings. (National Atomic Museum)

Gay in preparation for transfer of the pieces to its storage and restoration facility at Suitland (MD). The components were moved to the Suitland facility on 21 July 1961, where they lay in storage for the next 23 years.

Restoration of 44-86292 at the Paul E. Garber Preservation, Restoration, and Storage Facility in Suitland did not begin until 5 December 1984. On 28 June 1995 the forward section of the fuselage and other pieces of the *Enola Gay* were put on display at the National Air and Space Museum in Washington (DC). The display remained open to the public until 18 May 1998, when the pieces were returned to the Garber facility in Suitland. Restoration of *Enola Gay* has now been completed and it is on display fully assembled at the Steven F. Udvar-Hazy Center adjacent to Dulles Airport outside Washington, D.C.

Disposition: Dropped from USAAF inventory in August 1946 because of its transfer to the Smithsonian Institution.

B-29-50-MO-44-86346   Delivered to USAAF: 15 June 1945   Phase 3

44-86346 was one of the fifteen Silverplate B-29s used by the 509th Composite Group on Tinian. Built at the Glenn L. Martin Aircraft plant in Omaha (NE), it was flown from Omaha to Wendover Army Air Field (UT) in early July 1945 by one of the crews of the 393rd Bombardment Squadron, where it was assigned to airplane commander Herman S. Zahn and crew C-12.

On 27 July 1945, after being used for training and practice bombing missions at Wendover, it was flown by Zahn and crew C-12 from Wendover to Kirtland Army Air Field in Albuquerque (NM) on the first leg of its journey to Tinian. Two other Silverplate B-29s and crews accompanied 44-86346 to Kirtland that day.

One of the other B-29s was 44-86347 from the 393rd Bombardment Squadron, manned by crew A-2 with Edward M. Costello as airplane commander. It, along with Zahn's aircraft, were the last two of the 509th B-29s to move from Wendover to Tinian. The third B-29 in the group was 42-65386 from the 216th Air Base Unit at Wendover, with William Hartshorn as airplane commander. Hartshorn and his B-29 were assigned to the 216th at Wendover to provide test support to the Manhattan Project.

The reason for the B-29s stopping at Kirtland overnight was to load three Fat Man atomic bomb assemblies into their front bomb bays for transport to Tinian. The units loaded carried the designations F-31, F-32, and F-33. None of the assemblies included the plutonium core. Fat Man unit F-31, with arming, fuzing, and firing equipment and the plutonium core added on Tinian, was used for the Nagasaki mission. There are no records as to which Fat Man unit was carried in which B-29 on the trip from Kirtland to Tinian.

44-86346 and the other two B-29s flew from Kirtland to Mather Army Air Field (CA) the next day, 28 July 1945, for overseas preparation and processing. After an overnight stay, the three B-29s departed Mather on 29 July 1945 for the long trip across the Pacific. After refueling and rest stops in Hawaii and Kwajalein, 44-86346 and the other two B-29s arrived on Tinian on 2 August 1945.

After the three Fat Man assemblies were off-loaded, 44-86346 and 44-86347 joined the thirteen Silverplate B-29s of the 509th already in position on Tinian. Hartshorn and his crew departed Tinian to return to Wendover in 44-65386 either the next day or two days later. After joining the 509th on Tinian, 44-86346 was assigned call sign Victor 94. Because of its late arrival on Tinian, it was not used in any training, practice bombing, or pumpkin bombing missions. In addition, it was not given a name and nose art was not applied.

After only a week on Tinian, it was assigned to Thomas J. Classen and crew A-5 and departed Tinian on 9 August 1945, headed for Wendover on a special mission directed by 509th Operations Order number 41. Also flying this mission was 44-27303, manned by crew B-6 with John A. Wilson as airplane commander. The ground crews for both airplanes accompanied the air crews on the mission. Zahn and crew C-12 were then assigned 44-27354, the B-29 formerly used by Classen and crew A-5.

44-86346 was flown from Wendover to Roswell Army Air Field in November 1945 at about the same time that the 13 Silverplate B-29s remaining on Tinian were flown to Roswell, the new home of the 509th. At Roswell, it was given the nickname *Luke the Spook*.

In April 1946 it was deployed to Tinker Army Air Field (OK) for a short period of time and then assigned to Task Force 1.5 for use in the Operation Crossroads

101. Silverplate B-29 44-86346 as *Luke the Spook*. (Steve Pace)

atomic bomb tests at Bikini Atoll. It is not known if 44-86346 actually participated in atomic bomb Test Able on 1 July 1946. In August 1946 it was reassigned to the 509th (now a Bombardment Group) at Roswell, with deployments to Rome Army Air Field (NY) and Davis-Monthan Army Air Field (AZ).

In June 1949 it was assigned to the 97th Bombardment Group (later a Wing) at Biggs Air Force Base (TX). It was then assigned to the Oklahoma City Air Materiel Area at Tinker Air Force Base (OK) via Kelly Air Force Base (TX) in April 1950 where it underwent modification and was redesignated as a TB-29.

Subsequent assignments for 44-86346 included the 10th Radar Calibration Squadron at Yokota Air Base in Japan in August 1952 and the 6023rd Radar Evaluation Flight at Yokota AB in March 1954. It was then assigned to Johnson AB in Japan in May 1957, with deployments to Hickam Air Force Base (HI) and Itazuke AB in Japan. In November 1958 it was reassigned to Naha AB on Okinawa, with an assignment to the 6431st Air Base Group at Naha in December 1959. In July 1960 it was assigned to the 51st Air Base Group at Naha.

Disposition: Dropped from inventory at Naha as surplus in July 1960 (scrapped).

B-29-50-MO-44-86347   Delivered to USAAF: 15 June 1945   Phase 3

44-86347 was one of the fifteen Silverplate B-29s used by the 509th Composite Group on Tinian. Built at the Glenn L. Martin Aircraft plant in Omaha (NE), it was flown from Omaha to Wendover Army Air Field (UT) in early July 1945 by one of the crews of the 393rd Bombardment Squadron, where it was assigned to airplane commander Edward M. Costello and crew A-2.

On 27 July 1945, after being used for training and practice bombing missions at Wendover, it was flown by Costello and crew A-2 from Wendover to Kirtland Army Air Field in Albuquerque (NM) on the first leg of its journey to Tinian. Two other Silverplate B-29s and crews accompanied 44-86347 on the flight to Kirtland that day. One of the other aircraft was 44-86346 from the 393rd Bombardment Squadron, manned by crew C-12 with Herman S. Zahn as airplane commander. It and Costello's B-29 were the last two of the 509th B-29s to move from Wendover to Tinian. The third B-29 in the group was 42-65386 from the 216th Air Base Unit at Wendover, with William Hartshorn as airplane commander. Hartshorn and his B-29 were assigned to the 216th at Wendover to provide test support to the Manhattan Project.

The reason for the B-29s stopping at Kirtland overnight was to load three Fat Man atomic bomb assemblies into their front bomb bays for transport to Tinian. The units loaded carried the designations F-31, F-32, and F-33. None of the assemblies included the plutonium core. Fat Man unit F-31, with arming, fuzing, and firing equipment and the plutonium core added on Tinian, was used for the Nagasaki mission. There are no records to indicate which Fat Man unit was carried in which B-29 on the trip from Kirtland to Tinian.

44-86347 and the other two B-29s flew from Kirtland to Mather Army Air Field (CA) the next day, 28 July 1945, for overseas preparation and processing. After an overnight stay, the three B-29s departed Mather on 29 July 1945 for the trip across the Pacific.

102. Silverplate B-29 44-86347 Laggin' Dragon. (Steve Pace)

On take-off from Mather, 44-86347 was involved in an incident which almost ended in disaster for Costello and crew A-2. Shortly after liftoff from the runway at Mather, a door covering the life raft compartment popped open and the life raft ejected. The raft wrapped around the horizontal stabilizer and made the B-29 extremely difficult to control. After nearly crashing into the ocean, Costello and his co-pilot, Harry B. Davis, were able to recover control of the aircraft and return to Mather for a safe landing. The bombardier on the crew, John L. Downey, has stated that disaster was averted only through the extreme physical effort of Costello and Davis in regaining control of the aircraft. After repairs, 44-86347 departed Mather a short time later and was able to join up with the other two B-29s in Hawaii.

After refueling and rest stops in Hawaii and Kwajalein, it and the other two B-29s arrived on Tinian on 2 August 1945. After the three Fat Man assemblies were off-loaded, 44-86347 and 44-86346 joined the thirteen Silverplate B-29s of the 509th already in position on Tinian. Hartshorn and his crew departed Tinian either the next day or two days later to return to Wendover in 44-65386.

Upon joining the 509th on Tinian, 44-86347 was assigned call sign Victor 95. It was named *Laggin' Dragon* and nose art was applied after the atomic bombing missions.[24] On the Nagasaki atomic bombing mission on 9 August 1945, it was used by Charles F. McKnight and crew B-8 to scout the weather over Nagasaki. In August 1945 after the war had ended, it was used by Costello and crew A-2 on two training missions. Listings showing the dates, crews, airplane commanders, and purposes of the missions in which it was used on Tinian are included in chapter 3 and Appendix B.

In November 1945 it was flown back to the U.S. and assigned to the 509th Composite Group at Roswell Army Air Field (NM). It was assigned to Task Force 1.5 in April 1946 for use in Operation Crossroads, and was deployed for a short period of time to Tinker Army Air Field (OK) for modifications. The records indicate that 44-86347 was deployed to the Pacific for the atomic bomb Test Able on 1 July 1946, although it not known for what purpose it might have been used. In August 1946 it was reassigned to the 509th at Roswell, where it was used on a deployment to Rome Army Air Field (NY). In August 1949 it was assigned to the 97th Bombardment Group (later Wing) at Biggs Air Force Base (TX).

44-86347 was assigned to the Oklahoma City Air Materiel Area at Tinker Air Force Base (OK) in April 1950 via Kelly Air Force Base (TX) where it was modified and redesignated as a TB-29. It was then assigned to the 10th Radar Calibration Squadron at Yokota Air Base in Japan in September 1952, and then to the 6023rd Radar Evaluation flight at Yokota in March 1954. In July 1956 it was reassigned to Johnson AB in Japan and then in July 1958 to Naha AB on Okinawa. It was assigned to the 6431st Air Base Group at Naha, and then to the 51st Air Base Group at Naha in July 1960.

Disposition: Dropped from inventory at Naha as surplus in July 1960 (scrapped).

B-29-55-MO-44-86382   Delivered to USAAF: 26 July 1945   Phase 4

44-86382 was one of the last eight B-29s produced in the Silverplate configuration at the Glenn L. Martin Aircraft Plant in Omaha (NE). It was flown to Wendover Army Air Field (UT) in August 1945 and assigned to the 509th Composite Group to serve as a reserve aircraft in case the 509th on Tinian needed a replacement B-29.

It remained at Wendover until it was flown to Roswell Army Air Field (NM) after the war with Japan ended. It was used at Wendover on training and practice missions by crews of the 509th that did not deploy to Tinian and by crews of the 216th Base Unit in support of the Manhattan Project drop test program.

It was flown to Roswell in November 1945 and then deployed to the 4136th Base Unit at Tinker Army Air Field (OK) in February 1946 for modifications. In March 1946 it was assigned to Task Force 1.5 for use in Operation Crossroads and was flown to the Pacific in June 1946 for use in the atomic bomb Test Able on 1 July 1946. It is not known for what purpose it was used in Operation Crossroads.

In August 1946 it was reassigned to the 509th at Roswell where it was used in a deployment to Rome Army Air Field (NY). It was involved in a minor landing accident at Mitchel Army Air Field (NY) on 18 April 1947 and sustained some damage. The damage was repaired and 44-86382 was returned to full operational status.

It was assigned to the 97th Bomb Group at Walker Air Force Base (formerly Roswell) in June 1949 and then moved to the 97th at Biggs Air Force Base (TX) in July 1949. In April 1950 it was assigned to the San Antonio Air Materiel Area at Kelly Air Force Base (TX) and was deployed to Tinker Air Force Base (OK) where it was modified and redesignated as a TB-29. It was then assigned to the 106th Radar Calibration Squadron at Sioux City Air Force Base (IA) in October 1952, and then to the 7th Radar Calibration Squadron at Sioux City in October 1953.

On 18 December 1953, 44-86382 was involved in a landing accident at Ogden Municipal Airport (UT) in which the aircraft was almost totally destroyed by fire. The Aircraft Accident Report shows that the pilot and co-pilot mistook the Ogden airport runway for a runway at nearby Hill Air Force Base, and with a much shorter runway at the Ogden airport and excess landing speed they could not get the B-29 stopped in time. The aircraft ran off the end of the runway, crossed a deep ditch and a 10-foot wide canal, bounced over a highway, and came to a stop in several pieces 527 feet from the end of the runway. Fire broke out immediately. There was one fatality and two other members of the crew suffered injuries.[25] See chapter 5 for more information on this accident.

Disposition: Removed from inventory at Hill in December 1953 as lost to crash.

B-29-55-MO-44-86383   Delivered to USAAF: 30 July 1945   Phase 4

44-86383 was one of the last eight B-29s produced in the Silverplate configuration at the Glenn L. Martin Aircraft Plant in Omaha (NE). It was flown to Wendover Army Air Field (UT) in August 1945 and assigned to the 509th Composite Group to serve as a reserve aircraft in case the 509th on Tinian needed a replacement B-29.

It remained at Wendover until it was flown to Roswell Army Air Field (NM) after the war with Japan ended. It was used at Wendover on training and practice bombing missions by crews of the 509th that did not deploy to Tinian and by crews of the 216th Base Unit in support of the Manhattan Project drop test program.

It was flown to Roswell in November 1945 and then deployed to the 4136th Base Unit at Tinker Army Air Field (OK) in February 1946 for modifications. In March 1946 it was assigned to Task Force 1.5 for use in Operation Crossroads and was flown to the Pacific in June 1946 for use in the atomic bomb Test Able on 1 July 1946. It is not known for what purpose it was used in Operation Crossroads. In August 1946 it was reassigned to the 509th at Roswell where it was used in a deployment to Rome Army Air Field (NY).

On 12 August 1948, as part of a group of 509th B-29s deploying to Goose Bay Air Base in Labrador, 44-86383 departed Roswell with 21 crew members and passengers on board. Immediately after liftoff from the runway it lost altitude and impacted the ground. It bounced back into the air and then crashed six tenths of a mile from the point of first contact with the ground. The aircraft disintegrated and burned. The Aircraft Accident Report indicates that there were seven fatalities and major injuries to other members of the crew and to the passengers.[26] See chapter 5 for more information on this accident.

Disposition: Removed from inventory at Roswell in August 1948 as lost to crash.

103. Silverplate B-29 44-86383 Near Kwajalein. (Milford L. Foley)

B-29-55-MO-44-86384   Delivered to USAAF: 27 July 1945   Phase 4

44-86384 was one of the last eight B-29s produced in the Silverplate configuration at the Glenn L. Martin Aircraft Plant in Omaha (NE). It was flown to Wendover Army Air Field (UT) in August 1945 and assigned to the 509th Composite Group to serve as a reserve aircraft in case the 509th on Tinian needed a replacement B-29. It remained at Wendover until it was flown to Roswell Army Air Field (NM) after the war with Japan ended. It was used at Wendover on training and practice bombing missions by crews of the 509th that did not deploy to Tinian and by crews of the 216th Base Unit in support of the Manhattan Project drop test program.

44-86384 was flown to Roswell in November 1945 and then deployed to the 4136th Base Unit at Tinker Army Air Field (OK) in February 1946 for modifications. In March 1946 it was assigned to Task Force 1.5 for use in Operation Crossroads and was flown to the Pacific in June 1946 for use in the atomic bomb Test Able on 1 July 1946. It is not known for what purpose it was used in Operation Crossroads. In August 1946 it was reassigned to the 509th at Roswell where it was used in a deployment to Rome Army Air Field (NY). 44-86384 was assigned to the 97th Bomb Group at Biggs Air Force Base (TX) in June 1949.

In April 1950 it was assigned to the Oklahoma City Air Materiel Area where it was modified and redesignated as a TB-29. It was then assigned to the Boeing factory in Seattle (WA) in April 1951 where it was converted into a tanker version and redesignated as a KB-29. It was then assigned back to the 509th Bomb Wing at Walker (formerly Roswell) Air Force Base (NM) and was used in deployments to RAF Upper Heyford and RAF Burtonwood in the United Kingdom and to Hawaii. In July 1954 it was assigned to the 407th Strategic Fighter Wing at Malmstrom Air Force Base (MT) and was deployed to Elmendorf Air Force Base (AK). It was assigned to the Oklahoma City Air Materiel Area at Tinker Air Force Base (OK) in June 1957.

Disposition: Removed from inventory at Tinker as surplus in July 1957 (scrapped).

B-29-55-MO-44-86394   Delivered to USAAF: 24 July 1945   Phase 5

44-86394 was one of 19 B-29s produced in the regular B-29 configuration and later modified to the Silverplate version a year after the end of World War II when the U.S. atomic strike force was expanded. Produced at the Glenn L. Martin Aircraft Plant in Omaha (NE), it was flown to March Army Air Field (CA) in July 1945 where it was assigned to the 420th Base Unit. In November 1945 it was assigned to the 4196th Base Unit at Victorville Army Air Field (CA) for storage.

Removed from storage in August 1946, it was assigned to the 4127th Base Unit of the Air Depot at McClellan Army Air Field (CA) for conversion to the Silverplate configuration. After completion of the modifications, it was assigned to the 509th Bomb Group at Roswell Air Force Base (NM) in December 1947 and then deployed to Davis-Monthan Air Force Base (AZ) for a period of time. It was reassigned to the 97th Bomb Group at Biggs Air Force Base (TX) in July 1949.

In April 1950 it was assigned to the Oklahoma City Air Materiel Area at Tinker Air Force Base (OK) where it was modified and redesignated as a TB-29. 44-86394 was then assigned to the 3510th Basic Pilot Training Wing at Randolph Air Force Base (TX) in September 1950, and then to the 3510th Combat Crew Training Wing at Randolph in March 1952. In March 1956 it was reassigned to the Oklahoma City Air Materiel Area at Tinker.

Disposition: Removed from inventory at Tinker as surplus in July 1956 (scrapped).

B-29-55-MO-44-86401   Delivered to USAAF: 30 July 1945   Phase 5

44-86401 was one of 19 B-29s produced in the regular B-29 configuration and later modified to the Silverplate version a year after the end of World War II when the U.S. atomic strike force was expanded. Produced at the Glenn L. Martin Aircraft Plant in Omaha (NE), it was flown to Topeka Army Air Field (KS) in August 1945. In November 1945 it was assigned to the San Antonio Air Materiel Area at Kelly Army Air Field (TX), and then to the 4105th Base Unit at Davis-Monthan Army Air Field (AZ) for storage in December 1945.

Removed from storage in July 1946, it was assigned to the 4127th Base Unit of the Air Depot at McClellan Army Air Field (CA) for conversion to the Silverplate configuration. After completion of the modifications, it was assigned to the 509th Bomb Group at Roswell Army Air Field (NM) in March 1947 with a deployment to

104. Silverplate B-29 44-86401 in 1947. (Milford L. Foley)

Biggs Army Air Field (TX). It was reassigned to the 97th Bomb Group at Biggs Air Force Base in August 1949. In April 1950 it was assigned to the Oklahoma City Air Materiel Area at Tinker Air Force Base (OK) where it was modified and redesignated as a TB-29. It was then assigned to the Boeing factory in Seattle (WA) where it was again modified and redesignated as a KB-29.

In August 1951 it was reassigned to the 509th Bomb Wing at Walker (formerly Roswell) Air Force Base (NM), with deployments to RAF Upper Heyford in the United Kingdom and to Andersen Air Base on Guam. In April 1954 it was assigned to the 407th Strategic Fighter Wing at Malmstrom Air Force Base (MT), and then to the 429th Air Refueling Squadron at Langley Air Force Base (VA) in September 1954. In this last assignment, it was used on deployments to Goose AB in Labrador, Larson AFB (GA), Ernest Harmon AB in Newfoundland, and Aviano AB in Italy.

Disposition: Removed from inventory in September 1956 by transfer to the U.S. Army, probably for use at the Aberdeen Army Proving Ground (MD) for tests.

B-29-60-MO-44-86430   Delivered to USAAF: 27 August 1945   Phase 4

44-86430 was one of the last eight B-29s produced in the Silverplate configuration at the Glenn L. Martin Aircraft Plant in Omaha (NE). It was flown from Omaha to the 4000th Base Unit at Wright Army Air Field (OH) for modifications in August

105. Silverplate B-29 44-86430 at Roswell Army Air Field. (Milford L. Foley)

1945, and then to Wendover Army Air Field (UT) in October 1945. At Wendover, it was briefly assigned to the 216th Base Unit before being reassigned to the 509th Composite Group at Roswell Army Air Field (NM) in November 1945.

In March 1946 it was assigned to Task Force 1.5 for use in Operation Crossroads and was flown to the Pacific in June 1946 for use in the atomic bomb Test Able on 1 July 1946. In August 1946 it was reassigned to the 509th at Roswell where it was used in deployments to McClellan Army Air Field (CA), Rome Army Air Field (NY), and Biggs Army Air Field (TX).

It was assigned to the 97th Bomb Group at Biggs Air Force Base in June 1949. In April 1950 it was assigned to the Oklahoma City Air Materiel Area at Tinker Air Force Base (OK) where it underwent modification and was redesignated as a TB-29.

It was assigned to the 10th Radar Calibration Squadron at Yokota Air Base in Japan in September 1952, and to the 6023rd Radar Evaluation Flight at Yokota in March 1954. In July 1956 it was reassigned to Johnson Air Base in Japan, and then to the 3rd Tactical Bomb Wing at Johnson in April 1958.

Disposition: Removed from inventory at Johnson as surplus in October 1958 (scrapped).

B-29-60-MO-44-86431   Delivered to USAAF: 28 August 1945   Phase 4

44-86431 was one of the last eight B-29s produced in the Silverplate configuration at the Glenn L. Martin Aircraft Plant in Omaha (NE). It was flown to Wendover Army Air Field (UT) in August 1945 and assigned to the 509th Composite Group to serve as a reserve aircraft in case the 509th on Tinian needed a replacement B-29. It remained at Wendover until it was flown to Roswell Army Air Field (NM) after the war with Japan ended. It was used at Wendover on training and practice bombing missions by crews of the 509th that did not deploy to Tinian and by crews of the 216th Base Unit in support of the Manhattan Project drop test program.

It was flown to Roswell in November 1945 and then deployed to the 4136th Base Unit at Tinker Army Air Field (OK) in January 1946 for modifications. While no Accident Report has been found, it is believed that 44-86431 was involved in an accident at Tinker AAF that resulted in major damage to the aircraft.

Disposition: Removed from inventory at Tinker in August 1947 as surplus.

B-29-60-MO-44-86432   Delivered to USAAF: 30 August 1945   Phase 4

44-86432 was one of the last eight B-29s produced in the Silverplate configuration at the Glenn L. Martin Aircraft Plant in Omaha (NE). It was flown from Omaha to the 4000th Base Unit at Wright Army Air Field (OH) for modifications in August 1945, and then to Wendover Army Air Field (UT) in October 1945. It was assigned to the 216th Base Unit at Wendover for use in support of Manhattan Project bomb drop tests.

In November 1945 it was assigned to the 509th Composite Group at Roswell Army Air Field (NM). In March 1946 it was assigned to Task Force 1.5 for use in Operation Crossroads, but was deployed to Tinker Army Air Field (OK) and Robins Army Air Field (GA) without being used in the Pacific for atomic bomb Test Able. In August 1946 it was reassigned to the 509th Bomb Group at Roswell. In March 1949 it was assigned to the 97th Bomb Wing at Biggs Air Force Base (TX).

In April 1950 it was assigned to the Oklahoma City Air Materiel Area at Tinker Air Force Base (OK) where it was modified and redesignated as a TB-29. It was then assigned to the 2nd Radar Calibration Flight at Elmendorf Air Force Base (AK) in March 1953. In September 1954 it was assigned to the 5039th Air Base Wing at Elmendorf, and then to the 5015th Radar Evaluation Flight at Elmendorf in October 1954. In August 1955 it was reassigned to the Oklahoma City Air Materiel Area at Tinker.

Disposition: Removed from inventory at Tinker as surplus in October 1955 (scrapped).

B-29-60-MO-44-86437   Delivered to USAAF: 24 August 1945   Phase 5

44-86437 was one of 19 B-29s produced in the regular B-29 configuration and later modified to the Silverplate version a year after the end of World War II when the U.S. atomic strike force was expanded. Produced at the Glenn L. Martin Aircraft Plant in Omaha (NE), it was flown to the Oklahoma City Air Depot at Tinker Army Air Field (OK) in August 1945. It was then reassigned to the San Antonio Air Technical Service Center at Kelly Army Air Field (TX) in October 1945.

In November 1945 it was assigned to the 4105th Base Unit at Davis-Monthan Army Air Field (AZ) for storage. Removed from storage in July 1946, it was assigned to the 4127th Base Unit at McClellan Army Air Field (CA) for conversion to the Silverplate configuration. After completion of the modifications, it was assigned to the 509th Bomb Group at Roswell Army Air Field (NM) in May 1947. After a deployment to Biggs Air Force Base (TX), it was assigned to the 97th Bomb Wing at Biggs in June 1949.

In May 1950 it was assigned to the Oklahoma City Air Materiel Area at Tinker Air Force Base (OK) where it was modified and redesignated as a TB-29. It was then assigned to the 3510th Basic Pilot Training Wing at Randolph Air Force Base (TX) in October 1950, and then to the 3510th Combat Crew Training Wing at Randolph in March 1952.

Disposition: Dropped from inventory by transfer to the U.S. Navy in June 1957. It was probably flown to the Naval Ordnance Test Station at China Lake (CA) and used as a ground target for Navy gunnery and bombing training.

B-29-60-MO-44-86439   Delivered to USAAF: 24 August 1945   Phase 5

44-86439 was one of 19 B-29s produced in the regular B-29 configuration and later modified to the Silverplate version a year after the end of World War II when the U.S. atomic strike force was expanded.

Produced at the Glenn L. Martin Aircraft Plant in Omaha (NE), it was flown to the Oklahoma City Air Depot at Tinker Army Air Field (OK) in August 1945. It was then reassigned to the San Antonio Air Technical Service Center at Kelly Army Air Field (TX) in September 1945.

In October 1945 it was assigned to the 488th Base Unit at Chico Army Air Field (CA), and then to the 4196th Base Unit at Victorville Army Air Field (CA) for storage in November 1945. It was removed from storage in June 1946 and assigned to the

106. Formation of Silverplate B-29's Near Roswell Army Air Field. (Milford L. Foley)

4127th Base Unit of the Air Depot at McClellan Army Air Field (CA) for conversion to the Silverplate configuration. After completion of the modifications, it was assigned to the 509th Bomb Group at Roswell Army Air Field (NM) in January 1947. It was deployed to Biggs Army Air Field (TX) for a period of time and was then assigned to the 97th Bomb Group at Biggs in August 1949.

In April 1950, 44-86439 was assigned to the Oklahoma City Air Materiel Area at Tinker Air Force Base (OK) where it was modified and redesignated as a TB-29. It was then assigned to the 105th Radar Calibration Flight at Greenville Air Force Base (SC) in May 1950. 44-86439 moved with the unit to Laon AB in France in July 1952.

Subsequent assignments included Neubiberg AB in Germany in October 1952, Furstenfeldbruck AB in Germany in December 1952, Sidi Silimane AB and Nouasseur AB in Morocco in February 1953, and back to Furstenfeldbruck AB in April 1953. It was assigned to RAF Upper Heyford in the United Kingdom in October 1953, and then flown back to the U.S. for assignment to the 3040th Aircraft Storage Squadron at Davis-Monthan Air Force Base (AZ) for storage in February 1954.

Six Silverplate B-29s can be seen in Photograph 106. 44-86439 is at the upper left, 44-86430 is at the upper right, and 44-27302 is at the lower center of the photograph.

Disposition: 44-86439 was declared surplus and scrapped at Davis-Monthan in May 1954.

B-29-60-MO-44-86440   Delivered to USAAF: 28 August 1945   Phase 5

44-86440 was one of 19 B-29s produced in the regular B-29 configuration and later modified to the Silverplate version a year after the end of World War II when

107. Silverplate B-29 44-86440 Over New Mexico. (Milford L. Foley)

the U.S. atomic strike force was expanded. Produced at the Glenn L. Martin Aircraft Plant in Omaha (NE), it was flown to the San Antonio Air Technical Service Center at Kelly Army Air Field (TX) in September 1945.

It was then assigned to the 488th Base Unit at Chico Army Air Field (CA) in October 1945, and to the 4196th Base Unit at Victorville Army Air Field (CA) for storage in November 1945. It was removed from storage in May 1946 and assigned to the 4127th Base Unit of the Air Depot at McClellan Army Air Field (CA) for conversion to the Silverplate configuration. After completion of the modifications, it was assigned to the 509th Composite Group at Roswell Army Air Field (NM) in January 1947.

After a deployment to Davis-Monthan Air Force Base (AZ) for a short period of time, it was assigned to the 97th Bomb Group at Biggs Air Force Base (TX) in July 1949. In April 1950 it was assigned to the Oklahoma City Air Materiel Area at Tinker Air Force Base (OK) where it was modified and redesignated as a TB-29. 44-86440 was then assigned to the 3510th Basic Pilot Training Wing at Randolph Air Force Base (TX) in September 1950, and then to the 3510th Combat Crew Training Wing at Randolph in March 1952. In October 1956 it was assigned to the Air Research and Development Command for testing at Aberdeen Proving Ground (MD).

Disposition: Removed from inventory in October 1956 after being tested to destruction at Aberdeen Proving Ground.

B-29-60-MO-44-86443   Delivered to USAAF: 30 August 1945   Phase 5

44-86443 was one of 19 B-29s produced in the regular B-29 configuration and later modified to the Silverplate version a year after the end of World War II when the U.S. atomic strike force was expanded. Produced at the Glenn L. Martin Aircraft Plant in Omaha (NE), it was first flown to the Oklahoma City Air Depot (OK) in August 1945 and then to the San Antonio Air Technical Services Center at Kelly Army Air Field (TX) in September 1945. Assigned to the 488th Base Unit at Chico Army Air Field (CA) in October 1945, it was then flown to the 4196th Base Unit at Victorville Army Air Field (CA) for storage in November 1945.

Removed from storage in July 1946, 44-86443 was assigned to the 4117th Base Unit at Robins Army Air Field (GA) and then immediately reassigned to the 4127th Base Unit of the Air Depot at McClellan Army Air Field (CA) in August 1946 for conversion to the Silverplate configuration. After modification, it was assigned to the 509th Composite Group at Roswell (later Walker) Air Force Base (NM) in December 1947. In August 1949 it was assigned to the 97th Bomb Group at Biggs Air Force Base (TX).

44-86443 was assigned to the Oklahoma City Air Materiel Area at Tinker Air Force Base (OK) in April 1950 where it was modified and redesignated as a TB-29. It was then assigned to the 104th Radar Calibration Flight at Sewart Air Force Base (NY) in July 1952. It then began duty overseas when the unit moved to Sidi Silimane Air Base in Morocco and Wiesbaden Air Base in Germany in September 1952. It was reassigned to the 15th Radar Calibration Flight at Wiesbaden Air Base in October 1952 and moved with the unit to Furstenfeldbruck Air Base in Germany in December 1952.

Subsequent assignments included the 7366th Radar Evaluation Squadron at Furstenfeldbrook in June 1954 (including deployments to Keflavik Airport in Iceland and Rhein Main Air Base in Germany), the 36th Fighter-Day Wing at Bitburg Air Base in Germany in October 1957, and the 36th Tactical Fighter Wing at Bitburg in July 1958.

Disposition: The notation on the Aircraft Record Card indicates that 44-86443 was dropped from inventory at Bitburg by transfer to an unidentified school.[27]

B-29-60-MO-44-86444   Delivered to USAAF: 29 August 1945   Phase 5

44-86444 was one of 19 B-29s produced in the regular B-29 configuration and later modified to the Silverplate version a year after the end of World War II when the U.S. atomic strike force was expanded. Produced at the Glenn L. Martin Aircraft Plant in Omaha (NE), it was flown to the San Antonio Air Technical Services Center at Kelly Army Air Field (TX) in September 1945. It was then assigned to the 488th Base Unit at Chico Army Air Field (CA) in October 1945, and then to the 4196th Base Unit at Victorville Army Air Field (CA) for storage in November 1945.

It was removed from storage in April 1946 and assigned to the 4117th Base Unit at Robins Army Air Field (GA), but was reassigned in August 1946 to the 4127th Base Unit of the Air Depot at McClellan Army Air Field (CA) for conversion to the Silverplate configuration. After completion of the modifications, it was assigned to the 428th Base Unit at Kirtland Army Air Field (NM) in June 1947. It was used in atomic bomb testing programs of both the Army Air Forces (later U.S. Air Force and Department of Defense) and the Manhattan Project (later the Atomic Energy Commission).

In January 1949 it was assigned to the 2758th Air Base Group at Kirtland and redesignated as an EB-29. It was assigned to the Sacramento Air Materiel Area at McClellan in April 1949 for modifications, and then back to the 3078th Air Base Group at Kirtland in July 1949. It was assigned to the 4925th Special Weapons Wing at Kirtland in December 1949. In April 1950 it was assigned to the Oklahoma City Air Materiel Area at Tinker AFB (OK) where it was modified and redesignated as a TB-29.

In September 1950 it was assigned to the 3510th Basic Pilot Training Wing at Randolph Air Force Base (TX), and then to the 3510th Combat Crew Training Wing at Randolph with deployments to Yuma Air Force Base (AZ) and Amarillo Air Force Base (TX). In April 1956 it was assigned to the Oklahoma City Air Materiel Area at Tinker Air Force Base (OK).

Disposition: Removed from inventory as surplus at Tinker in July 1956 (scrapped).

B-29-60-MO-44-86445   Delivered to USAAF: 29 August 1945   Phase 5

44-86445 was one of 19 B-29s produced in the regular B-29 configuration and later modified to the Silverplate version a year after the end of World War II when the U.S. atomic strike force was expanded. Produced at the Glenn L. Martin Aircraft Plant in Omaha (NE), it was flown to the San Antonio Air Technical Services Center at Kelly Army Air Field (TX) in October 1945. It was then assigned to the 488th Base Unit at Chico Army Air Field (CA) in November 1945, and then immediately thereafter to the 4196th Base Unit at Victorville Army Air Field (CA) for storage.

It was removed from storage in July 1946 and assigned to the 4117th Base Unit at Robins Army Air Field (GA), but was immediately reassigned in August 1946 to the 4127th Base Unit of the Air Depot at McClellan Army Air Field (CA) for conversion to the Silverplate configuration. After completion of the modifications, it was assigned to the 509th Bomb Group at Roswell Army Air Field (NM) in July 1947 for operational use. After a deployment to Davis-Monthan Army Air Field (AZ), it was assigned to the 97th Bomb Group at Biggs Air Force Base (TX) in April 1949.

In May 1950, 44-86445 was reassigned to the Oklahoma City Air Materiel Area at Tinker Air Force Base (OK) where it was modified and redesignated as a TB-29. In September 1950 it was assigned to the 3510th Basic Pilot Training Wing at Randolph Air Force Base (TX), and then in March 1952 it was assigned to the 3510th Combat Crew Training Wing at Randolph.

Disposition: Removed from inventory in October 1956 by transfer to the U.S. Army. It was probably flown to the Army Aberdeen Proving Ground (MD) for tests that resulted in its destruction.

B-29-60-MO-44-86447   Delivered to USAAF: 10 September 1945   Phase 5

44-86447 was one of 19 B-29s produced in the regular B-29 configuration and later modified to the Silverplate version a year after the end of World War II when the U.S. atomic strike force was expanded. Produced at the Glenn L. Martin Aircraft Plant in Omaha (NE), it was flown to the 488th Base Unit at Chico Army Air Field (CA) in October 1945, and then to the 4196th Base Unit at Victorville Army Air Field (CA) in November 1945 for storage.

In April 1946 it was removed from storage and assigned to the 4117th Base Unit at Robins Army Air Field (GA), but was reassigned in August 1946 to the 4127th Base Unit of the Air Depot at McClellan Army Air Field (CA) for conversion to the Silverplate configuration. After completion of the modifications, it was assigned to the 428th Base Unit at Kirtland Army Air Field (NM) in June 1947. It was used in atomic bomb testing programs of both the Army Air Forces (later U.S. Air Force and Department of Defense) and the Manhattan Project (later the Atomic Energy Commission).

In January 1949 it was assigned to the 2758th Air Base Group at Kirtland and redesignated as an EB-29. It was assigned to the 3078th Air Base Group at Kirtland in July 1949, and to the 4925th Special Weapons Wing at Kirtland in December 1949. In April 1950 it was assigned to the Oklahoma City Air Materiel Area at Tinker Air Force Base (OK) where it was modified and redesignated as a TB-29. In September 1950 it was assigned to the 3510th Basic Pilot Training Wing at Randolph Air Force Base (TX), and then to the 3510th Combat Crew Training Wing at Randolph in March 1952.

Disposition: Declared surplus at Randolph in November 1955 and scrapped.

B-29-60-MO-44-86448   Delivered to USAAF: 31 August 1945   Phase 5

44-86448 was one of 19 B-29s produced in the regular B-29 configuration and later modified to the Silverplate version a year after the end of World War II when the U.S. atomic strike force was expanded. Produced at the Glenn L. Martin Aircraft Plant in Omaha (NE), it was flown to the Oklahoma City Air Depot at Tinker Army Air Field (OK) in August 1945. It was then assigned to the San Antonio Air Technical Services Center at Kelly Army Air Field (TX) in September 1945, to the 488th Base Unit at Chico Army Air Field (CA) in October 1945, and to the 4196th Base Unit at Victorville Army Air Field (CA) for storage in November 1945.

It was removed from storage in April 1946 and assigned for modifications to the 4117th Base Unit of the Air Depot at Robins Army Air Field (GA). It was then reassigned in August 1946 to the 4127th Base Unit of the Air Depot at McClellan Army Air Field (CA) for conversion to the Silverplate configuration. After completion of the modifications, it was assigned to the 4121st Base Unit of the Air Depot at Kelly Army Air Field (TX) in September 1946 for further modifications and then to the 509th Bomb Group at Roswell Army Air Field (NM) in January 1947. In June 1949 it was assigned to the 97th Bomb Group at Biggs Air Force Base (TX).

In April 1950 it was assigned to the Oklahoma City Air Materiel Area at Tinker Air Force Base (OK) where it was modified and redesignated as a TB-29. It was then assigned to the 3510th Basic Pilot Training Wing at Randolph Air Force Base (TX) in September 1950. It was assigned to the 3510th Combat Crew Training Wing at Randolph in March 1952. In August 1953 it was assigned to the 3040th Aircraft Storage Squadron at Davis-Monthan Air Force Base (AZ) for storage.

Disposition: Declared surplus and scrapped at Davis-Monthan in July 1954.

B-29-60-MO-44-86451   Delivered to USAAF: 31 August 1945   Phase 5

44-86451 was one of 19 B-29s produced in the regular B-29 configuration and later modified to the Silverplate version a year after the end of World War II when the U.S. atomic strike force was expanded. Produced at the Glenn L. Martin Aircraft Plant in Omaha (NE), it was flown to the Oklahoma City Air Technical Services Center at Tinker Army Air Field (OK) in September 1945. In October 1945 it was assigned to the San Antonio Air Technical Services Center at Kelly Army Air Field (TX), and then to the 4196th Base Unit at Victorville Army Air Field (CA) in November 1945 where it was placed in storage.

It was removed from storage in July 1946 and assigned for modifications to the 4117th Base Unit of the Air Depot at Robins Army Air Field (GA). It was next assigned to the 4136th Base Unit at the Oklahoma City Air Depot in August 1946, and then to the 4127th Base Unit of the Air Depot at McClellan Army Air Field (CA) for conversion to the Silverplate configuration. After completion of the modifications, it was assigned to the 509th Bombardment Group at Roswell Army Air Field (NM) in August 1947. In August 1949 it was assigned to the 97th Bombardment Group at Biggs Air Force Base (TX).

In April 1950, 44-86451 was assigned to the Eighth Air Force at Carswell Air Force Base (TX). It was reassigned to the Wright Air Development Center at Wright-Patterson Air Force Base (OH) in April 1952. In August 1952 it was assigned to the 307th Aerial refueling Squadron at Walker (formerly Roswell) Air Force Base (NM) and was used in a deployment to Kwajalein Atoll.

It was then assigned to Bergstrom Air Force Base (TX) in February 1953 and redesignated as a TB-29. In December 1953 it was assigned to the 27th Aerial Refueling Squadron at Bergstrom and used in a deployment to Westover Air Force Base (MA). It was assigned to the 3040th Aircraft Storage Squadron at Davis-Monthan Air Force Base (AZ) for storage in February 1954.

Disposition: Declared surplus and scrapped at Davis-Monthan in May 1954.

B-29-60-MO-44-86472   Delivered to USAAF: 2 October 1945   Phase 4

44-86472 was one of the last two Silverplate B-29s produced at the Glenn L. Martin Aircraft Plant in Omaha (NE). In fact, it is probably one of the last B-29s of any configuration produced at the Martin Omaha plant. It was flown to Wendover Army Air Field (UT) in October where it was assigned to the 509th Composite Group and used on training missions by crews of the 509th that did not deploy to Tinian. It was flown to Roswell Army Air Field (NM) in November 1945 to join the rest of the 509th B-29s that returned from Tinian to Roswell at the same time.

In January 1946 it was assigned to the 4136th Base Unit of the Oklahoma City Air Depot at Tinker Army Air Field (OK) for modifications. It was then assigned to Task Force 1.5 in March 1946 for use in Operation Crossroads and was deployed to the Pacific for use in the atomic bomb Test Able. It is not known for what purpose it was used in Operation Crossroads. In August 1946 it was reassigned to the 509th Bombardment Group at Roswell Army Air Field and was used in a deployment to Rome Army Air Field (NY).

Although the proper records have not been located, the early demise of 44-86472 makes it very likely that it was involved in an accident while at Roswell or elsewhere and suffered damages sufficient to result in a decision not to repair the aircraft.

108. Silverplate B-29 44-86472 in Operation Crossroads Markings. (Robert W. Krauss)

Disposition: Dropped from inventory at Roswell as surplus in June 1947 (scrapped).

B-29-60-MO-44-86473   Delivered to USAAF: 2 October 1945   Phase 4

44-86473 was one of the last two Silverplate B-29s produced at the Glenn L. Martin Aircraft Plant in Omaha (NE). In fact, it is probably one of the last B-29s of any configuration produced at the Martin Omaha plant. It was flown to Wendover Army Air Field (UT) in October 1945 where it was assigned to the 509th Composite Group and used on training missions by crews of the 509th that did not deploy to Tinian.

It was flown to Roswell Army Air Field (NM) in November 1945 to join the rest of the 509th B-29s that returned from Tinian to Roswell at the same time. In January 1946 it was assigned to the 4136th Base Unit of the Oklahoma City Air Depot at Tinker Army Air Field (OK) for modifications. It was then assigned back to the 509th at Roswell in February 1946. In March 1946 it was deployed to Kirtland Army Air Field (NM) for bomb drop test activities.

On 1 March 1946, it was involved in a ground taxiing accident that resulted in considerable damage to 44-86473 and another Silverplate B-29, 44-27296. Someone undertook to taxi 44-86473 on the Kirtland tarmac without properly energizing the hydraulic system for the landing gear brakes. Once in motion, the aircraft could only be stopped by running into another object, which happened to be the parked 44-27296. The damage to both aircraft was considerable and neither B-29 was ever used operationally again. 44-86473 was reassigned to the 428th Base Unit at Kirtland in April 1946 for disposition. See chapter 5 for more information on this incident and the disposition of aircraft 44-27296.

Disposition: 44-86473 was dropped from inventory (salvaged) at Kirtland as surplus in April 1946 as a result of the accident.

B-29-90-BW-44-87752   Delivered to USAAF: 10 July 1945   Phase 5

44-87752 was one of 19 B-29s produced in the regular B-29 configuration and later modified to the Silverplate version a year after the end of World War II when the U.S. atomic strike force was expanded. It was also one of the seven Silverplate B-29s not produced at the Glenn L. Martin Aircraft Plant in Omaha (NE).

Built at the Boeing plant in Wichita (KS), it was flown to Topeka Army Air Field (KS) in July 1945, and then assigned to the San Antonio Air Technical Services Center at Kelly Army Air Field (TX) in October 1945. It was assigned to the 4105th Base Unit at Davis-Monthan Army Air Field (AZ) for storage in November 1945.

In July 1946 it was removed from storage and assigned to the 4127th Base Unit of the Air Depot at McClellan Army Air Field (CA) for conversion to the Silverplate configuration. After completion of the modifications, it was assigned to the 509th Bombardment Group at Roswell (later Walker) Air Force Base (NM) in September 1947. It was deployed to Carswell Air Force Base (TX) for a period of time and then assigned to the 97th Bombardment Group at Biggs Air Force Base (TX) in June 1949.

44-87752 was assigned to the Oklahoma City Air Materiel Area at Tinker Air Force Base (OK) in April 1950 where it was modified and redesignated as a TB-29. It was then assigned to the 3510th Basic Flying Training Wing at Randolph Air Force

Base (TX) in September 1950, and then to the 3510th Combat Crew Training Wing at Randolph in March 1952. In July 1954 it was assigned to the 3040th Aircraft Storage Squadron at Davis-Monthan Air Force Base (AZ) for storage.

Disposition: Declared surplus and scrapped at Davis-Monthan in September 1954.

B-29-90-BW-44-87771   Delivered to USAAF: 17 July 1945   Phase 5

44-87771 was one of 19 B-29s produced in the regular B-29 configuration and later modified to the Silverplate version a year after the end of World War II when the U.S. atomic strike force was expanded. It was also one of the seven Silverplate B-29s not produced at the Glenn L. Martin Aircraft Plant in Omaha (NE). Built at the Boeing plant in Wichita (KS), it was flown to the Oklahoma City Air Depot at Tinker Army Air Field (OK) in July 1945. It was then reassigned to the Warner Robins Air Technical Services Center at Robins Army Air Field (GA) in September 1945. In November 1945 it was assigned to the 4105th Base Unit at Davis-Monthan Army Air Field (AZ) for storage.

44-87771 was removed from storage in July 1946 and assigned to the 4127th Base Unit of the Air Depot at McClellan Army Air Field (CA) for conversion to the Silverplate configuration. After completion of the modifications, it was assigned to the 509th Bombardment Group at Roswell Army Air Field (NM) in August 1947.

It was deployed to RAF Lakenheath and RAF Mildenhall in the United Kingdom for a period of time and was then assigned to the 9th Bombardment Wing at Travis Air Force Base (CA) in November 1951. After a deployment to Ernest Harmon Air Base in Newfoundland, it was assigned to the 9th Bombardment Wing at Mountain Home Air Force Base (ID) in May 1953. It was then used on deployments to Hunter Air Force Base (GA), Andersen Air Base on Guam, March Air Force Base (CA), and Carswell Air Force Base (TX).

In August 1954 it was assigned to the 3040th Aircraft Storage Squadron at Davis-Monthan Air Force Base (AZ) for storage. It was removed from storage in September 1955 and assigned to the Oklahoma City Air Materiel Area at Tinker Air Force Base (OK). There it was modified and redesignated as a TB-29. It was then assigned to the 3rd Tow Target Squadron at Goose Bay Air Base in Labrador in March 1956 and was used on a deployment to Ernest Harmon Air Base in Newfoundland.

Disposition: Dropped from inventory by transfer to the U.S. Army in July 1956. It was probably flown to the Army Aberdeen Proving Ground (MD) for tests that resulted in its destruction.

B-29-90-BW-44-87774   Delivered to USAAF: 18 July 1945   Phase 5

44-87774 was one of 19 B-29s produced in the regular B-29 configuration and later modified to the Silverplate version a year after the end of World War II when the U.S. atomic strike force was expanded. It was also one of the seven Silverplate B-29s not produced at the Glenn L. Martin Aircraft Plant in Omaha (NE).

Built at the Boeing plant in Wichita (KS), it was flown to the Oklahoma City Air Depot at Tinker Army Air Field (OK) in July 1945. In August 1945 it was assigned to the San Antonio Air Technical Services Center at Kelly Army Air Field

(TX). In November 1945 it was stored by the 4105th Base Unit at Davis-Monthan AAF (AZ).

Removed from storage in July 1946, it was assigned to the 4127th Base Unit of the Air Depot at McClellan Army Air Field (CA) for conversion to the Silverplate configuration. After completion of the modifications, it was assigned to the 509th Bombardment Group at Roswell Army Air Field (NM) in March 1947.In August 1949 it was assigned to the 97th Bombardment Group at Biggs Air Force Base (TX).

Less than a year later, in April 1950, it was assigned to the Oklahoma City Air Materiel Area at Tinker Air Force Base (OK) where it was modified and redesignated as a TB-29. It was then assigned to the 3510th Basic Pilot Training Wing at Randolph Air Force Base (TX).

Disposition: Declared surplus and scrapped at Randolph in March 1952.

B-29-90-BW-45-21707   Delivered to USAAF: 26 July 1945   Phase 5

45-21707 was one of 19 B-29s produced in the regular B-29 configuration and later modified to the Silverplate version a year after the end of World War II when the U.S. atomic strike force was expanded. It was also one of the seven Silverplate B-29s not produced at the Glenn L. Martin Aircraft Plant in Omaha (NE). Built at the Boeing plant in Wichita (KS), it was flown to March Air Force Base (CA) in July 1945 where it was assigned to the 239th Base Unit. In November 1945 it was assigned to the 4196th Base Unit at Victorville Army Air Field (CA) for storage.

Removed from storage in September 1946, it was assigned to the 4126th Base Unit of the Air Depot at McClellan Army Air Field (CA) for conversion to the Silverplate configuration. After completion of the modifications, it was assigned to the 509th Bombardment Group at Roswell (later Walker) Air Force Base (NM) in December 1947. During this assignment it was deployed for a period of time to Davis-Monthan Air Force Base (AZ). In March 1949 it was assigned to the 509th Maintenance Support Group at Walker Air Force Base (NM).

Although confirming documentation has not yet been located, it is highly probable that 45-21707 was involved in an accident or was in such condition that it was removed from operational service when it was assigned to the Maintenance Support Group at Walker. See chapter 5 for more information on this suspected accident.

Disposition: Dropped from inventory as salvage at Walker in August 1949.

B-29-90-BW-45-21736   Delivered to USAAF: 1 August 1945   Phase 5

45-21736 was one of 19 B-29s produced in the regular B-29 bomber configuration and later modified to the Silverplate version a year after the end of World War II when the U.S. atomic strike force was expanded. It was also one of the seven Silverplate B-29s not produced at the Glenn L. Martin Aircraft Plant in Omaha (NE).

Built at the Boeing plant in Wichita (KS), it was flown to Kearney Army Air Field (NE) in August 1945. In November 1945 it was assigned to the Warner Robins Air Technical Services Center at Robins Army Air Field (GA). It was then assigned to the 4105th Base Unit at Davis-Monthan Army Air Field (AZ) for storage in December 1945.

Removed from storage in July 1946, it was assigned to the 4126th Base Unit of the Air Depot at McClellan Army Air Field (CA) for conversion to the Silverplate configuration. After completion of the modifications, it was assigned to the 509th Bombardment Group at Roswell Army Air Field (NM) in May 1947. About one year later, in April 1948, it was assigned to the Boeing Modification Center in Wichita (KS) for modifications.

44-21707 was then assigned to the 4127th Base Unit at McClellan Air Force Base (CA) in August 1948 for further modifications. It was reassigned to the 509th Bombardment Group at Walker (formerly Roswell) Air Force Base (NM) in February 1949 where it was used in a deployment to RAF Marham in the United Kingdom. Although confirming documentation has not been located, it is likely that it was involved in an accident at some point in time during its assignment to Walker or RAF Marham and that the accident was of such severity that it was taken out of operational service. See chapter 5 for more information on this suspected accident.

Disposition: Dropped from inventory as salvage at Walker in August 1950.

B-29-90-BW-45-21739   Delivered to USAAF: 3 August 1945   Phase 5

45-21739 was one of 19 B-29s produced in the regular B-29 bomber configuration and later modified to the Silverplate version a year after the end of World War II when the U.S. atomic strike force was expanded. It was also one of the seven Silverplate B-29s not produced at the Glenn L. Martin Aircraft Plant in Omaha (NE).

Built at the Boeing plant in Wichita (KS), it was flown to Kearney Army Air Field (NE) in August 1945. In November 1945 it was assigned to the Warner Robins Air Technical Services Center at Robins Army Air Field (GA). It was then assigned to the 4105th Base Unit at Davis-Monthan Army Air Field (AZ) for storage in December 1945. Removed from storage in July 1946, it was assigned to the 4126th Base Unit of the Air Depot at McClellan Army Air Field (CA) for conversion to the Silverplate configuration.

After completion of the modifications, it was first assigned to the 307th Bombardment Group at MacDill Army Air Field (FL) in September 1947 and then to the 509th Bombardment Group at Roswell Air Force Base (NM) in October 1947. It was reassigned to the 97th Bombardment Group at Biggs Air Force Base (TX) in August 1949.

In May 1950 it was assigned to the Oklahoma City Air Materiel Area at Tinker Air Force Base (OK) where it was modified and redesignated as a TB-29. It was then assigned to the 3510th Basic Pilot Training Wing at Randolph Air Force Base (TX) in June 1951. In March 1952 it was assigned to the 3510th Combat Crew Training Wing at Randolph.

Disposition: Dropped from inventory by transfer to the U.S. Navy in October 1956. It was probably flown to the Naval Ordnance Test Station at China Lake (CA) and used as a ground target for Navy gunnery and bombing training.

B-29-90-BW-45-21818   Delivered to USAAF: 28 August 1945   Phase 5

45-21818 was one of 19 B-29s produced in the regular B-29 bomber configuration and later modified to the Silverplate version a year after the end of World War II when the U.S. atomic strike force was expanded. It was also one of the seven Silverplate B-29s not produced at the Glenn L. Martin Aircraft Plant in Omaha (NE).

Built at the Boeing plant in Wichita (KS), it was flown to the Oklahoma City Air Depot at Tinker Army Air Field (OK) in August 1945. In October 1945 it was assigned to the Warner Robins Air Technical Services Center at Robins Army Air Field (GA), and then in December 1945 it was assigned to the 4105th Base Unit at Davis-Monthan Army Air Field (AZ) for storage.

It was assigned to the 4126th Base Unit of the Air Depot at McClellan Army Air Field (CA) in July 1946 for conversion to the Silverplate configuration. After completion of the modifications, it was assigned to the 428th Base Unit at Kirtland Army Air Field (NM) in July 1947. It was used in atomic bomb testing programs of both the Army Air Forces (later U.S. Air Force and Department of Defense) and the Manhattan Project (later the Atomic Energy Commission). It was assigned to the 2758th Air Base Group at Kirtland in March 1949 and was redesignated as an EB-29.

In July 1949 it was reassigned to the 3078th Air Base Group at Kirtland, and in December 1949 it was assigned to the 4925th Special Weapons Wing at Kirtland. In this assignment it was used in a deployment to Wright-Patterson Air Force Base (OH), but was returned to the 4925th Test Group at Kirtland in July 1951. It was assigned to the Oklahoma City Air Materiel Area at Tinker Air Force Base (OK) in February 1953 for modifications, and then assigned to the Air Force Missile Center at Patrick Air Force Base (FL) in June 1953.

Disposition: 45-21818 was dropped from inventory in September 1955 by transfer to the U.S. Army. It was probably flown to the Army Aberdeen Proving Ground (MD) for use in tests that resulted in its destruction.

Chapter Notes

Preface

1. The term actually used in the directive of 1 December 1943 to modify the first B-29 bomber was "Silver Plated Project." The code word evolved into "Silverplate" over a period of time and was used as an expression of the project's priority. The project was given the name "Pullman" at Wright Field.

2. *Enola Gay* was put on display in December 2003 at the new Steven F. Udvar-Hazy Center of the Smithsonian Air and Space Museum near Dulles Airport. *Bockscar* has been on display at the Air Force Museum near Dayton, Ohio, for many years.

3. The National Atomic Museum Foundation invited the 509th to hold its 50th anniversary reunion in Albuquerque at the time the 509th was holding its Chicago reunion in 1994. The offer included support for trips to the Trinity site, Los Alamos, and the National Atomic Museum. The 509th named Frederick C. Bock as chairman of the reunion planning committee for the Albuquerque reunion and the Foundation Board of Trustees appointed the author as chairman of the Foundation support committee. Bock then named the author as his co-chairman for Foundation support.

4. The majority of the research was conducted during visits to the Air Force Historical Research Agency at Maxwell Air Force Base in Montgomery; Alabama; the archives at Los Alamos National Laboratory; the Research Division at the Air Force Museum near Dayton, Ohio; and the archives at the National Atomic Museum in Albuquerque, New Mexico. Additional material was gathered from individuals with historical collections and from the author's personal collection of books, documents, and photographs.

5. This book's division of deliveries and operations of the Silverplate B-29s into phases is simply this author's method of describing the increments of production and activities throughout the course of the project. Such phase terminology is not found in official documents pertaining to Silverplate.

Chapter 1

1. Einstein's letter was drafted at his home on Long Island with the assistance of Leo Szilard and Edward Teller. Szilard gave the letter to Dr. Alexander Sachs on 15 August 1939 for delivery to President Roosevelt, but Sachs did not get to see the president and deliver the letter until 11 October 1939. For more details on the preparation of the letter and its delivery, see Rhodes' *The Making of the Atomic Bomb*, pp. 303–309.

2. The full text of Einstein's letter can be found in *The Manhattan Project: A Documentary Introduction to the Atomic Age*, edited by Stoff, Fantan, and Williams, pp. 18–19. President Roosevelt's reply to Einstein, dated 19 October 1939, is on p. 20.

3. Rhodes (in *The Making of the Atomic Bomb*, p. 450) explains that the first choice for the laboratory site selected by the Corps of Engineers officer responsible for recommending locations was Oak City, Utah. The second choice, visited by Oppenheimer and Groves on 16 November 1942, was a site near Jemez Springs, a small community northwest of Santa Fe, New Mexico. Groves did not like the location, so he and Oppenheimer traveled to the top of the nearby mesa and inspected the property occupied by the Los Alamos Ranch School. This was the site chosen for the facility that became known as Los Alamos Laboratory (also known as Site Y). Since Oppenheimer had previously traveled in this part of New Mexico in his younger days and liked the area very much, it is possible that he had already made up his mind where the laboratory should be located.

4. Ramsey's unpublished report, "History of Project A," and Dike's paper, "Atomic-Bomb Project Aircraft."

5. Several different figures have been published as the total number of B-29s produced. The total of 3,965 seems to be the most often quoted number. Final assembly of B-29s took place at Boeing's plants in Wichita, Kansas, and Renton, near Seattle in Washington; at the Omaha, Nebraska, plant operated by the Glenn L. Martin Company; and at the Bell plant in Marietta, Georgia.

6. See the discussion of costs at the end of chapter 9.

Chapter 2

1. From Fenwick's Silverplate history. The directive was a letter from Army Air Forces Headquarters to the Commanding General of Materiel Command, subject: Silver Plated Project, dated 1 December 1943.

2. Due to the length of the Thin Man bomb (17 feet), the nose section was actually in the front bomb bay area and the tail section in the rear bomb bay area when the bomb was mounted in the aircraft.

3. Documentation included in Fenwick's Silverplate history shows that Semple was assigned to the Materiel Command (probably to the Engineering Division). It is reasonable to assume that Shields was also assigned to the same organization. Shields and Semple were later assigned to the 216th Base Unit at Wendover Army Air Field when the Los Alamos test program was moved from Muroc to Wendover in the fall of 1944. After the end of World War II, when the test program was moved to Kirtland Army Air Field in New Mexico, Shields and Semple were reassigned to the 428th Base Unit at Kirtland.

4. Due to a malfunction in the controls for the bomb release mechanism, the Thin Man unit was inadvertently released before the bomb bay doors were opened. The crew was eventually able to jettison the bomb and land at a nearby field for temporary repairs before returning to Muroc.

5. Los Alamos scientists determined that the muzzle velocity required for a plutonium projectile in a gun-type weapon could not be achieved. Any velocity less than the calculated minimum would result in a premature explosion, or a "poof" instead of a "bang."

6. The 216th Base Unit was an organizational element of Wendover Army Air Field and was not a part of the 509th Composite Group. Many of the personnel assigned to the 216th were former members of the unit that had supported the P-47 training program that preceded the 509th at Wendover.

7. From Dike's report, p. 128. Major Charles Sweeney was the pilot for the test mission in which 42-6259 was damaged during landing. The date of the accident is not specified in Dike's report, but it is apparent from his description that it occurred in the fall of 1944.

8. There is some confusion over where the turrets and armor were removed. Tibbets implies in his book (pp. 174–175) that they were removed after the aircraft were delivered to Wendover. It is possible that the turrets were removed at the Martin-Omaha modification center before delivery at the direction of Tibbets. In discussions in 2003 between Tibbets and the author regarding preparation of the Foreword to this book, Tibbets insisted that the turrets were removed at the modification center, notwithstanding the language in his book.

9. The 509th Composite Group was constituted (established on paper) on 9 December 1944.

10. The Daily Diaries of Shields note numerous instances of 393rd crews flying test missions.

11. From the Daily diaries of Shields, dated 15 March 1945.

12. The decision-makers concluded that new aircraft could be delivered quicker than the modified aircraft could be delivered, that providing new aircraft was less expensive than a odification program, and that the 509th needed the best B-29s that could be built.

13. As explained in chapter 7, Captain Parsons of Los Alamos and Dr. Lauritsen of Cal Tech are credited with coining the "pumpkin" name.

14. The electronics test officers were members of the 1st Ordnance Squadron. The officers who filled this position were Morris R. Jeppson on the Hiroshima mission, Philip M. Barnes on the Nagasaki mission, and Leon D. Smith on Test Able in Operation Crossroads.

15. Credit for discovering the block number change from 35 to 36 is due David Menard, who was with the Air Force Museum at the time he advised the author that the identification plate mounted in *Bockscar* (in the museum) reflected the change. It was his conclusion that the entire group of Silverplate B-29s produced in block 35 were changed to block 36. Entries in accident reports concerning other Silverplate B-29s in this group of aircraft confirm his position.

16. From Fenwick's Silverplate history.

17. Document included in Fenwick's Silverplate history.

18. From Fenwick's Saddletree history.

Chapter 3

1. Each crew was given combat mission credit for the pumpkin missions it completed and for participation in either of the two atomic bombing missions. After the Nagasaki mission, when nose art was allowed, each crew had a fat man symbol painted on the nose of their assigned airplane for each credited combat mission. These fat man symbols can be seen in Appendix G in the photographs of the aircraft that were on Tinian. Although not readily discernible in the black and white photographs, a black fat man symbol represented a pumpkin mission and a red symbol represented participation in one of the atomic missions. For example, the photograph of *Some Punkins* (44-27296) in Appendix G shows the five symbols for the five pumpkin missions flown by crew B-7.

2. No documentation has been found to explain what system was used to judge the results of a pumpkin mission (e.g., poor, fair, excellent, etc.). The "unobserved" notation was undoubtedly used when the target was cloud covered and the strike cameras could not record the impact of the bomb.

3. The records indicate that engine trouble caused the crew to abort the mission and that the aircraft returned to Tinian and landed with the pumpkin bomb still in the bomb bay.

4. There is some confusion regarding where the mission was aborted. It may have occurred over Japanese territory, in which case the crew probably got credit for a combat mission. In any case, the pumpkin

bomb was jettisoned into the ocean near Iwo Jima on the way back to Tinian.

5. The crews of the 509th were not supposed to bomb the Emperor's palace. Had the Emperor been killed by the pumpkin bomb dropped by Eatherly and his crew, the outcome of the war with Japan might have been totally different.

6. There was concern on Tinian that there were Japanese soldiers hiding in remote areas of the island and that they observed 509th activities and reported them to Tokyo by radio. Because of this concern, the normal tail markings for the 509th aircraft, an arrow in a circle, were changed in order to disguise the identification of the unit carrying out the atomic missions. These different markings are described in chapter 2. In addition, the normally used radio call sign for *Enola Gay*, Victor 82, was changed to Dimples 82 for the Hiroshima mission.

7. The airplane commander (Tibbets) was basically responsible for getting the airplane to and from the target area and for any decisions affecting the operation of the airplane. The bomb commander (Parsons) was responsible for the bomb and any decisions regarding its release.

8. The term used for the function Parsons performed, "bomb commander," is taken from Ramsey's report on Project Alberta. Other terms used for this role included weaponeer, weapon officer, and weapon commander. The term "electronics test officer" for the Jeppson role is also from Ramsey's report. This position was also called the weapon test officer.

9. See note 8 above regarding the terms used for the roles fulfilled by Ashworth and Barnes.

10. The fuel shortage was supposedly aggravated by a malfunctioning fuel transfer pump that would not move fuel from the bomb bay tank to the main wing tanks. Fred Bock told the author at one time that his flight engineer checked the pump on Bockscar after the Nagasaki mission and could not find anything wrong with it. There have also been reports that Sweeney's flight engineer, John Kuharek, later admitted that they were able to use the fuel in the bomb bay tank.

11. The Nagasaki mission was a success in that the Fat Man bomb was dropped on an authorized target and it detonated as planned. Yet, the mission almost ended in disaster because of a number of problems, some mechanical and some caused by the ground rules for the use of the bombs and the split responsibilities of the airplane and bomb commanders, Sweeney and Ashworth (see note 7 above). First, there was the confusion over the availability of the 600 gallons of fuel in the aft bomb bay tank (see note 10). Second, the delay at the rendezvous point should have been no more than 15 minutes according to the orders given to Sweeney by Tibbets before takeoff, but he waited 45 minutes for the airplane carrying the photographic equipment in the mistaken belief that photographs of the were necessary for mission success. Third, when *Bockscar* arrived at Kokura, the weather conditions were no longer acceptable for visual bombing as they had been when reported earlier by the crew of the weather reconnaissance aircraft (*Enola Gay*). An additional burden was the directive that the bomb had to be dropped on one of the authorized targets (no targets of opportunity) and that it had to be dropped using visual sightings. This led to the mistake of making three fuel-consuming runs over Kokura before diverting to Nagasaki, the secondary target. The second or third bomb run at Kokura and the diversion to Nagasaki might have been unnecessary had a radar bomb run been authorized as an alternative method when the safety of the airplane and crew were in danger (by virtue of the fuel shortage). As it was, Ashworth and Sweeney finally agreed to the use of radar bombing at Nagasaki as a last resort, and this deviation from the rules probably saved the lives of all on board *Bockscar*. In the last minute of the run on Nagasaki, a break in the clouds allowed bombardier Beahan to drop the bomb visually. The return to Okinawa almost ended in disaster. *Bockscar* ran out of fuel on the taxiway after landing safely.

12. See Lawren's *The General and the Bomb*, p. 255.

Chapter 4

1. *Critical Assembly* by Hoddeson, Henriksen, Meade, and Westfall provides an excellent description of the formation and activities of the Ordnance Division of Group E-7 in chapter 19, beginning on page 378. See also Project Alberta in Appendix E herein.

2. *Critical Assembly*, p. 380.

3. Rowe complains frequently in his book about the demanding test schedule imposed on his unit by the mysterious visitors from some unknown place and the lack of information regarding the objectives of the test program.

4. See chapter 5.

5. See chapter 5.

Chapter 5

1. Of the 16 accidents, 14 occurred while the airplanes were in the Silverplate configuration and two happened after the airplanes had been converted to other uses.

2. Locating an accident report for a specific aircraft at the Air Force Historical Research Agency is difficult unless very precise dates and locations are known. As was the case for several accidents described in this chapter, an accident report could not be located even though it probably existed.

3. Accident Report 46-3-7-6 includes a statement that "Pieces that became detached in flight were scattered as far as sixteen (16) miles southeast of the main crash." The accident occurred at about 1:00 in the afternoon. Eyewitness accounts indicate that the aircraft was spinning (and maybe tumbling end over end) when it disintegrated. The main section of the airplane struck the ground in an inverted position with all engines intact. Just prior to the incident, the radio operator had informed a ground station that "The drop was lousy, we're coming home, having some prop trouble, 387 out."

4. In a bailout situation, crew members in the forward pressurized compartment would normally exit the aircraft through an opening in the floor of the flight deck and the nose gear opening after the nose gear was lowered. If a crew member dove through the opening head first, there was always the possibility that he would hit his head on a piece of the nose gear operating mechanism.

5. *Jabit III* hit the boundary fence and concrete numeral and arrow at the approach end of runway 4-C. After hitting the fence, the aircraft landed with the left wing low and the left outboard engine caught fire. The aircraft left the runway and stopped in the nearby grassy area.

Chapter 6

1. Silverplate B-29s of the 509th were based temporarily at several locations. The Naval Air Station at the Naval Ordnance Test Station (NOTS) at Inyokern, California was used for a considerable number of Los Alamos drop test missions. Ten 509th crews and aircraft were temporarily based at Batista Field near Havana, Cuba, in January 1945 for long-range navigational training. After World War II, 509th crews and aircraft from Roswell would periodically deploy to Goose Bay Air Base in Labrador for polar navigation and operational training.

2. It is believed that Fred Bock's father, Wyman C. Bock, played a central role in resolving the confusion by writing a letter to *Life* magazine in 1950. In his letter, the elder Mr. Bock noted that *Bockscar* was piloted by Sweeney and that his son, Fred, had piloted *The Great Artiste*.

3. See the chronology in Appendix A for additional events associated with Roswell (later Walker Air Force Base).

4. The town of Roswell was named by an early settler, Van C. Smith, in honor of his father, Roswell Smith.

5. After the United States took over Tinian, all of the roads were named after streets and avenues in Manhattan.

6. An effort has been made to combine Wendover with West Wendover in Nevada. Action in the U.S. Congress to permit the adjustment of the boundary between Utah and Nevada to facilitate this change has been considered but unsuccessful to date.

Chapter 7

1. Bowens history of Project Silverplate, p. 96.

2. Coster-Mullen has never knowingly had access to any classified information regarding the Little Boy and Fat Man bombs. The amazing thing about his book is that it is based totally on unclassified sources, and yet it is probably the most detailed description of the bombs ever published.

3. The information on the use of general purpose (GP) high explosive bombs by the 509th was taken from 509th Operations Orders.

4. The island targets for the practice bombing missions were written on copies of the 509th Operations Orders after they were typed, except in two cases.

5. The term "pumpkin" was probably used because of the appearance of the fat, round shape of the bomb. There have been suggestions that the name came about because the bombs were painted yellow-orange, but this is probably not true since it is believed the pumpkin bombs were painted an olive drab or khaki color.

6. The original list of atomic targets included Kyoto, Hiroshima, Kokura, and Niigata. Kyoto was removed from the list at the direction of Secretary of War Stimson and was replaced with Nagasaki. The pumpkin targets were selected because of their proximity to the atomic targets on the original list.

7. These radar units were also known as "Archies."

8. The loading process began with the bomb being moved to one of the loading pits on a special transport trailer towed by a truck. The bomb rested on a cradle on the trailer with the cradle held in place by four large pins. At the loading pit, the trailer was positioned across the pit on two rails, then a hydraulic lift (similar to devices used in auto service bays) lifted the trailer so that the rails could be removed. The trailer, cradle, and bomb were then rotated 90 degrees and lowered to the bottom of the pit. Next, *Enola Gay* (or *Bockscar* for Fat Man and the Nagasaki mission) was backed over the pit with the front bomb bay positioned over the pit. The four pins holding the cradle to the trailer were removed and the bomb on the cradle was raised up into the bomb bay and attached to the bomb shackle. Sway braces were then positioned and the various electrical and mechanical connections were completed.

Chapter 8

1. See chapter 1.

2. Tibbets provides an excellent account of his interview in *Return of the Enola Gay*, pp. 158–164.

3. The primary reason for using a "composite group" concept was the concern for secrecy. By providing the unit with all the resources it needed to accomplish its mission, there was no need for the involvement of other organizations; therefore there would be less chance of the mission of the unit being compromised. An additional benefit of this organizational structure was that all of the elements essential to mission success were under the direction of the group commanding officer.

4. The 320th Troop Carrier Squadron was inactivated at Roswell on 19 August 1946. It was replaced by the 1st Air Transport Squadron, which was activated on 13 August 1946.

5. The 1st Ordnance Squadron (Special) Aviation was redesignated as the 1st Ordnance Squadron Aviation on 30 July 1946 and reassigned from the 509th at Roswell to Kirtland Army Air Field under the 58th Bombardment Wing of the 15th Air Force, Strategic Air Command.

6. There is no direct parallel between the 509th Composite Group on Tinian and the current 509th Bomb Wing at Whiteman because of intervening reorganizations. The unit comparisons are:

Tinian	Whiteman
393rd Bombardment Squadron (VH)	393rd Bomb Squadron
509th Composite Group	509th Operations Group
313th Bombardment Wing	509th Bombardment Wing
Twentieth Air Force	Eighth Air Force
U.S. Army Strategic Air Forces, Pacific	Air Combat Command
U.S. Army Air Forces	U.S. Air Force

7. Paul Tibbets was awarded the Distinguished Service Cross by General Spaatz immediately after *Enola Gay* landed following the Hiroshima mission. Others participating in the mission were awarded medals at a later date, as were those individuals involved in the Nagasaki mission.

8. Department of the Air Force Special Order GB-294, dated 2 September 1999, which read, "By direction of the Secretary of the Air Force, the 509th Composite Group has been awarded the Air Force Outstanding Unit Award (with Valor) for exceptionally outstanding achievement in combat for the period 1 July 1945 to 14 August 1945."

Chapter 9

1. See Phase One and Phase Two in chapter 2.
2. See Phase Three in chapter 2.
3. Chapter 4.
4. Chapter 4.
5. The navigator was Jack Widowsky (see crew B-8 in Appendix C).
6. *Wendover Memories: 509th Composite Group* by Robert W. Krauss, p. 63.
7. This aircraft was dropped from inventory in April 1956 by transfer to the U.S. Army. It was probably flown to the Army's Aberdeen Proving Ground in Maryland for use as a test article.
8. After being assigned to Carswell Air Force Base, 44-86451 was based at several other locations. It was finally declared surplus and scrapped at Davis-Monthan in May 1954.
9. 44-87771 was involved in several additional assignments after its basing at Travis Air Force Base before being converted to a TB-29 at Tinker in September 1955. It was dropped from inventory by transfer to the U.S. Army in July 1956. Like 42-65386, it probably ended up at the Aberdeen Proving Ground for use as a test vehicle.
10. Inflation factors used were 10.51 (1945 dollars to 2004 dollars), 8.72 (1945 to 1996), and 1.21 (1996 to 2004). These factors for converting different year dollars were derived from the U.S. Bureau of Labor Statistics inflation calculator on its web site (stats.bls.gov).
11. Estimates of the cost of World War II for the United States vary considerably according to the factors included in various sources. The figure used here was taken from "World War II," Microsoft Encarta® Online Encyclopedia 2004 (http://encarta.msn.com© 1997–2004, Microsoft Corporation — All Rights Reserved).
12. Hewlett and Anderson in *The New World*, p. 724.

13. The Brookings Institution study edited by Schwartz includes a total B-29 program cost of $27 billion in 1996 dollars for 3,960 airplanes and spare parts (p. 112, footnote 17). The equivalent cost in 2004 dollars would be $32.6 billion. In 1945 dollars, the figure would be $3.1 billion. The total program cost figure equates to $6.818 million per airplane in 1996 dollars, $8.250 million per airplane in 2004 dollars, and about $782,000 per B-29 in 1945 dollars. Comparable figures from other sources are $639,000 per airplane (Air Force Museum web site, *www.wpafb.af.mil/museum*) and $756,620 (Muelen). The figures from the Brookings Institution study are used herein.

14. The cost to modify a B-29 to the Silverplate configuration was $285,000 in 1996 dollars (from The Brookings Institution study edited by Schwartz, p. 112, footnote 17). This figure equates to $32,700 in 1945 dollars. The modification cost information in The Brookings Institution study was derived from *A History of the Air Force Atomic Energy Program, 1943–1953*, vol. 3: *Building an Atomic Force, 1949–53* by Lee Bowen, Robert D. Little, and others (issued by the U.S. Historical Division in 1959).

15. From the Bureau of Labor Statistics inflation calculator, the factor for converting 1945 dollars to 2004 dollars is 10.51.

16. The total cost of the Silverplate B-29s is $814,700 times the 65 aircraft produced (approximately $53 million in 1945 dollars). The logistical support cost was determined using figures cited in The Brookings Institution study edited by Schwartz, p. 112, footnote 17. This study cites a total Silverplate project cost of $76 million to modify 46 aircraft and provide the logistical support. Deleting the modification costs leaves $62.9 million for the logistical support costs (in 1996 dollars). Conversion to 1945 dollars produces a logistics cost of about $7 million.

Appendix G

1. Interpretation of the original entries on an aircraft record card by an uninformed person is almost impossible. Knowledge of the codes used to indicate locations and transactions is required. The translation of the record card data for 65 Silverplate B-29 aircraft to meaningful information by Archie DiFante of the Air Force Historical Research Agency was a tremendous effort.

2. The delivery date was the date on which the Army Air Forces representative at the manufacturer's plant accepted the aircraft. Acceptance was preceded by one or more test flights by the manufacturer and the Army Air Forces to prove the airworthiness of the plane and to identify any problems that required fixing before the government would accept the airplane.

3. See note 4 in chapter 2.
4. See note 7 in chapter 2.
5. The loading pit at Kirtland Air Force Base was originally constructed in July 1945 in order to load the Fat Man units transported to Tinian in 42-65386, 44-86346, and 44-86347. See the individual histories for these aircraft.

6. According to the Daily Diaries of Shields, the pilot of 42-65235 that day was George Marquardt.

7. From *Albuquerque Journal*, "B-29 Crash a Mystery Since '47," Section B, 26 January 1997.

8. Hartshorn was assigned to the 216th Base Unit at Wendover. His primary duty was to fly test missions in support of Los Alamos.

9. Accident Report 46-3-7-6, Air Force Historical Research Agency.

10. The name *Some Punkins* chosen by crew B-7 came from a comic strip of the same name that was popular at the time.

11. For example, Fenwick's Silverplate history.

12. The name *Bockscar* chosen by crew C-13 was a play on words to honor the airplane commander of the crew, Frederick C. Bock.

13. The confusion began with New York Times correspondent William L. Laurence, who was an observer on *The Great Artiste* flown by Bock and crew C-13. Since Sweeney was flying the aircraft carrying the bomb and his normal B-29 was *The Great Artiste*, Laurence erroneously concluded that the bomb-carrying airplane was the one Sweeney would normally be flying. He was unaware that a switch of *Bockscar* and *The Great Artiste* had been made because of the blast instrument configuration already installed in *The Great Artiste*.

14. Accident Report 49-5-25-3, Air Force Historical Research Agency.

15. The name *Straight Flush* referred to the gambling habits of Eatherly, the airplane commander.

16. The name *Top Secret* was a reference to the secrecy of the activities of the 509th Composite Group.

17. It is unknown whether nose art was ever actually painted on the aircraft. A rendition of a probable version of *Jabit III* nose art was included in Bock's 1997 reunion booklet, but there are no known photographs of the art work on a Silverplate B-29.

18. Accident Report 46-9-29-1, Air Force Historical Research Agency.

19. The artist who painted the nose art on *Up an' Atom* was Hal Olsen, who was in the Navy and stationed on Tinian at the time. He presently lives in Albuquerque, New Mexico. He has done several paintings involving 509th subject matter, including a replica of the *Bockscar* nose art on a sheet of aluminum.

20. The name *The Great Artiste* was a reference to unspecified talents of the bombardier on crew C-15, Kermit K. Beahan.

21. Accident Report 48-C-9-3-4, Air Force Historical Research Agency.

22. The name *Necessary Evil* was probably in reference to the use of the atomic bombs.

23. The normal Airplane Commander for 44-86292, Robert A. Lewis, was reportedly upset that someone had painted a name on "his" airplane. When he complained to Tibbets, he was told who had directed the painting of *Enola Gay* on the airplane and why. Lewis no longer complained.

24. According to a member of crew A-2, the name *Laggin' Dragon* was selected because the Airplane Commander, Edward Costello, always did everything by the book and the crew and airplane were always behind whatever schedule was being followed. There is also a reference to the dragon used in the 393rd insignia (which was never officially approved).

25. Accident Report 52-12-18-1, Air Force Historical Research Agency.

26. Accident Report (number illegible), Air Force Historical Research Agency.

27. The Aircraft Record Card indicates that this airplane was transferred to a museum in September 1958, but there is no notation to identify the museum. Present day records of B-29s still in existence do not include this serial number; therefore the ultimate disposition of 44-86443 is a mystery.

BIBLIOGRAPHY

Alberts, Don E., and Allen E. Putnam. *A History of Kirtland Air Force Base, 1928–1982*. Kirtland Air Force Base, New Mexico, 1985.
Allen, Thomas B., and Norman Polmar. *Code-Name Downfall: The Secret Plan to Invade Japan and Why Truman Dropped the Bomb*. Simon & Schuster, 1995.
Berger, Carl. *B-29: The Superfortress*. Ballantine Books, 1970.
Beser, Jacob. *Hiroshima and Nagasaki Revisited*. Global Press, 1988.
Birdsall, Steve. *Saga of the Superfortress*. Doubleday, 1980.
_____. *Superfortress: The Boeing B-29*. Squadron Signal Publications, 1980.
Bock, Frederick C., ed. *509th Composite Group: 50th Anniversary Reunion Commemorative Booklet*. Self-published, 1995.
_____. *509th Composite Group: 50th Anniversary Reunion Commemorative Booklet* (revised and corrected). Self-published, 1997.
Bowen, H. L. *A History of the Air Force Atomic Energy Program, 1943–1953*. Volume 1, "Project Silverplate, 1943–1946." U.S. Air Force, 1958.
Bowers, Peter M. *Boeing B-29 Superfortress*. Warbird Tech Series Volume 14. Specialty Press, 1999.
Campbell, John M. *Boeing B-29 Superfortress*. Schiffer Military/Aviation History, 1997.
Campbell, Richard H. *A Brief History of the Enola Gay*. National Atomic Museum Foundation, 1998.
Caron, George R., and Charlotte A. Mearer. *Fire of a Thousand Suns*. Web, 1995.
Christman, Al. *Target Hiroshima*. Naval Institute Press, 1998.
Collison, Thomas. *The Superfortress Is Born*. Duell, Sloan & Pierce, 1945.
Coster-Mullen, John. *Atom Bombs: The Top Secret Inside Story of Little Boy and Fat Man*. Self-published, 2003.
Craven, Wesley Frank, and James Lee Cate, eds. *The Army Air Forces in World War II: Volume Five, The Pacific: Matterhorn to Nagasaki; June 1944 to August 1945*. University of Chicago, 1953.
Davis, Larry. *B-29 Superfortress in Action*. Squadron/Signal Publications, 1997.
Dike, Sheldon H. "Atomic-Bomb Project Aircraft." Declassified extract of Chapter 5, Volume 23 of Los Alamos Technical Series, *Nuclear Weapons Engineering and Delivery (U)*, LA-1161-DEL (EXTRACT). Los Alamos Scientific Laboratory, 1946.
Felchlia, Albert O. *Into the Wild Blue Yonder with A.O. Felchlia, Navigator*. Self-published, 1995.
Fenwick, Amy C. *History of Saddletree Project*. Air Force Material Command, May 1953.
_____. *History of Silverplate Project*. Air Force Material Command, June 1952.
Gibson, James N. *The History of the U.S. Nuclear Arsenal*. Brompton Books, 1989.
_____. *Nuclear Weapons of the United States*. Schiffer, 1996.
Goldstein, Donald N., Katherine V. Dillon, and J. Michael Wenger. *Rain of Ruin: A Photographic History of Hiroshima and Nagasaki*. Brassey's, 1995.
Groves, Leslie R. *Now It Can Be Told*. Harper & Row, 1962.
Gurney, Gene. *Journey of the Giants: The Story of the B-29 "Superfort"— The Weapon That Won the War in the Pacific*. Coward, 1961.
Hansen, Chuck. *U.S. Nuclear Weapons: The Secret History*. Aerofax, 1988.
Hawkins, David, Edith C. Truslow, and Ralph Carlisle Smith. *Project Y: The Los Alamos Story. Part I— Toward Trinity. Part II— Beyond Trinity*. Tomash, 1983.
Hewlett, Richard G., and Oscar E. Anderson, Jr. *The New World, 1939/1946: A History of the United States Atomic Energy Commission, Vol. 1*. Pennsylvania State University, 1962.
Hoddeson, Lillian, Paul W. Henriksen, Roger A. Meade, and Catherine Westfall. *Critical Assembly*. Press Syndicate of the University of Cambridge, 1993.

Hooker, Roger D. *History of the 509th Bomb Wing: 1944–1993.* 509th Bomb Wing History Office, 1994.
Jones, Vincent C. *Manhattan: The Army and the Atomic Bomb.* United States Army in World War II, Special Studies. Center of Military History (U.S. Army), 1985.
Keenan, Richard M. *The 20th Air Force Album.* 20th Air Force Association, 1982.
Krauss, Robert W. *Wendover Memories: 509th Composite Group.* Self-published, 2002.
_____, ed. *The 509th Remembered.* Self-published, 2003.
Lawren, William. *The General and the Bomb.* Dodd, Mead, 1988.
LeMay, General Curtis E., and Bill Yenne. *Superfortress.* McGraw-Hill, 1988.
Lloyd, Alwyn T. *B-29 Superfortress: Part 1, Production Versions.* Detail & Scale TAB Books, 1983.
_____. *B-29 Superfortress: Part 2, Derivatives.* Detail & Scale TAB Books, 1987.
_____. "Silverplate Aircraft by Serial Number." Unpublished manuscript, not dated.
Maurer, Maurer. *Air Force Combat Units of World War II.* U.S. Government Printing Office. Reprint, Chartwell Books, 1961.
_____. *World War II Combat Squadrons of the United States Air Force.* Smithmark (prepared by Historical Division, Air University), 1992.
Meulen, Jacob Vander. *Building the B-29.* Smithsonian Institution Press, 1995.
Miller, Merle, and Abe Spitzer. *We Dropped the A-Bomb.* Thomas Y. Crowell, 1946.
Norris, Robert S. *Racing for the Bomb: General Leslie R. Groves, the Manhattan Project's Indispensable Man.* Steerforth Press, 2002.
Olivi, Fred J. *Decision at Nagasaki: The Mission That Almost Failed.* Self-published, 1999.
Osborne, Richard E. *World War II Sites in the United States: A Tour Guide & Directory.* Riebel-Roque, 1996.
Ossip, Captain James J., ed. *509th Pictorial Album.* 509th Composite Group, 1945.
Pace, Steve. *Boeing B-29 Superfortress.* The Crowood Press, 2003.
Pacific War Research Society, The. *Japan's Longest Day.* Kodansha International, 1968.
Pimlott, John. *B-29 Superfortress.* Bison Books Limited, 1980.
Ramsey, Norman F. "History of Project A." Unpublished report, Los Alamos Scientific Laboratory, not dated.
Rhodes, Richard. *Dark Sun: The Making of the Hydrogen Bomb.* Simon & Schuster, 1995.
_____. *The Making of the Atomic Bomb.* Simon & Schuster, 1986.
Rowe, James Les. *Project W-47.* JA A RO, 1978.
Russ, Harlow. *Project Alberta: The Preparation of Atomic Bombs for Use in World War II.* Exceptional Books, 1990.
Rust, Kenn C. *Twentieth Air Force Story.* Historical Aviation Album, 1979.
St. John, Philip M. *B-29 Superfortress.* Turner, 1994.
Schwartz, Stephen I., ed. *Atomic Audit: The Costs and Consequences of U.S. Nuclear Weapons Since 1940.* The Brookings Institution, 1998.
Shields, Major Clyde S., daily diaries, 2 February 1945 through 31 July 1945. Flight Test Section, 216th Base Unit, Wendover Army Air Field, Utah.
Sinclair, W.B. *The Big Brothers: The Story of the B-29.* Naylor Press, 1972.
Smyth, Henry DeWolf. *Atomic Energy for Military Purposes: The Official Report on the Development of the Atomic Bomb Under the Auspices of the United States Government, 1940–1945.* U.S. Government Printing Office, August 1945.
Stoff, Michael B., Jonathan F. Fantan, and R. Hal Williams, eds. *The Manhattan Project: A Documentary Introduction to the Atomic Age.* Temple University Press, 1991.
Sweeney, Maj Gen Charles W., USAF (Ret). *War's End.* Avon Books, 1997.
Thole, Lou. *Forgotten Fields of America: World War II Bases and Training Then and Now.* Pictorial Histories, 1996.
Thomas, Gordon, and Max Morgan Witts. *Enola Gay: Mission to Hiroshima.* White Owl Press, 1995.
Tibbets, Paul W. *Return of the Enola Gay.* Mid Coast Marketing, 1998.
U.S. Air Force. Aircraft Record Cards. Air Force Historical Research Agency, Maxwell Air Force Base, Montgomery, Alabama.
_____. *A History of the Air Force Atomic Energy Program, 1943–53.* Chapter III (Silverplate, The Initial AAF Program) and Chapter IV (Project Silverplate, 1943–1946). Agency unknown, not dated.
U.S. Army Air Forces. "Final Report of Missions." 20 July–14 August 1945. Headquarters, 509th Composite Group, not dated.
_____. "Consolidated Statistical Summary of Combat Operations." Missions No. 1–12, Special Bombing Missions to Japan by 509th Bomb Group. Twentieth Air Force, 4 August 1945.
_____. "Consolidated Statistical Summary of Combat Operations." Missions No. 13 & 16, Special Bombing Missions to Japan by 509th Bomb Group. Twentieth Air Force, not dated.

_____. "Consolidated Statistical Summary of Combat Operations." Missions No. 14, 15, 17, & 18, Special Bombing Missions to Japan by 509th Group. Twentieth Air Force, 22 August 1945.

_____. *History of 509th Composite Group, Activation to 15 August 1945.* 509th Composite Group, 31 August 1945.

_____. Operation Orders, numbered 1 through 48. Headquarters, 509th Composite Group, 29 June–21 August 1945.

_____. *Tactical Mission Report: A Report of Activities of 509th Composite Group During July and August 1945.* Headquarters, Twentieth Air Force, not dated.

U.S. Strategic Bombing Survey. *The Effects of the Ten Thousand-Pound Bomb on Japanese Targets: A Report on Nine Incidents.* U.S. Government Printing Office, 1947.

Serial Number Index

B-29-5-BW-42-6259: accident of 47, 104; assignments and usage of 8, 44, 57, 59, 67, 68; history of 161

B-29-5-MO-42-65209: assignments and usage of 12, 57, 67; history of 162

B-29-10-MO-42-65216: assignments and usage of 12, 60, 67; history of 162-63

B-29-10-MO-42-65217: assignments and usage of 12, 60, 67; history of 163

B-29-15-MO-42-65234: assignments and usage of 12, 13, 44, 56, 59, 66, 67; history of 163

B-29-15-MO-42-65235: accident of 13, 47, 104; assignments and usage of 12, 44, 57, 67; history of, 163

B-29-20-MO-42-65236: assignments and usage of 12, 13, 44, 45, 60, 67; history of 164

B-29-20-MO-42-65237: assignments and usage of 12, 57, 67; history of 164-65

B-29-20-MO-42-65238: assignments and usage of 12, 13, 57, 67; history of 165

B-29-20-MO-42-65239: assignments and usage of 12, 57, 67; history of 165

B-29-20-MO-42-65240: assignments and usage of 12, 67; history of 165

B-29-20-MO-42-65258: assignments and usage of 12, 13, 44, 59, 60, 67; history of 165-66

B-29-20-MO-42-65259: assignments and usage of 12, 13, 44, 45, 60, 67; history of 166

B-29-20-MO-42-65260: assignments and usage of 12, 13, 44, 45, 57, 67; history of 166

B-29-20-MO-42-65261: assignments and usage of 12, 60, 67; history of 166

B-29-20-MO-42-65262: assignments and usage of 12, 13, 44, 61, 67; history of 166-67

B-29-20-MO-42-65263: assignments and usage of 12, 67; history of 167

B-29-25-MO-42-65264: assignments and usage of 12, 57, 67; history of 167

B-29-30-MO-42-65384: assignments and usage of 16, 45, 59, 66, 67; history of 167-68

B-29-30-MO-42-65385: accident of 48; assignments and usage of 16, 45, 59, 67; history of 168

B-29-30-MO-42-65386: assignments and usage of 16, 45, 59, 67; history of 168-69

B-29-30-MO-42-65387: accident of 48; assignments and usage of 16, 45, 59, 67; history of 169

B-29-36-MO-44-27295: assignments and usage of 16, 45, 56, 59, 66, 67; history of 169-71

B-29-36-MO-44-27296: accident of 48-49, 104; assignments and usage of 16, 18, 26, 62, 64, 67; crew of 129; history of 171-72; missions of 27, 113

B-29-36-MO-44-27297: assignments and usage of 16, 18, 46, 57, 62, 64, 67; crew of 138; history of 172-73; missions of 27, 32, 113-14

B-29-36-MO-44-27298: assignments and usage of 16, 18, 26, 56, 62, 64, 66, 67; crew of 119; history of 173-75; missions of 28, 30, 32, 114

B-29-36-MO-44-27299: accident of 50; assignments and usage of 16, 18, 26, 46, 56, 62, 64, 67; crew of 122; history of 175-76; missions of 28, 114

B-29-36-MO-44-27300: accident of 50-51; assignments and usage of 16, 18, 26, 57, 62, 64, 67, 104; crew of 123-24; history of 176-78; missions of 28, 114-15

B-29-36-MO-44-27301: assignments and usage of 16, 18, 26, 57, 62, 64, 66, 67; crew of 135; history of 178-79

B-29-36-MO-44-27302: assignments and usage of 16, 18, 26, 56, 62, 64, 66, 67; crew of 130; history of 180-81; missions of 28, 115

B-29-36-MO-44-27303: accident of 51, 104;

assignments and usage of 16, 18, 26, 46, 64, 67; crew of 127; history of 181–83; missions of 28, 30, 116

B-29-36-MO-44-27304: assignments and usage of 16, 18, 26, 56, 62, 64, 66, 67; crew of 134; history of 183–84; missions of 28, 116

B-29-40-MO-44-27353: accident of 51–52, 104; assignments and usage of 16, 18, 26, 62, 64, 67; crew of 141–42; history of 184–85; missions of 28, 30, 32, 116–17

B-29-40-MO-44-27354: assignments and usage of 16, 18, 26, 46, 56, 62, 64, 66, 67; crew of 126; history of 186–89; missions of 28, 30, 32, 117

B-29-40-MO-44-86263: assignments and usage of 22, 56, 62, 66; history of 189

B-29-45-MO-44-86291: assignments and usage of 16, 18, 26, 57, 62, 64, 66, 67; crew of 139; history of 189–91; missions of 29, 30, 117

B-29-45-MO-44-86292: assignments and usage of 16, 18, 26, 46, 58, 62, 64, 67; crew of 132; history of 194–96; missions of 29, 30, 32, 117–18

B-29-50-MO-44-86346: assignments and usage of 16, 18, 26, 57, 62, 64, 66, 67; crew of 136–37; history of 194–96; missions of 118

B-29-50-MO-44-86347: assignments and usage of 16, 18, 26, 32, 56, 62, 64, 66, 67; crew of 121–22; history of 196–98; missions of 118

B-29-55-MO-44-86382: accident of 52–53, 199; assignments and usage of 21, 56, 62, 66, 67; history of 198–99

B-29-55-MO-44-86383: accident of 53, 199; assignments and usage of 21, 62, 67; history of 199

B-29-55-MO-44-86384: assignments and usage of 21, 56, 62, 66, 67; history of 200–01

B-29-55-MO-44-86394: assignments and usage of 22, 56, 62, 66; history of 201

B-29-55-MO-44-86401: assignments and usage of 22, 57, 62, 66; history of 201–02

B-29-60-MO-44-86430: assignments and usage of 21, 57, 62, 66, 67; history of 202–03

B-29-60-MO-44-86431: accident of 53, 204; assignments and usage of 21, 62, 65, 67; history of 203–04

B-29-60-MO-44-86432: assignments and usage of 21, 56, 62, 66, 67; history of 204

B-29-60-MO-44-86437: assignments and usage of 22, 56, 62, 66; history of 204–05

B-29-60-MO-44-86439: assignments and usage of 22, 56, 62, 66; history of 205–06

B-29-60-MO-44-86440: assignments and usage of 22, 56, 62, 66; history of 206–07

B-29-60-MO-44-86443: assignments and usage of 22, 57, 62, 66; history of 207–08

B-29-60-MO-44-86444: assignments and usage of 22, 59, 66; history of 208

B-29-60-MO-44-86445: assignments and usage of 22, 57, 62, 66; history of 208–09

B-29-60-MO-44-86447: assignments and usage of 22, 59, 66; history of 209

B-29-60-MO-44-86448: assignments and usage of 22, 56, 62, 66; history of 209–10

B-29-60-MO-44-86451: assignments and usage of 22, 56, 62; history of 210–11

B-29-60-MO-44-86472: accident of 53–54, 211; assignments and usage of 21, 62, 67; history of 211–12

B-29-60-MO-44-86473: accident of 54, 104; assignments and usage of 21, 62, 67; history of 212

B-29-90-BW-44-87752: assignments and usage of 22, 56, 62, 66; history of 212–13

B-29-90-BW-44-87771: assignments and usage of 22, 62; history of 213

B-29-90-BW-44-87774: assignments and usage of, 22, 56, 62, 66; history of 213–14

B-29-90-BW-45-21707: accident of 54, 214; assignments and usage of 22, 62; history of 214

B-29-90-BW-45-21736: accident of 54–55, 215; assignments and usage of 22, 62; history of,214–15

B-29-90-BW-45-21739: assignments and usage of 22, 57, 62, 66; history of 215

B-29-90-BW-45-21818: assignments and usage of 22, 59, 66; history of 215–16

INDEX

Abbreviations used in the index include AAF for Army Air Field, AB for Air Base, and AFB for Air Force Base.

1st Ordnance Squadron, Special (Aviation) 99–100, 220n5
1st Technical Services Detachment 25, 97, 156
1027th Air Materiel Squadron 99
1227th Air Base Group 185
1395th Military Police Company 99
20th Air Force 25–27, 103
216th Base Unit 10, 21, 44, 48, 59, 61, 66, 97, 218n6
236th Base Unit 60, 162
2nd Air Force 13
2nd Marine Division 64
307th Aerial Refueling Squadron 210
313th Bombardment Wing 25, 64
320th Troop Carrier Squadron 25, 39, 98–99, 220n4
390th Air Service Group 99
393rd Bombardment Squadron 3, 11, 25–26, 57, 96, 105; activation of 97; description of 97–98
4000th Base Unit 61
4105th Base Unit 57–58, 161
4117th Base Unit 61
4141st Base Unit 60
428th Base Unit 49, 54, 59, 172, 208, 209, 212
468th Bombardment Group 161
4th Marine Division 64
504th Bombardment Group 66, 97
509th Bomb Wing 101
509th Bombardment Group 54, 62
509th Composite Group 3, 4, 10, 25, 43, 70, 103; activation of 7, 96–97; organization of 97–100; outstanding unit award for 101–02
509th Maintenance Group 54, 62
509th Pictorial Album 143
58th Bombardment Wing 22
603rd Air Engineering Squadron 99
715th Bombardment Squadron 62
7th Bombardment Group 161

8th Air Force 56
82nd Field Artillery 57
830th Bombardment Squadron 62
9th Bombardment Wing 62–63, 66
97th Bomb Wing 50, 56
97th Bombardment Group 62–63, 66

Aberdeen Proving Ground 22, 207, 209, 216
actuators 14
adapter 81
Aerospace Maintenance and Regeneration Center 58
Agnew, Harold 158
Air Force Flight Test Center 60
Air Force Historical Research Agency vii, 161
Air Force Museum 61, 173
Air Force Outstanding Unit Award 101–02
Air Force Test Pilot School 60
Air Materiel Command 22, 65, 103
Air Technical Service Command 60
Aircraft Record Card 62
Albuquerque AAF/AFB 59
Albuquerque Journal 48
Albuquerque, NM 3, 58
Albury, Charles D. 19, 26, 141
Albury crew *see* Crew C-15
Alvarez, Luis W. 157, 158
Amarillo AFB 208
amatol 71–72
Andersen AFB 213
AN-M64A1 70
AN-M65A1 71
antenna 83
anvil 82
Archies 220n7
arming & firing 92
Arnold, Henry H. 6, 96

Batista Field 13, 165
battery 83, 84

Begg, Charles F.H. 100, 143
Bergstrom AFB 210
beryllium 83
Big Stink (44-27354) 18, 28, 30, 32, 46, 127, 186; crew of 126; history of 186–89; missions of 117
Biggs, James B. 57
Biggs AAF/AFB 50, 63, 66, 94; assignments to 56–57; description of 56–57
Birch, A. Francis 80, 157
Bitburg AB 208
Blanchard, William H. 62
Bock, Frederick C. iv, 3, 4, 13, 19, 26, 33, 138, 172
Bock crew *see* Crew C-13
Bockscar (44-27297) 3, 27, 31, 36, 46, 57, 61, 138, 222n12; crew of 138; history of 171–73; missions of 113–14; Nagasaki mission and 31–34
Boeing 8, 106
Boeing B-29 Superfortress 4
Bonneville Salt Flats 68
Bono, Sam viii
Bontekoe, Jacob 104
breech plug 82
Brookley AAF 166
Brooks AAF 165
Building the B-29 4
Bureau of Ordnance 73

California Institute of Technology 44, 72, 73
Calipatria, CA 45, 104
capsule, nuclear 94
Carswell AFB 57, 210
Casey, Earl O. 99, 143
Casey, John J. 99, 143
Castle AAF/AFB 59, 165
Caver, Joe vii
Centerline Company 73
Cerrillos, NM 64
chain of command 102
Chanute AAF 165
Chateauroux AB 168
Chicago, IL 58
Chicago Municipal Airport 20, 51, 104, 182
Chico AAF 189, 207, 209
China Lake 20, 22, 175
Churchill, Prime Minister Winston 70
Classen, Thomas J. 11, 18, 26, 98, 126, 186, 195
Classen crew *see* Crew A-5
clock box 83
Clovis AAF 181
Colorado Springs AAF 190
Colorado Springs, CO 96
Columbia River 75

Composition B 20, 71–72, 74, 91
Consolidated Steel Co. 73
core 38, 92; composite 94; levitated 94
Corum 59
cost figures 107–08
Costello, Edward M. 26, 105, 121, 194, 196
Costello crew *see* Crew A-2
Coster-Mullen, John vii, 4, 70, 91
Cowell, CA 75
cradle 35
crew: A-1 26, 119–20; A-2 26, 121–22; A-3 26, 122; A-4 26, 123–24; A-5 26, 126; B-6 26, 127; B-7 26, 129; B-8 26, 130; B-9 26, 132; B-10 26, 134; C-11 26, 29, 135; C-12 26, 136–37; C-13 26, 138; C-14 26, 139; C-15 26, 141–42
Critical Assembly 4, 155
Curtiss Electric 14

Dahlgren Naval Proving Ground 42, 76
Dalhart AAF 97
Dave's Dream 18, 48, 169
Davis, Harry B. 105, 197
Davis, Samuel H. 58
Davis-Monthan AAF/AFB 13, 106; assignments to 57; description of 57–58
Dayton, OH 68, 70
Delivery Group 42
Derry, J.A. 38
detonator 91
Devore, Ralph N. 26, 122, 175
Devore crew *see* Crew A-3
DiFante, Archie vii, 161
Dike, Sheldon 6, 13, 47, 157, 169
Dimples 18
director, antenna 84
Distinguished Service Cross 101, 221n7
Doll, Edward B. 157
Douglas Aircraft Company 66
Downey, John L. 105, 197

Eatherly, Claude R. 26, 29, 135, 178
Eatherly crew *see* Crew C-11
Edwards, Glen W. 60
Edwards AFB 60, 161
Eielson AFB 177
Einstein, Professor Albert 5, 7, 96
El Paso, TX 50, 56–57
electronics test officer 14, 93
ellipsoidal 88
Elmendorf AFB 179, 181, 189, 201, 204
Engineering Division 68
Enola Gay (44-86292) 3, 18, 29, 32, 46, 58, 61, 85, 132, 192; crew of 132; display of 194, 217n2; Hiroshima mission and 30, 192; history of 191–94; missions of 117–18; Nagasaki mission and 32

Enola Gay: Mission to Hiroshima 4
Ernest Harmon AB 202, 213

Fairfield Aviation General Supply Depot 69
Fairfield-Suisun AAF 193
Fairmont AAF 66, 96, 97, 167
Farrell, B/Gen Thomas F. 100, 143, 156
Fat Man bomb 68; description of 87–93; F-13 46; F-18 46; F-31 38–39; F-32 38; F-33 38, 46; loading of 34–37; Model 1561 88; Nagasaki and 31–31; naming of 70
Ferebee, Thomas W. 19, 97, 133
fin, tail 81, 85, 90
Foley, Mel viii
Fort Bliss 57
Fort Worth AAF 11, 47, 57
Fort Worth, TX 57
Foundation, National Atomic Museum 3, 217n3
fuel injection 13–14
Fujikoshi 130
Fukushima 139
Full House (44-27298) 28, 30, 32, 120; crew of 119; history of 173–75; missions of 114
Furstenfeldbruck AB 167, 170, 206, 207

Geller, Guy 99, 143
GEM 23
General Purpose bomb 70–72
General Services Agency 60
Germany 64
Glen L. Martin Aircraft Plant 106
gold 83
Goose Bay AB 51–52, 53, 185, 199, 202, 213
Grand Isle AAF 167
The Great Artiste (44-27353) 28, 30, 32, 58, 142, 158, 172, 184, 222n20; accident of 51, 104, 185; crew of 141–42; history of 184–85; missions of 116–17
Green Hornet Line 98
Greenville AFB 167, 206
Griffiss AFB 170, 189, 190
Group E-7 6, 155
Groves, Leslie R. 6, 155
Grumman TBF Avenger 42
Guam 65, 103
Guguan 19, 26, 71
gun barrel 81

Hamamatsu 135
Hamilton AFB 184
Hanford 75, 77
Hanscom AFB 59, 169
Harvard AAF 165, 167
Hartshorn, William 168, 194, 196, 222n8
HE preassemblies 38

Headquarters and Base Services Squadron 97
Headquarters, 509th Composite Group 97
Herrington AAF 162
H-frame 14
Hickam AFB 177, 196
Hill AFB 52, 170, 174, 188, 199
Hiroshima 5, 18, 25–26, 29, 41, 133, 135, 136
Hitachi 127
Hooker, Roger viii
Hopkins, James I., Jr. 19, 33, 97, 104, 140
Hunter AFB 213
hydraulic lift 36

Imperial Palace 29
Industrial Soda Company 131
initiator 83
Inland Storage Area 75
Inyokern 44, 46
Iwo Jima 20, 46, 131

Jabit III (44-27303) 18, 28, 30, 46, 127, 181, 222n17; accident of 51, 104, 182–83, 220n5; crew of 127; history of 181–83; missions of 116
Jeppson, Morris R. 82, 86, 99
Johnson AB 163, 203
Johnston, Lawrence 158

Karl, Allan A. 192
Kashiwazaki 140
Kawasaki Locomotive and Car Company 140
Keflavik Airport 208
Kelly AAF/AFB 58, 167, 170, 196, 198
Kirkpatrick, Elmer E. 156, 157
Kirtland AAF/AFB 16; accidents at 48; assignments to 56, 59; bomb transportation from 38; description of 58–59
Kirtland, Roy C. 59
Kobe 132, 140, 142
Kokura 33, 41, 128, 135
Konopacki, Hubert J. 99
Korean 64
Koriyama 133, 140
Koromo 132, 139, 142
Krauss, Robert W. viii
Kwajalein 58, 61, 177, 193
Kyoto 220n6

Labrador 51, 53, 185, 199, 213
Laggin' Dragon (44-86347) 29, 32, 105, 122, 198, 222n24; crew of 121–22; history of 196–98; missions of 118
Lancaster, Avro 6
Langley AFB 202
Lansdale, John 96
Laon AB 167, 206

Larson AFB 202
Laurence, William C. 222n13
Lauritsen, Charles C. 72
Lewis, Robert A. 19, 26, 132, 191
Lewis crew *see* Crew B-9
Little Boy bomb 9, 43, 77; description of 78–86; Hiroshima and 29; L-1 46, 80; L-2 46, 80; L-5 46, 80; L-6 46, 80; L-11 80, 85; loading of 85; naming of 70
Lloyd, Alwyn T. vii
loading pit 34, 37, 59, 67
Los Alamos, NM 5, 9–10, 103
Los Alamos Ranch School 217n3
Los Lunas, NM 48, 169
Luke the Spook (44–86346) 18, 29, 137, 195; crew of 136–37; history of 194–96

MacDill AAF 215
Macon, GA 61
Maizuru 135
The Making of the Atomic Bomb 4, 39
Malmstrom AFB 201, 202
Manhattan Island 220n5
Manhattan Project 4, 5, 7, 18, 25, 58, 64, 96, 107
Marcus 19, 26, 71
Marianas Islands 19, 64
Marquardt, George W. 26, 47, 134, 183, 192
Marquardt crew *see* Crew B-10
Marshall, George C. 40
Martin Omaha 11–13, 67
Mathewson, Tom viii
Maxwell AAF/AFB 161, 164, 165, 166
McAlester, OK 74
McClellan AAF 22, 62, 106
McCook Army Air Field 163, 165, 166
McCook Field 63
McKnight, Charles F. 26, 130, 180
McKnight crew *see* Crew B-8
Meade, Roger A. viii
Menard, David viii, 218n15
Midwest Air Depot 66
Mitchel Field 52, 198
Mitsubishi Heavy Industries Plant 125
Mizner, Wilson 3
Mk-3 bomb 93–94
Mk-4 bomb 94–95
Mobile Air Materiel Area 175, 177
Monthan, Oscar 58
Morrison, Philip 157
Mountain Home AFB 213
Muroc AAF, 42, 67, 87; description of 59–60; prototype at 59, 161; testing at 76
MX-469, Project 8

Nagasaki 20, 25–26, 31, 33, 41, 51, 88, 135, 139, 141, 142

Nagoya 123, 126, 130, 132, 141
Naha Air Base 163, 196, 198
Nakajima Aircraft Engine Factory 139
National Air and Space Museum 194
National Atomic Museum 31, 217n3
National Cash Register Company 69
Naval Ammunition Depot 74
Naval Gun Factory 81
Naval Ordnance Test Station 44–45, 175, 220n1
Necessary Evil (44–86291) 29, 30, 140, 157, 189, 222n22; crew of 139; history of 189–91; missions of 117
Newhouse, Gerry viii
Next Objective (44–27299) 28, 46, 122; accident of 50, 176; crew of 122; history of 175–76; missions of 114
Niigata 41
Niihama 123, 139
Nippon Oil Company 128
Nippon Soda Plant 122
Nolan, James F. 157
Norden 43
Norris, Robert S. 4
North Field 25
nose section 81
Noussaur AB 178, 206
Now It Can Be Told 4
nuclear deterrent 96
Nuebiburg AB 167, 206

Oak Ridge 77, 80
Odessa, TX 60
Ogaki 130
Ogden Municipal Airport 52, 199
O'Hare International Airport 193
Okinawa 33
Oklahoma City Depot 22, 57, 59, 66, 106
Oklahoma City, OK 65, 66
Omaha Modification Center 12, 15
Omaha, NE 106
Operation Crossroads 18, 22, 48, 53, 61–62, 99, 188, 193
Oppenheimer, J. Robert 6, 74
oralloy 80, 82, 83
Orchard Place Air Field 58
Ordnance Division 6, 42, 44, 155
Osaka 123
Otsu 131, 135

Park Ridge 193
Parsons, Capt William S. 42, 72, 86, 96, 97, 143, 156
Patrick AFB 216
Patterson, Frank J. 69
Patterson, John H. 69

Patterson Field 69
Paul E. Garber Preservation, Restoration, and Storage Facility 194
Pawhuska, OK 60
Pearl Harbor 57
Pease AFB 100
Penney, William G. 157
Perkins, Clay viii
Phase One 8–11
Phase Two 11–13
Phase Three 14–21
Phase Four 21
Phase Five 21–23
Phase Six 23–25
plaster of paris 74
plug, pull-out 85, 93
plutonium 42, 75, 78
pneumatic 14
polonium 83
Port Chicago 75
Porter, John W. 99, 143
Potsdam 40
powder bags 82, 86
Price, James N., Jr. 26, 49, 129, 171
Price crew *see* Crew B-7
primary target 27
Project 98146-S 12
Project 98228-S 14
Project Alberta 17, 25, 97, 155, 157–58
Project Alberta: The Preparation of Atomic Bombs for Use in World War II 4, 143
Project DOM-515C 22
Project DOM-595C 23
Project DOM-599C 23
Project Y: The Los Alamos Story 4, 155
projectile 81, 83
prototype 8–11, 42, 57, 59; accident of 47; history of 161; Muroc and 8–10, 42, 59; Wendover and 10, 67
Pullman 8, 70
Pumpkin bomb 14, 19; description of 72–75; missions with 27; naming of 70, 218n13, 220n5
Purnell, R/Adm William R. 100, 143, 156
pusher 91
Pyote AAF 13, 106, 162; assignments to 60; description of 60
Pyote Tank, TX 60
Pyote, TX 60, 106

Racing for the Bomb 4
radar 83
RAF Brize Norton 51, 178
RAF Burtonwood 167, 201
RAF Lakenheath 213
RAF Marham 55, 62, 215
RAF Mildenhall 213
RAF Upper Heyford 201, 206
Rain of Ruin 4
Ramsey, Norman F. 6, 42, 70, 80, 96, 155
Randolph AAF/AFB 162, 165, 167, 201, 205, 207, 208, 209
Ray, Norman W. 26, 139, 189
Ray crew *see* Crew C-14
RDX 74
reflector, antenna 84
Return of the Enola Gay 4
Reunions 105
Rhein Main AB 208
Rhodes, Richard 4, 39
Robins, Augustine Warner 61
Robins AAF/AFB 61, 106, 167; assignments to 61; description of 60
Rogers Dry Lake 59
Rome AAF 176, 179, 181, 188
Roosevelt, President Franklin D. 5, 7, 70
Roswell AAF 20; accidents at 48, 50, 53, 54, 55; assignments to 62–63; description of 61–64
Roswell, NM 64, 220n4
Rota 19, 26, 71
Rowe, James A. 44
RT-34/APS-13 83
Russ, Harlow 4, 143

Sachs, Alexander 217n1
Sacramento Air Depot 62–63
Sacramento Air Material Area 22
Saddletree 4, 22, 23
safe/arm plugs 82
Saga of the Superfortress 4
Saipan 16, 65
Salt Lake City, UT 68
Salton Sea 13, 45, 161
San Antonio Air Technical Service Command 58, 208, 213
San Bernadino Air Depot 43
San Francisco, CA 75, 104
Sandia Base 93
Sandia National Laboratories 93
Sandy Beach 45–46
Schaffer, Louis 99, 143
secondary target 27
Semple, Dave 9, 18, 48, 187, 218n3
Serber, Robert 157
Sewart AFB 170, 207
sewer pipe bomb 76
shell, high explosive 91
Shields, Clyde S. 9, 44, 47, 49, 54, 218n3
Shimoda 130
Sidi Silimane AB 168, 206, 207
Signal Corps Aviation School 68

Silva, Peer de 39, 156
Silver Plated Project 7, 217n1
Sioux City AFB 52, 174, 188, 199
Smith, Bill 68
Smith, Elbert B. 19
Smith, Leon viii, 99
Smithsonian Institution 58, 193
Smoky Hill AAF 7, 8, 57, 68, 161
Some Punkins (44-27296) 27, 129, 222n10; accident of 49, 104; crew of 129; history of 171-72; missions of 113
sortie 26
Spaatz, Carl 101
Spain 64
sphere, high explosives 82
sphere, inner 88
Spiller, John viii
State Line Nugget Hotel and Casino 68
Stateline Club 68
Steven F. Udvar-Hazy Center 194, 217n2
Stevenson, Edward C. 157
Stimson, Henry L. 40
Straight Flush (44-27301) 28, 30, 135, 178, 222n15; crew of 135; history of 178-79; missions of 115
Strange Cargo (44-27300) 28, 104, 124, 176; accident of 50, 178; crew of 123-24; history of 176-78; missions of 114-15
Strategic Air Command 22
Sumitomo Aluminum Plant 139
Sumitomo Copper Refining Plant 120
Sumitomo Rayon Plant 123
Sweeney, Charles W. 19, 33, 47, 98, 99, 104, 142, 143, 218n7
Szilard, Leo 217n1

tail code: N in a triangle 19; P in a square 19; plain letter A 19; R in a circle 19
Taira 125, 128, 135
tamper 81, 91, 94
target assembly 81
Target Hiroshima 4
target of opportunity 27
Taylor, Ralph R. 26, 119, 173
Taylor crew *see* Crew A-1
Teller, Edward 217n1
Test Able 18, 48, 99
Test Section 44, 47, 67
Thin Man 6, 8, 42, 78; accident with 76, 104; description of 75-78; naming of 70; termination of 77; testing of 42
third bomb 37, 39
Three Igloo Job 75
Tibbets, Paul W. viii, 13, 18, 96, 133, 143, 191
Tinian 7, 16, 25-26, 46, 65; assignments to 64; description of 64-65; Hiroshima mission from 30-31; Nagasaki mission from 31-33
Tinker, Clarence L. 66
Tinker AAF/AFB 22, 106; accident at 65; assignments to 66; description of 65-66
TNT 71, 72
Tokushima 133
Tokyo-Musashino 139
Tokyo Railroad Station 135
Top Secret (44-27302) 28, 130, 180, 222n16; crew of 130; history of 180-81; missions of 115
The Top Secret Inside Story of Little Boy and Fat Man 4
Topeka AAF 184, 201, 212
Toyama 120, 122, 142
Toyo Rayon Factory 135
Toyoda Auto Works 132, 139, 142
transport trailer 35
Travis AFB 62, 66, 213
tritinal 72
Truk 19, 26, 71
Truman, President Harry S 40
Tsugami-Atagi Manufacturing Company 127
Tsugawa 135
Tsuruga 126
Tucson Municipal Airport 58
Type F release 10, 15
Type G attachment 10, 15

U-235 80
U-238 80
Ube 121, 128, 131
United Kingdom 55, 206
Up an' Atom (44-27304) 28, 134, 183; crew of 134; history of 183-84; missions of 116
uranium, highly enriched 43, 77, 78, 80
U.S. Air Corps 56
U.S. Army Air Forces 56, 103
U.S. Army Signal Corps 68
U.S. Army Strategic Air Forces 102
U.S. Naval Magazine 75
U.S. Strategic Bombing Survey 29, 75
Uwajima 128

Van Kirk, Theodore J. 19, 97, 133
Victor, call sign 18
Victorville Army Air Field 163, 189, 201, 207, 210
Villa, Pancho 57
Vincent AFB 184, 191

Wakayama 127
Wake Island 66
Waldman, Bernard 157
Walker, Kenneth Newton 64

Walker AFB 56, 61, 64, 94
Warner, Roger S., Jr. 157
Warner Robins Air Logistics Center 61
Warner Robins Air Materiel Area 61
Wendover AAF 43, 68, 96; accidents at 47; assignments to 67; description of 66–68; prototype at 47; tests at 46
Wendover, UT 66, 68
West Wendover, NV 68
Western Pipe and Steel Co. 73
Westover, Joseph E. 26, 104, 123
Westover crew *see* Crew A-4
Wheelus AB 178
Whiteman AFB 101
Wichita, KS 106, 214
Wiesbaden AB 170, 207
Wilbur Wright Field 68
Wilson, John A. 18, 26, 51, 127, 181, 195
Wilson crew *see* Crew B-6

Wright, Wilbur 68
Wright AAF 6, 10, 70, 87, 103; description of 68–69; prototype at 68
Wright Cyclone R-3350 103
Wright-Patterson AFB 58

X-Unit 45, 93

Yagi 84
Yaizu 121
Yokkaichi 130, 131, 136
Yokota Air Base 163, 196, 198, 203
Yontan AB 34
Yuma County Airport 175, 184, 191, 208

Z Division 93
Zahn, Herman S. 18, 26, 136, 194
Zahn crew *see* Crew C-12

www.ingramcontent.com/pod-product-compliance
Ingram Content Group UK Ltd.
Pitfield, Milton Keynes, MK11 3LW, UK
UKHW050533150426
5217IPUK00026B/1921